The Soviet Jewish Americans

Other Titles in
The New Americans Series
Ronald H. Bayor, Series Editor

The South Asian Americans
Karen Isaksen Leonard

The Cuban Americans
Miguel Gonzalez-Pando

The Dominican Americans
Silvio Torres-Saillant and Ramona Hernández

The Taiwanese Americans
Franklin Ng

The Korean Americans
Won Moo Hurh

The Soviet Jewish Americans

Annelise Orleck

Photographs by Elizabeth Cooke

THE NEW AMERICANS
Ronald H. Bayor, Series Editor

GREENWOOD PRESS
Westport, Connecticut • London

Library of Congress Cataloging-in-Publication Data

Orleck, Annelise.
    The Soviet Jewish Americans / Annelise Orleck ; photographs by
Elizabeth Cooke.
        p.   cm.—(The New Americans, ISSN 1092–6364)
    Includes bibliographical references and index.
    ISBN 0–313–30074–7 (alk. paper)
    1. Jews, Soviet—United States—Social conditions.   2. Jews—
Soviet Union—History.   3. Immigrants—United States—Social
conditions.   4. United States—Ethnic relations.   I. Title.
II. Series: New Americans
E184.J5068   1999
973'.04924047—dc21   98–22917

British Library Cataloguing in Publication Data is available.

Library of Congress Catalog Card Number: 98–22917
ISBN: 0–313–30074–7
ISSN: 1092–6364

First published in 1999

Greenwood Press, 88 Post Road West, Westport, CT 06881
An imprint of Greenwood Publishing Group, Inc.

Printed in the United States of America

The paper used in this book complies with the
Permanent Paper Standard issued by the National
Information Standards Organization (Z39.48–1984).

10 9 8 7 6 5 4 3 2 1

For Ruthie, in loving memory

Contents

Series Foreword

Oscar Handlin, a prominent historian, once wrote, "I thought to write a history of the immigrants in America. Then I discovered that the immigrants were American history." The United States has always been a nation of nations where people from every region of the world have come to begin a new life. Other countries such as Canada, Argentina, and Australia also have had substantial immigration, but the United States is still unique in the diversity of nationalities and the great numbers of migrating people who have come to its shores.

Who are these immigrants? Why did they decide to come? How well have they adjusted to this new land? What has been the reaction to them? These are some of the questions the books in this "New Americans" series seek to answer. There have been many studies about earlier waves of immigrants—e.g., the English, Irish, Germans, Jews, Italians, and Poles—but relatively little has been written about the newer groups—those arriving in the last thirty years, since the passage of a new immigration law in 1965. This series is designed to correct that situation and to introduce these groups to the rest of America.

Each book in the series discusses one of these groups, and each is written by an expert on those immigrants. The volumes cover the new migration from primarily Asia, Latin America, and the Caribbean, including: the Koreans, Cambodians, Filipinos, Vietnamese, South Asians such as Indians and Pakistanis, Chinese from both China and Taiwan, Haitians, Jamaicans, Cubans, Dominicans, Mexicans, Puerto Ricans (even though they are already U.S. citizens), and Jews from the former Soviet Union. Although some of these people, such as Jews, have been in America since colonial times, this series concentrates on their recent migrations, and thereby offers its unique contribution.

These volumes are designed for high school and general readers who want to learn more about their new neighbors. Each author has provided information about the land of origin, its history and culture, the reasons for migrating, and the ethnic culture as it began to adjust to American life. Readers will find fascinating details on religion, politics, foods, festivals, gender roles, employment trends, and general community life. They will learn how Vietnamese immigrants differ from Cuban immigrants and, yet, how they are also alike in many ways. Each book is arranged to offer an in-depth look at the particular immigrant group and to enable readers to compare one group with the other. The volumes also contain brief biographical profiles of notable individuals and a short bibliography of readily available books and articles for further reading. Many contain a glossary of foreign words and phrases.

Students and others who read these volumes will secure a better understanding of the age-old questions of "who is an American" and "how does the assimilation process work?" Similar to their 19th- and early 20th-century forebears, many Americans today doubt the value of immigration and fear the influx of individuals who look and sound different from those who had come earlier. If comparable books had been written 100 years ago they would have done much to help dispel readers' unwarranted fears of the newcomers. Nobody today would question, for example, the role of those of Irish or Italian ancestry as Americans; yet this was a serious issue in our history and a source of great conflict. It is time to look at our recent arrivals, to understand their history and culture, their skills, their place in the United States, and their hopes and dreams as Americans.

The United States is a vastly different country than it was at the beginning of the twentieth century. The economy has shifted away from industrial jobs; the civil rights movement has changed minority-majority relations and, along with the women's movement, brought more people into the economic mainstream. Yet one aspect of American life remains strikingly similar—we are still the world's main immigrant-receiving nation and, as in every period of American history, we are still a nation of immigrants. It is essential that we attempt to learn about and understand this long-term process of migration and assimilation.

Ronald H. Bayor
Georgia Institute of Technology

Acknowledgments

I could not have written this book without the generous and spirited guidance of three generations of Soviet immigrant writer/scholars. Tamara Truskanova, Semyon Kommissar, Alexander Sirotin, Natasha Zaretsky, and Shirley Sperling each opened doors for me into a community whose members are, for very good reason, not always happy to share their life stories with a stranger. I am very grateful for their insights, for the time they devoted to this project, and for the opportunity to get to know them.

Shirley Sperling and Towfik Al Swaidi daily performed research miracles, ferreting out journal articles and psychological studies, gathering and processing statistics, and tracking down contacts at immigrant organizations across the United States. I owe them far more than the few lunches I was able to buy.

Thanks are due as well to Jennifer Wood, Barbara Rader, Terry Park, and the staff at Greenwood for their support of and work on this project.

Seventeen years ago, Liz Cooke and I returned home from college to our childhood haunts in Brighton Beach and began photographing and interviewing elderly Polish, Hungarian, Czech, and Soviet Jewish immigrants. This book has its roots and much of its heart in that youthful endeavor. My thinking about Brighton Beach and about the three waves of Jewish immigrants who have lived there has developed over more than a decade and a half of conversation and collaboration with Liz.

My mother, Thelma, provided love and warmth, joy and laughter throughout this process as she has always done. Also, she and my brother Jerry and my nephews Larry and Jon were always willing to spend an evening on the boardwalk eating *shashlyk* and drinking vodka "in the name of research." I am grateful to them for those nights of fun and more deeply for a lifetime of support.

To Alexis Jetter—my life partner, editor, and muse—I owe more than I can ever squeeze into these little paragraphs. So too our little daughter Evann, whose delighted grin is my daily inspiration. They are my rock in this world, my grounding in everything I do.

My aunt, Ruth Orleck, wandered the streets of Brighton with me in the early days, drank tea in many immigrants' apartments, and translated from the Yiddish so that I could conduct interviews with those who preferred to speak their *mamaloshn* (mother tongue). Her love, her wisdom, her irrepressible joy, and wise-cracking sense of humor lightened those first years of research, as they did so much of my life. I still miss her every day.

Introduction: The Third and Fourth Waves of East European Jewish Immigration

One summer night in 1975 I took a long, slow walk on the Brighton Beach boardwalk, soaking up some Brooklyn flavor before leaving home to attend college. A cool sea breeze hit the warm city air, creating a light mist that hung over the scene like a curtain. Elderly immigrant Jews walked slowly arm in arm, speaking an animated mixture of Yiddish and English. Silent old men and women lined the wooden benches facing the sea, silhouetted against a glowing urban night sky. Sounds of mandolin, accordion, and *balalaika* filled the air as old musicians played and sang Yiddish songs with a smattering of Russian thrown in. I could see the lined, intent faces of the musicians in the gassy orange light of the street lamps behind them. A handful of homeless people danced to the music; they were well-known neighborhood characters whose craziness had a Yiddish accent. Some sang in cracking voices with a great deal of verve. It all felt very poignant, fragile, temporal—this world of retired garment workers, union activists, Holocaust survivors. The people around me were very old; many were frail. I had the feeling, as I prepared to leave my childhood home, that the boardwalk would never look or feel quite this way again.

I was both right and wrong. In the five years between the time I moved away from Brooklyn and the time I returned, my old neighborhood was entirely transformed. Many of the elderly East European Jews among whom I was raised had died, moved into nursing homes, or left Brighton for the warmer seascape of Miami Beach. Their places had been taken by a new group of immigrants, Jews from the Soviet Union. By 1980, there were upward of 30,000 Soviet Jewish emigres living in and around the narrow little seaside neighborhood known as Brighton Beach. The crowded streets now rang with conversations in Russian. The old kosher delicatessens, dairy restaurants, and appetizing stores were being replaced by "international food" emporia selling a dazzling array of East European food and by glitzy nightclubs with Russian names, pulsing disco rhythms, and strangely opaque facades. The dominant culture of Brighton was no longer shaped by old Jews who had once fled tsarist repression and Cossack violence. These new arrivals were an entirely different kind of East European Jewish immigrant. Or so I thought at first.

During the past 15 years I've interviewed scores of Soviet Jewish emigres living in and around New York. I've read psychological, sociological, and journalistic accounts of their lives both before and after they emigrated from the former Soviet Union. I've spent a great deal of time observing life in Brighton, as well as other Soviet Jewish immigrant communities. All of it has convinced me that the more than 400,000 Soviet Jews who have immigrated to this country since the 1970s *are* quite different from, but are also intimately related to, the more than 2 million East European Jews who streamed into the United States from 1881 to 1924, and the 100,000 or so survivors of Nazi death camps who came after World War II. Having spent 70 years living under a dictatorial and anti-religious regime, most of these Soviet Jews have only faded and tenuous ties to the Jewish religion. Few but the elderly among them can speak Yiddish or Hebrew, and those old enough to have been raised with those languages had to dust them off here after half a century of disuse. In the main, these Soviet emigres are highly educated, fairly well assimilated, and quite a bit more urban than their predecessors. Their dress and their manners seem to distinguish them from older Jewish immigrants.

And yet, many of these Soviet Jews come from the same cities and towns in Russia, Lithuania, Byelorussia, Moldavia, and the Ukraine that sent earlier waves of Jewish immigrants to the United States. Indeed, some came from the very same families. In 1980 I interviewed a Soviet immigrant shopkeeper in Brighton Beach who made this comment: "From this side of the Atlantic it might look like three different kinds of immigrants. From the other side I saw it this way. My grandfather left before the First World War. My uncle, who was in the Red Army, escaped after the Second. And I came thirty years after him." The major waves of East European Jewish immigration to this country were, to this shopkeeper, just family history. That observation is the underpinning for one of the major themes in this book.

These more recent Soviet Jewish immigrants have too often been treated as though they were fundamentally different and separate from earlier waves of Jewish immigrants from Russia and other parts of Eastern Europe. It is my contention that, as the shopkeeper strongly affirms, they are inextricably bound up with the main currents of 20th-century East European Jewish life. Therefore the first two chapters, which explore why so many Soviet Jews have chosen to leave their homeland during the past quarter-century, examine that exodus in the context of a larger Eastern European Jewish history, stressing both the important continuities as well as the differences in experience between these immigrants and those who left Eastern Europe before them. The third and fourth chapters, which look closely at Soviet immigrant communities on this side of the Atlantic, similarly stress both the divisions and essential ties between Soviet and earlier Jewish emigres to the United States who have, since the 1970s, co-existed uneasily in aging urban neighborhoods from New York to Los Angeles.

This book also seeks to place Soviet Jews in the larger context of the massive post-1965 immigration to the United States, including the newest waves of Filipinos, Chinese, West Indians, and Koreans. Like many of these post-1965 immigrants, a large proportion of Soviet Jewish emigres have not been rural agrarians but educated urban professionals who are able to adapt quickly to life in fast-paced American cities. They fare less well, however, in the competitive U.S. job market. Many, if not most, Soviet Jewish emigres have experienced a sudden and dramatic loss of status and income. These losses have exacerbated the natural mourning process that is part of leaving an old home for a new one and have taken a profound psychological and emotional toll on immigrants of all ages. Depression, anxiety, high blood pressure, and psychosomatic illnesses are common among this and other recent immigrant groups—at least during the first few years.

But the Soviet emigres have not all responded in exactly the same ways to the pressure and pleasures of American life. This is a highly diverse group of immigrants and their processes of adaptation and acculturation have been strongly colored by sex, age, class, education, and region of origin. The second part of this book will explore the varied ways that men and women, old and young, big-city dwellers and those from smaller towns have made their peace with American life. Where they settle in the United States has made a big difference as well. The experience of Soviet Jews now living in Los Angeles has been quite distinct from that of their countrymen and women who have settled in Chicago; similarly, Chicagoans' lives have diverged in many ways from those of former Soviet Jews who have made their homes in the suburbs surrounding Boston. While there is not enough space to explore these varied communities in detail, some key distinctions and similarities will be highlighted. Finally there are some important differences between so-called Third

Wave immigrants—those Soviet Jews who came to the United States in the 1970s—and the Fourth Wave—those who left after the dissolution of the Soviet Union.

Stressing the diversity of this immigration is a major goal of this study. Like most immigrant groups, Soviet Jews have been subject to stereotyping. They have been described as rude, overly ambitious, in love with white-collar crime. The truth, as one might expect, is far more complex. It is difficult to generalize about this highly varied immigrant group, and simply impossible to make claims about the whole of "Soviet Jewish America." This book therefore examines a range of different communities, historical and cultural experiences, political and social persuasions. It is a patchwork held together by the few central threads that bind these immigrants—their love-hate relationship with Russian culture, their experience of Soviet Communism, and the terrible, violent history of Russian Jewry before and since the Russian Revolution.

This book draws from historical and social science literature, the statistics and annual reports of Jewish immigrant aid and resettlement agencies, Internet postings and clippings from newspapers across the United States. But its lifeblood is an array of immigrant voices set within a larger social, historical, and political context. Thematically and stylistically, this book represents a departure from most earlier studies of Soviet Jews in the United States. Though there is a growing body of literature on the so-called Third and Fourth Waves of East European Jewish immigration to the United States, it has been social scientific in nature, focusing mostly on social service delivery, psychological, and medical strategies for treatment and, to a lesser extent, on U.S. and Soviet engagements over the issue of free emigration. A smaller qualitative literature has been generated largely by journalists in the Russian-language and mainstream U.S. press. There have been, as far as I know, a handful of ethnographic studies of particular Soviet Jewish communities, but there have been few attempts to examine the immigration as a whole.

Some of the recent literature has explored the complex and tense relationship between Soviet emigres and American Jews. However, there has been little discussion of the fact that many of the American Jews among whom Soviet Jews have settled—in Brighton Beach, Brooklyn; West Hollywood, California; and West Rogers Park, Illinois, to name the most important examples—were immigrants themselves 50 to 75 years ago. And though these older emigres have been profoundly influenced by decades in the United States and consider themselves Americans, they were also deeply imprinted by the experience of persecution as Jews in Eastern Europe. In the process of becoming "American," Soviet Jewish immigrants are learning not from native Americans, but from other immigrants with whom they have much in common. This book will examine the complicated encounters between these different waves of Jewish immigrants. It will also illustrate the ways that these interactions have shaped Soviet Jews' experience of becoming "American."

The following pages focus not only on the outpouring of Jews from the Soviet Union between 1967 and 1981, but also on the much larger exodus from the former Soviet Union since 1991. I divide the Soviet Jewish emigration into four phases. The first period, coming after the Arab-Israeli Six-Day War in 1967, saw the most Jewish-identified, Zionist and religious Jews leave the Soviet Union for Israel. The second period began in 1976, when American Jewish resettlement agencies decided to provide assistance to Soviet emigres wishing to settle in the United States. From 1976 to 1981 the majority of Jews leaving the Soviet Union chose to come to the United States. They left the Soviet Union for two major reasons: decreasing opportunity for Jews as a result of official government anti-Semitism; and a disintegrating economy, overtaxed by a half-century arms race, that was no longer able to provide even the most basic comforts for its citizens. Between 1981 and 1987, the doors to the Soviet Union were once again slammed shut. During this third phase, only a handful of Jews were allowed to leave. Emigres already living in the United States and Israel scanned news and Jewish agency reports anxiously during those years for hopeful signs that their family members might soon be allowed to leave. Suddenly in 1987, under the leadership of Mikhail Gorbachev, the doors opened again. A new immigration began that gathered tremendous force with the fall of the Communist regime in 1991. More than a million Jews have left the former Soviet Union since 1987, approximately 300,000 settling in the United States.

Jews have fled the former Soviet Union for a complex array of reasons. Many cite resurgent anti-Semitism of the old-fashioned, pre-Communist kind. As in other parts of Eastern Europe, the re-emergence of nationalist political parties in the republics of the former Soviet Union has been partially fueled by a politics of blame that points to Jews as prime carriers of the infectious disease of Western cosmopolitanism. A slightly different strain of anti-Semitism has appeared in the Central Asian republics, Uzbekistan being a prime example. There, some Islamic nationalists have targeted Jews as both agents of Russian imperialism and religious infidels. In the Ukraine and Byelorussia, which have sent more immigrants to this country than any other part of the former Soviet Union, another terror is driving the exodus. There, the devastating effects of the 1986 Chernobyl nuclear power plant accident have left thousands of emaciated and balding children, skyrocketing rates of thyroid cancer, heart and lung disease, birth defects and miscarriages.

Particularly in the cities, economic chaos and a political power vacuum have created a staggering increase in violent crime. Rising unemployment rates and continued food shortages have made life especially hard in the second cities of the former Soviet Union, including Minsk, Kiev, Kharkov, and Gomel. Many of the newest immigrants are from these areas. They share with earlier Soviet emigres an abhorrence of the Soviet Communist system, but they are less sure that free-market capitalism is the answer to all of their problems.

From the perspective of the post–World War II United States, where anti-Communism has been woven into the very fabric of political and cultural life, it has been all too easy to assume that most of the Soviet Jews who came to the United States between 1972 and 1989 came primarily to escape Communist repression. While that is certainly part of the truth, the rapid increase in emigration since the fall of the Soviet Union reflects a more complicated set of motivations. Many Soviet Jews who have emigrated since the fall of the Soviet Union in 1991 believe that Russian anti-Semitism is more deeply rooted than Bolshevik ideology. The persistence of both official and unofficial anti-Semitism in today's Commonwealth of Independent States reveals the deep roots of anti-Semitism in Russian culture and Slavic Christianity. Economic and political chaos has also ignited the volatile mix of Russian anti-Semitism and the indigenous anti-Semitic strains that had long circulated underground in many Soviet republics. As in other parts of Eastern Europe—the former Yugoslavia being the most horrific example—ethnic hatreds were not eradicated in the Soviet Union but rather recast to serve a variety of political purposes during 70 years of Communist rule. Jews suffered greatly during the brutal 30-year reign of Joseph Stalin, and they did not fare well under his successors. However, the dissolution of the Soviet Union has not eliminated politically organized anti-Semitism in its former republics. Instead, old ethnic and religious hatreds have re-entered political discourse, appearing now as resurgent nationalism.

Here in the United States, the end of the Cold War and the partisan politics of the post-Reagan era have wrought some important changes in Soviet immigrant communities. Many, if not most, of the Soviet Jews who came to the United States in the 1970s were passionately anti-Communist. They translated that into strong support for President Ronald Reagan, who, they thought, had a clear-eyed understanding of the dangers of real-life Communism. One afternoon in the early 1980s, I was having tea with a refined teacher from Leningrad and I made a crack about the extremism that I felt underlay Reagan's labeling of the Soviet Union as "the evil empire." She stirred her tea and then eyed me with a trace of amusement at my naivete. "Ah, my dear," she said softly, "but it is!" Soviet immigrant support for the Republican Party was intensified by an abhorrence that these refugees from authoritarianism felt toward the "lawlessness" of this free society. "In Russia they imprisoned innocent people," one immigrant told me throwing up his hands. "Here they let the criminals run free." Nostalgia for physically safe cities and well-behaved children (whether those memories were rose-colored or not) drew many Soviet Jews to vote for candidates perceived as being tough on crime and moral issues. For all of those reasons, some historically Jewish and Democratic districts in New York City voted Republican for the first time in the 1980s as large numbers of Soviet immigrants became citizens and cast their ballots.

The 1990s has seen those loyalties shift yet again. As the Republican Party has spearheaded legislation to limit immigration, to restrict the numbers of people who can acquire refugee status, to cut foreign aid, and to eradicate social services both to legal immigrants and U.S. citizens, Soviet emigres have begun to vote for Democratic candidates. The Personal Responsibility and Work Opportunity Act of 1996, better known as "welfare reform," sent shivers through many Soviet emigre communities in the United States, for the most recent and the most elderly among Soviet Jewish immigrants have been heavily dependent on Supplemental Security Income, Medicaid, and federally subsidized housing. Soviet immigrant groups have also joined for the first time with organizations representing Mexican Americans, Asian Americans, and Central American emigres to lobby against proposed Republican legislation to dramatically limit the number of legal immigrants permitted into the United States. Comfortable enough now to be critical of the U.S. government, sure enough of their place in a pluralist society to join broad multiethnic coalitions, Soviet Jewish immigrants are beginning to seem more and more American.

PART I

WHAT THEY LEFT BEHIND AND WHY THEY LEFT

1

Remembering Soviet Jewish Life

PROLOGUE: MEMORY AND IDENTITY

Soviet Jewish emigres living in the United States carry with them a profound ambivalence toward the land of their birth. Many are deeply Russian—infused to the core with passionate love and affection for Russian language, literature, music, theater, and dance. Whether they are from Russia proper or the Ukraine, Byelorussia, Lithuania, or Moldova, most Soviet Jewish emigres call themselves Russians and think of themselves that way. But even the most Russian-identified immigrant would admit that Russian Jews were always strangers in their own country. In times of crisis, of which there were so many during the turbulent 20th century, Jews were inevitably the first targets of nationalist demagogues and discontented soldiers, easily labeled as the enemies within. So, at the heart of Soviet Jewish immigrants' strained relationship to the United States is their conflicted attachment to Russia and things Russian. Having never known security it is difficult to feel it even now. Never having had a home, they are unsure whether they have finally found one.

The elderly in particular carry heavy emotional baggage: memories both of a Russian Jewish world that is largely gone and of periodic reigns of terror that took the lives of parents, siblings, friends, and other loved ones. Cossack rampages (known as pogroms), Nazi slaughters, Stalin's prison camps—these nightmares sometimes bleed through the thin tissue separating a happier present from a more troubled past. Bits of random memories surface suddenly in the conversations of aged immigrants who bundle up for afternoons in the little asphalt and tar parks that dot New York, Boston, Chicago, and Los Angeles.

In the free air of the United States, where these emigres need no longer be afraid to talk of their lives as Jews, these spontaneous recollections are often happy ones. There are images of warm family gatherings in small Jewish villages from the years before Stalin stamped out most vestiges of traditional Russian Jewish culture. Old men and women remember themselves as children in the loving embrace of their parents, who were deeply religious Jews or, less often, passionately committed Bolshevik revolutionaries. The eldest remember their own brief hopes that Communism would work, that it would lift Russian Jews and others out of poverty and fear. Robust men and women in their 70s recall their Red Army years, when all Soviet citizens united to "save the Motherland" from the Nazi invaders. They speak assertively, voices full of color and emotion, as if to reverse decades of enforced silence, as if to revive the spirits of those long gone.

These memories of Soviet Jewish life are not just the province of the elderly. They color the intimate and loving relations between parents and children, grandparents and grandchildren here in the United States, where deep closeness and unshakeable loyalty are marks of the Soviet immigrant family. In an emigre community that includes approximately 150,000 elderly, family life in many homes is conducted against a backdrop of revolution, war, and repression. Among the Soviet elderly, even reminiscences that begin with happier times usually drift sooner or later to tales of loss. The identities of middle-aged emigres, even of the youngest Soviet Jewish children, have been forged in the heat of this complex history of hope and violence. Those who can no longer speak Russian, who have never spoken Yiddish or prayed in Hebrew, struggle to imagine what their grandparents went through. They are both proud of and saddened by what they learn of Jewish life in Russia and the Soviet Union—where fierce anti-Semitism dates back to the tsars and has outlived the Communists. To be a Soviet Jew is to be the inheritor of that legacy. To understand Soviet Jewish life in the United States it is necessary first to know something of where they came from. What follows is not intended to be a complete history of Jewish life in the Soviet Union. It is rather a tapestry of immigrant reminiscences woven together with some scholarly threads. All of the narrators in the pages below were interviewed in New York City between 1980 and 1996. (See the bibliography for full citations of all author's interviews quoted in this book.)

THE BACKGROUND: JEWISH LIFE IN RUSSIA ON THE EVE OF THE REVOLUTION

At the dawn of the first great exodus of Jews from Russia, nearly 3 million out of 4 million Russian Jews lived in a region known as the Pale of Jewish settlement. The Pale evolved in the late 18th century after Russia's conquest of Poland expanded the borders of the Russian Empire, bringing hundreds of thousands of Jews under the rule of the tsars. Created to keep Jewish merchants out of the mercantile centers of Moscow and Smolensk, the Pale became a reservation for Russian Jews. In the 1870s, Tsar Alexander II began easing restrictions on where Jews could live and what work they could perform. He hoped to normalize the legal status of Russian Jews and begin their integration into Russian society. But his assassination by revolutionary anarchists in 1881 led instead to a period of intense legal and violent backlash against the Jewish population of the Russian Empire. Forced evictions of Jews from their homes and years of mob violence sparked the first mass exodus of Jews from Russia.

Between 1881 and 1921 two million Russian and Polish Jews left for the United States. Most came from the 15 provinces of the Ukraine, Byelorussia, Lithuania, Bessarabia, and Russia known as the Pale. They came to be known as the "First Wave," the first Russian Jews to settle in the United States. After World War II, small numbers of Soviet Jews who had left the former Pale to serve in the Red Army and, at war's end found themselves outside Soviet borders, joined more than 100,000 Jewish Holocaust survivors in the Second Wave of immigration to this country. In the 1970s, '80s, and '90s, the Pale would again send hundreds of thousands of Soviet Jews to the United States (Howe, 1976: p. xix).

Cyclical outbreaks of anti-Semitic violence in the late 19th and early 20th centuries precipitated the First Wave of Jewish emigration from Russia and laid the groundwork for all later Jewish emigrations. These pogroms were fueled by anti-Semitic beliefs that persisted from the tsarist era to the Stalinist terror. Even today, in the 1990s nationalist revival that has targeted Jews in many republics of the former Soviet Union, one can hear echoes of these hate-filled folk mythologies. The war cries have remained eerily consistent. As they charged on horseback into Jewish city neighborhoods and small *shtetlakh* (villages), the Cossacks in 1881, the Black Hundreds in 1905, and the White Armies in 1919 shouted the rallying cry that would later incite Russian and Ukrainian Christians to aid the Nazis during World War II and neo-Nazis to burn Jewish synagogues after the collapse of the Soviet Union: "Beat the Yids and Save Russia" (Klier, 1992: 13–38; Lambroza, 1992: 195–247).

The Ukraine, which would send more Jews to the United States in the early and late 20th century than any other region, was the center of anti-Jewish violence in tsarist Russia. Odessa, the Ukraine's major seaport, was the city most prone to pogroms. By the late 19th century, Jews made up one third of Odessa's population, more than in any other Russian city. Jews had migrated to the port city on the Black Sea from other parts of the Pale searching for economic opportunity. During the 19th century Jews established a large and comfortable community with synagogues, businesses, trade unions, schools, and cultural centers. Odessan Jews were more prosperous and more assimilated than most other Jews in the Russian Empire, but their complacency was shattered by periodic outbreaks of violence that usually occurred around the closely linked spring festivals of Easter and Passover. These spring riots were often fueled by blatantly false ritual murder accusations that charged Jews with draining the blood of Christian children to use in Passover matzohs. Though it is not clear what role police and governors played in these cases, their silence gave Jews and non-Jews the feeling that the authorities approved (Weinberg, 1992: 248–289).

In March 1881, after the assassination of Tsar Alexander II by a revolutionary group that included at least one Jew, anti-Jewish violence swept through the Ukraine, hitting the cities of Odessa and Kiev hardest. It began with an Easter week tavern brawl in the Ukrainian city of Elisavetgrad. But, amid rumors that the new tsar was urging good Russians to beat the Jews for having murdered his father, and with some big-city newspapers publishing inflammatory, anti-Semitic articles, spontaneous riots grew into a pogrom movement. Posters openly called for violent attacks on Jews. Populist revolutionary groups sent mixed messages throughout the period of violence, condemning anti-Semitism while affirming peasant anger at the Jew who "plunders the people and sucks the blood of working men." That ambivalence foreshadowed Russian Socialism's view of Jews and anti-Semitism. It would be echoed hundreds of times in official Soviet publications after the Revolution (Aronson, 1992: 44–61; Haberer, 1992: 98–134).

Historians no longer believe that the 1881–1883 pogroms were orchestrated by the administration of Tsar Alexander III, for the new tsar feared that popular violence of any kind might quickly move beyond the ability of government authorities to control. Still, the new government sought to assuage peasants' anger at how little they had been given since the freeing of Russia's serfs in 1863. The interior minister, N. P. Ignatiev, led a commission to investigate the pogroms. He declared that Ukrainian Jews were at fault, claiming that they had drawn peasant ire because of their revolutionary activities, religious zeal, clannishness, and exploitation of the peasants to whom

they sold shoes, clothing, and liquor. Soon thereafter, the national government passed what came to be known as the May Laws, which restricted
Jewish trade and commerce, especially trade in liquor, a traditional Jewish
franchise in the Pale. Local police were free to interpret the May laws as they
chose. Hundreds of thousands of *shtetl* Jews were forced from their homes,
by police order. Though anti-Jewish violence subsided quickly, and there was
almost none for the next two decades, legal repression and rapid industrial-
ization wrought havoc on Russia's Jews. The 1897 census found that nearly
three quarters of them earned no regular income. Hundreds of thousands
saw little other choice but to leave for America (Schwartz, 1951: 72).

The years from 1883 to 1900 were relatively quiet, but with the resump-
tion of revolutionary agitation in Russia early in the 20th century, mob
violence against Jews returned. Between 1903 and 1906, thousands of
Ukrainian Jews became the victims of pogroms. This time the violence was
sparked by the upheavals associated with the 1905 revolution, along with
widespread crop failure and the displacement of millions caused by indus-
trialization. Leaders of nationalist organizations loyal to the tsar blamed Jews
for all of these problems. In the province of Bessarabia, the influential and
government-funded daily newspaper *Bessarabets* charged Jews with killing a
young Christian boy, and urged local patriots to "Crusade Against the Hated
Race!" The bishop of Kishinev publicly declared that Jews committed ritual
murder as part of Passover observance. And once again, the revolutionary
organizations straddled the fence, asserting the brotherhood of all workers
while sputtering rage at "Jewish exploiters."

On April 19 and 20, 1903, starting on Easter Sunday, a pogrom swept
the city of Kishinev that shocked the world. It left 47 dead, 424 wounded,
700 houses burned, and 600 shops looted. On the first day, artisans, students,
and laborers led the violence. On the second day, peasants rushed into town
from small surrounding villages to join the looting. Neither the governor nor
the local garrison commander intervened. In some areas police and troops
participated. Rumors of Jewish revolutionary activities deepened their ire.
Five months later, an argument between a Jewish fishmonger and a Christian
peasant sparked a similar riot in the heavily Jewish town of Gomel. Hundreds
of railroad workers surged through a Jewish neighborhood beating people
and burning homes, but strong Jewish self-defense squads had been organized
in the wake of the Kishinev attack. International newspaper accounts reported heavy hand-to-hand combat in which women as well as men fought
the rioters. When 1,600 Russian troops were called to restore peace, they
broke ranks, some joining in the assault, some genuinely attempting to restore
peace. The death toll might have been worse had not so many Jews resisted.

In the end ten Jews and eight Christians were killed. Observers called Gomel a turning point: No more would Jews greet their attackers passively (Lambroza, 1992: 195–247).

Still, Gomel did not end the violence. Each time the Russian army suffered losses in the disastrous 1904–1905 war against Japan, demobilized soldiers attacked Jewish villages and urban neighborhoods, falsely charging all Jews with collaboration and war profiteering. There were 24 draft riots in 1904 alone that targeted Ukrainian Jews; there were 43 pogroms between 1903 and 1904. The violence escalated dramatically in 1905, with 657 pogroms and more than 3,000 deaths. Jews were blamed by different factions for Russia's loss in the war with Japan, for being instigators of revolutionary agitation, for unfair competition in the workplace, and for high prices. That October, mobs of Ukrainian peasants and workers rampaged against any Jews they could find in hundreds of cities, towns, and villages. Thousands were killed or injured. In Odessa, police reported the deaths of 400 Jews and 100 non-Jews in one pogrom alone. Later historical estimates cited casualties of between 800 and 2,500 (Weinberg, 1992: 248–89).

Rose Kaplan, a fierce, dark-eyed emigre from Odessa, recalls that the highly assimilated Odessan Jewish population was caught off-guard by these early 20th-century pogroms. Many Jews were genuinely shocked to be the object of such fierce hatred. In the twenty years of relative peace since Tsar Alexander's assassination, many middle-class Jews, like Kaplan's family, had come to think of themselves as Russian first and Jewish second. In the aftermath of the pogroms, Odessan Jews began to form self-defense groups which Kaplan believes brought a generation of young Jewish men into the revolutionary movement.

Like thousands of other young Jews, Kaplan's brother moved from a Jewish self-defense organization to a revolutionary cell. Anti-Semitic nationalists, says Kaplan, worked as informers for the Odessan police, helping them to uncover these underground groups. Kaplan's brother was turned in by an informer inside his organization and sentenced to a lengthy prison term.

"My brother was not even 18 years old when they sent him to Siberia," she says. "He was just walking in the middle of the city when they stopped him and arrested him. My mother used to travel along to see him in jail. She would say to my brother: 'Your father says that God said that the tsar will be here forever.' So my brother said: 'Mama, if it will not be in my time, it will be in my children's, my grandchildren's, my great grandchildren's time. There will come a time when there will be a revolution in Russia.' That was less than 10 years before the Revolution came."

THE RUSSIAN REVOLUTION AND ITS AFTERMATH

World War I had a profound impact on the Jews of the Russian Empire. Much of the fighting took place in the Pale of Jewish settlement. As many as 600,000 Jews were displaced from their homes and another 500,000 Jews served in the tsar's army. The poorly fed and clothed Russian army fared miserably in the war, and charges of Jewish draft evasion and collaboration with the enemy were once again heard in the taverns where demobilized Russian veterans drank. The tsar's government helped to incite greater tensions by issuing a warning that, because so many Russian Jews had relatives in other countries, they could not be trusted to remain true to Russia. Watch them, tsarist propaganda urged, for they might be functioning as agents of Russia's enemies. All correspondence and all publications in Yiddish and Hebrew were banned for the duration of the war (Kenez, 1992: 243–313; Ettinger, 1970: 15–30).

The 1917 Revolution and withdrawal of Russia from the war effort made matters worse. Ukrainian nationalists, in open rebellion against the Bolsheviks, blamed Jews for being both pro-revolutionary and pro-Russian. In 1919, as the civil war between Bolsheviks and White Army forces raged, Russian Jewry experienced the worst violence in its history, second only to the Nazi Holocaust of World War II. With the start of the new year, an independent Ukrainian nationalist force under S. V. Petliura began to slaughter Jews indiscriminately. They killed tens of thousands before the winter of 1919 was over. After an abortive Bolshevik rising in the Western Ukraine, Petliura's forces slaughtered 2,000 Jewish noncombatants in three hours. The White Army under Generals L. G. Kornilov and A. I. Denikin was no better. From looting villages and raping women in the early summer of 1919, organized Cossack violence escalated to mass murder. In groups of five they would enter the villages, break into houses, and demand property. Jews were shot, bayoneted, hanged, burned, or buried up to their necks in the sand to be run over by Cossack horses. Kiev researcher Gusev Orenburgskii estimates that 200,000 died. More conservative scholars estimate 10 percent of the Ukrainian Jewry was killed that year. This was the era in which the oldest Soviet emigres to the United States came of age (Kenez, 1992: 297–302).

Riva Rabinowitz, born in a village near Kiev, remembers growing up in the midst of a "storm in the life" of small-town Russian Jews. Sitting in her immaculate Brighton Beach apartment, she recalled long-ago terror, her soft voice and carefully coiffed white hair trembling as she spoke:

The First World War came in 1914. And then we had a revolution in 1917 and then a civil war in our part of Russia. That's how long already we had a storm in the life of the *shtetl.* It was a storm for all Russia but especially the *shtetl* because we were so traditional there and because we were so easy to pick out. I cannot possibly forget the time when the war was already over and the Revolution was already raging a long time, how every little group of ragged soldiers was killing Jews, killing young girls, raping and killing. The *pogromchiks* were not like regular soldiers. They were ex-soldiers who weren't part of a regiment anymore. And without leaders they made themselves crazy. Mostly they were from the White Army. And they were running away from the Red Army and they would stop along the way to make pogroms against the Jews and to take all of their possessions. I remember one night they raped maybe 40, 50 girls in our small town. And in the morning we found them all laying dead.

The 1919 pogroms darkly illustrate the persistence of rabid anti-Semitism among average people in the Soviet Union. Ukrainian nationalists and officers of the White Army spread the false charge that Jews were primarily responsible for the Revolution, for the Soviet state, for Russia's domination. This came on the heels of tsarist government propaganda blaming Jews for Russia's military failures in World War I. The government claimed Jews were the source of all Russia's problems, the germ that had infected the body politic with strange, modern ideologies. Jews were "cosmopolitans" with no national loyalties. They were never to be trusted.

For those Russian Jews who could not escape to the United States in the terrible years after the Revolution, there was no haven in the villages of the former Pale. Yenta Katz was five years old when Ukrainian soldiers stormed her small town of Kozimick, near the city of Minsk. Fearing attack, the men had evacuated the town's women and children. Katz's brother survived to tell her how their father and 17 other Jewish men died that day. Yenta Katz an animated, diminutive woman, gestured angrily as she told the story of her father's murder:

The massacres came when the Ukrainian soldiers had to escape the Red Army. They were everywhere killing Jews. All month we were hearing about how there was a pogrom in this town near us and that one. We knew that it would soon be coming to us, this pogrom lust. So the women with the children left to go to another town. My mother and I were among them. It was early morning and all the men were in synagogue. One of the Ukrainians shot a pistol in the air to warn the others to come. They came in on horses. They pogromized. My father died in that pogrom. He was running through the streets and they shot his head full of holes. They murdered 18 Jews in our town that day.

Yenta Katz in her Brighton Beach apartment.

With few other options and little hope, many small-town Russian Jews came to see the Bolshevik army as their saviors. This view was reinforced when the Red Army liberated the small towns in the wake of White Army pogroms. Young Jewish men and women who had joined the Red Army to fight for the Revolution would speak in Yiddish to the gathered villagers, promising to build a new country in which Jews would be full citizens. Smiling, as if flushed with the relief she felt so many years ago Riva Rabinowitz recalled: "So when the Red Army would march in and say, 'Come out. It's just us. Don't be afraid,' we came out. It was something for us not to be afraid because at that time everybody was killing Jews. But there were a lot of Jewish boys in the Red Army and so we were not afraid. That was still before the Red Army changed." Overcome with gratitude, many young people pledged themselves to the Revolution. Sometimes whole villages would follow the Red Army, moved less by their zeal for socialism than by their fear that the White Army might return.

Though nearly 90, Pearl Itsky, a retired seamstress for Slutsk, vividly remembered the day her town was liberated by the Red Army. A deeply religious woman, Itsky was observing the Jewish fast day of Tisha B'av on the hot August afternoon she related her story. She served her visitors ice water but would not allow herself any.

After the war *pogromchiks* came to our town and we would have to hide in our cellars and under our roofs. Then the Red Army came to our town and they sang a revolutionary song: 'Who is the world for? The world is for us, the workers!' We had all suffered so much from the war and from the tsar. And then the Red Army gave us what to wear and what to eat. They weren't mean or violent like the tsar's soldiers. They gave out a couple of pounds of sugar and milk and flour to everyone. Do you know what it means when you're starving? At the time the Communists weren't bothering Jews yet. So, many Jewish people in my town joined the movement. Some even became Communist leaders.

There were many reasons for Jewish enthusiasm about the Bolshevik Revolution. One of the first things that the provisional government did when tsarism fell in March 1917 was to grant Russian Jews legal equality. Over the next few years, there was a blossoming of Jewish political and social activity all across Russia. Towns and villages were encouraged to elect local governments, and many Jews were elected to municipal office. All restrictions on Yiddish and Hebrew publishing were lifted and there was a veritable explosion of Jewish newspaper and book publishing. The Bolshevik leadership also supported the creation of a system of secular Jewish education with locally run kindergartens, secondary schools, teachers' seminaries, and colleges. Yiddish was recognized as the national language of Soviet Jewry. Classroom instruction in the national mother tongue was not only permitted but encouraged (Ettinger, 1978).

For many Jews in the most remote villages of the old Pale it would take years before they were touched by either the hope or the terror of the revolutionary years. Nechama Sirotina, one of Soviet Russia's most famous Yiddish actresses, was born in Dobryanka, on the border of Byelorussia and the Ukraine in 1917, the year of the Bolshevik takeover. Into the early 1920s her village life continued as it had for centuries—Jews, Byelorussians, and Ukrainians living together in relative peace and deep poverty. "In our town there was only one stone building. The rest were made of wood. All the people were farmers and all the land was bad." Jews and non-Jews alike were fairly sympathetic to the Bolsheviks, she says. Everyone was hoping for an easier life. In 1922, when she was five, the first Bolshevik officials arrived in her town to celebrate the new holidays of May 1 (International Workers Day) and October 8 (the symbolic birthday of the Revolution). As a daughter of the Revolution, she was chosen to greet them. It was the beginning of a lifetime of public speaking and performance. "I was young and I had a pretty face and a very nice voice," she recalls. "I was to symbolize the new Russia, the young country. It was beautiful for just a while. But soon times got bad. The Ukrainian soldiers found us. They dragged rabbis and religious men through the streets by their beards. Jews could not live any longer in our town. So with everything on our backs, we decided to try and find a better place." During this period of cyclical violence, between 1881 and 1921, over 2 million Russian and Polish Jews emigrated, seeking that "better place" in the United States. Those who remained became citizens of the new Soviet state.

THE OKTYEBRAWNOK GENERATION: CHILDREN OF THE REVOLUTION, 1919–1937

We who were born in Russia before the Second War were raised to believe in the spirit of equality, that all people are the same. It was really good when people believed we were all the same, when nobody cared about nationality, when we helped each other as if there were no differences between people. OK. You know what? I would like it to have been like that. I wish it was. But I know it wasn't.
—*Sophie Spector, English teacher, Brighton Beach YM-YWHA senior center*

During the early 1920s it still seemed possible for Jews to find both safety and freedom in the new Soviet Union. Vladimir Ilyich Lenin and his inner circle, while insisting on the supremacy of the Communist Party elite, recognized that the success of their new government would depend on their ability to win the allegiance of the disparate ethnic and national groups formerly ruled by the tsars. To convince restive Ukrainians, Armenians, Georgians, and other nationalities that the Bolsheviks didn't intend simply to reassert Russian dominance, Lenin authorized Article 2 of the 1917 Declaration of the Rights of the Peoples of Russia, which guaranteed to all peoples under Bolshevik rule "the right of self determination." This declaration laid the groundwork for a new multinational state, the Union of Soviet Socialist Republics. In theory at least, the Bolsheviks promised limited self-government as well as linguistic and cultural autonomy for the diverse population they now set out to rule. Though neither Lenin nor his successor, Joseph Stalin, considered Jews a "legitimate nationality"—because they lacked territory and because they were geographically dispersed—Soviet Jews benefited to some extent from this stated Bolshevik commitment to multiculturalism and decentralized government (Sawyer, 1979: 1–25).

Most Jewish religious schools, theaters, libraries, and synagogues were unmolested for at least a decade after the Revolution. In some small towns they remained open until the outbreak of World War II. Jews were granted equal rights with all other Soviet citizens. And Lenin, building on Karl Marx's axiom that a country's treatment of its Jews was an index of its modernity, argued forcefully and publicly that anti-Semitism had no place in a socialist state. In 1919 he wrote an article, "Concerning Jewish Pogroms," in which he insisted that "Jews are not the enemy of the workers. . . . They are our brothers of oppression by capitalism, our comrades in the struggle for socialism. . . . The shame is for them who sow animosity toward the Jews, who sow hate toward other people" (Lenin cited in Sawyer, 1979: 13).

By the mid-1920s there was an attempt by some in the Soviet leadership, like President Mikhail Kalinin, to transform the Jews into a full-fledged Soviet nationality. Kalinin encouraged Jews to abandon their lives in towns and cities and become farmers. By the mid-1930s there were 500 Jewish collective farms in the Soviet Union, with 225,000 Jews engaged in agriculture in Byelorussia, Crimea, and the Ukraine. And in 1927 Stalin created the "autonomous" region of Birobidzhan, which, he claimed, would finally make real Jewish claims of "nationhood" by giving them what they had always lacked: a territory of their own. Stalin's not-so-secret ulterior motive, as he moved to consolidate power and to isolate supporters of his main rival Leon Trotsky, was to resettle the Jewish Communist leadership as far from Moscow and Leningrad as possible. Very few took the bait. Removed as it was from the traditional centers of Jewish settlement in Western Russia and the Ukraine, Birobidzhan was a complete failure (Abramsky, 1978: 64–77).

Communist Party leaders were far more successful in recruiting young Jewish artists and teachers to proselytize for the growth of a nonreligious "proletarian" Jewish culture in the Jewish towns and cities of the Ukraine, Moldavia, and Byelorussia. Jewish Communists tapped into the rich secular Jewish culture that had developed in many small towns during the revolutionary era, producing a vital body of literature, theater, and political theory in the vernacular Yiddish rather than in the sacred Hebrew language. This new revolutionary secular Judaism was particularly strong in the Ukraine, where approximately one-third of Soviet Jews lived by the 1930s. In the 1925, the Ukraine boasted 250 Jewish schools, an institute of Jewish culture that was part of the Ukrainian academy of sciences, and Jewish theatrical companies. As late as 1935 there were 10 Yiddish newspapers in the Ukraine. It was the center of Jewish cultural life in post-revolutionary Russia (Levenberg, 1978: 30–46).

During her childhood in Tchorny Ostrov in the Ukraine, Lyuba Halberstam saw both the destruction of Jewish religious culture and the promotion of secular Jewish identity. A strongly built woman with thick white hair, Halberstam showed traces of her Red Army past in the formality of her bearing and speech. She recalled:

I remember when I was a very little child we still had some synagogues. They weren't synagogues as you might see in a big town. They were very very tiny. But it was the policy of the government that the Jewish religion had to vanish. So they closed these synagogues, and in one they made a power station. Still the big one stayed until the beginning of the Second World War.

But while there was an all-out assault on religion, there was lip-service paid to allowing ethnic minorities to develop revolutionary versions of their national cultures, at least until the Stalinist purges of the late 1930s. After 1937, said Halberstam, when Stalin's intense anti-Semitism had begun to manifest in bloody purges and show trials, all Jewish content was eliminated from these schools. Students were still taught in the Yiddish language but the content was completely culture-neutral. "In Yiddish school," she recalled, "we learned the Yiddish, Russian, and Ukrainian languages. We had geography and the general history of the country. Specifically Jewish history was not taught because it was considered to be connected to religious studies. But there was math, chemistry, and physics. For all of these subjects they had textbooks in Yiddish."

As a young girl Nechama Sirotina also felt the freedom to develop a proud, if secular Jewish identity. Perhaps the most famous of Soviet Jewish cultural institutions during the prepurge years was Solomon Mikhoels' Moscow Yiddish Theater. In 1933, the renowned director was given permission to travel to small Jewish towns throughout Byelorussia and the Ukraine to seek bright young children for his theater school in Moscow. "He came to Gomel," Sirotina recalled, "because he heard there was talent there." Sirotina, then 15, was among the lucky few chosen for the new revolutionary Yiddish theater company. Excited and hopeful, she left family and friends behind and boarded the train for the roughly 400-mile trek north to Moscow. That same evening, half asleep, she thought she heard the wheels of the train chanting, "gayen di yidn; gayen di yidn" (the Jews are going). "The Jews are always going someplace else," Sirotina thought. "And I have become one of those wandering Jews."

She arrived in Moscow during an exciting cultural moment for Soviet Jews. One night in January, 1935, at a gala event at the Bolshoi Theater, Stalin himself led a standing ovation for Mikhoels and his leading man, Binyamin Zuskin. Some observers believe that Stalin's public lauding of these and other Jewish artists was a cover for purges of Stalin's Jewish political rivals that had already begun. Later, Mikhoels and Zuskin too would become targets of Stalin's rage, but on this heady night in Moscow, the city's Jewish cultural elite was understandably elated (Vaksberg, 1994: 67–68).

Many young Jews continued to believe well into the 1930s that the Revolution would bring positive changes. Lyuba Halberstam was a devout Com-

Lyuba Halberstam in her Brighton Beach apartment.

munist in her youth until local leaders decided that having close relations in America made her no longer trustworthy. She was angry, though she thought it was all rather silly.

I was a true *Oktyebrawnok*. That means child of the Revolution. That's what they called the first generation born after the 1917 Revolution. And that's what they called the political organization for children. It was like what is here called the Scouts. In high school I was a *Komsomol* [the Communist youth organization]. But I had a problem politically. My mother's parents and her brothers all lived in America. They had moved before the Revolution. They used to send us packages to help out. Somehow the people in *Komsomol* found out about this. They had a special meeting to decide what to do about me and they decided that I was the relative of a capitalist. And so they threw me out. After they threw me out I never joined again.

Disillusionment came hard for Jews who had believed in the Communist ideal, but Riva Rabinowitz said that she could see it coming even before Stalin's systematic persecutions. Rabinowitz's young husband had been imprisoned and threatened with execution for speaking out against abuses by local party leaders in the late 1920s. The two later staged a daring escape from the country at a time when almost no one could get out. Interviewed more than a half century later, Rabinowitz's eyes grew dark and her elegant features hardened as she described the Bolshevik betrayal:

I'll tell you something about Communism. In my town we did think it was the right thing, that the Revolution was true and ideal. They wanted everyone should live together and be together in their hearts and share together in brother-love. It was a wonderful idea. It's not what happened after the Revolution finally ended. But it was a wonderful idea. Unfortunately, once the Bolsheviki were in power they became big shots like everybody else. If you spoke against them they killed you. It was all black and white to them. Either you were with them or you were a counter-revolutionary and they killed you. We suffered, the Jews suffered again, just like before the Revolution.

"THE TERRIBLE YEARS," 1937–1945

The terrible years began in 1937 to 38 when we cannot sleep every night because we can feel that another neighbor has been taken.
—*Dr. Bertha Klimkovich of Borisov, Minsk, now retired and living in Brooklyn*

Like earlier Russian revolutionary movements, the Bolsheviks had always carried mixed messages to the Soviet people about Russian Jewry and anti-

Semitism. On the one hand they condemned racism and nationalist ideologies that asserted the cultural, religious, or biological superiority of any one group. On the other they adapted and revitalized old-fashioned Slavic anti-Semitism. Though his visceral hatred of Jews was rooted in his Georgian childhood, Joseph Stalin did not need to turn to "reactionary" nationalist tracts, or to the forbidden Orthodox Church to affirm his anti-Semitism. The foundational literature of Soviet Communism is rife with many of the most poisonous of 19th-century European stereotypes of Jews and the Jewish religion. Stalin could turn to the theoretical father of Communism himself to validate his personal prejudices.

The son of a Jewish lawyer who converted to Lutheranism, Karl Marx seemed in some of his writings to have swallowed European anti-Semitic iconography whole. The most venomous of his works in this regard was his fantasy, *A World Without Jews*, in which he portrayed his grandparents' co-religionists as the symbol and embodiment of capitalist money-lust: "What is the object of the Jew's worship in this world: Usury. What is his worldly God? Money. . . . Money is the zealous one God of Israel besides which no other God may stand. . . . The social emancipation of Jewry is the emancipation of society from Jewry" (Marx cited in Sawyer, 1979: 4–5).

Like the Russian populists of the late 19th century, Marx insisted that he was speaking figuratively about a certain kind of Jew whom he was using to symbolize the worst abuses of capitalism and who was the enemy of working-class Jews as much as of working-class Christians. But his choice of symbol is telling. And one can easily imagine the inflammatory effect that such words might have on men and women raised with the historic image of the Jew as a literal sucker of Christian blood.

While not anti-Semitic in the way that Stalin was, the Bolsheviks' first ruler, Lenin, certainly provided his protégé with ideological grounds for the repression of Jewish religious and cultural expression in the Soviet Union. Lenin condemned as "manifestly reactionary" any claims to Jewish nationhood, and argued that the only "progressive" course of action for Jews was total assimilation. "Assimilation can be cried down only by the reactionary Jewish petty bourgeois who want to turn the wheel of history back," he wrote (Lenin, 1961: 139). On such politically unassailable foundations it was relatively easy for the deeply anti-Semitic Stalin to convince many Soviet citizens that Jews were, by definition, dangerous enemies of the revolution. Even as he continued to mouth a "progressive" line, publicly repudiating all forms of nationalism and racism, Stalin systematized persecution of Soviet Jewry, beginning in the late 1930s with a series of purges that wiped out many of the best-known leaders of the revolutionary generation.

Living in the sheltered and privileged world of the Moscow Yiddish Theater School, Nechama Sirotina did not see political trouble coming until 1937, when Stalin began to arrest anyone who might have been perceived as a political rival. After a series of well-publicized show trials he imprisoned and quickly executed most of the Jews who had attained high positions in the Communist Party. Then he moved on to high-ranking military officers, decimating the top command of the Red Army. Finally he turned to intellectuals, artists and writers. Suddenly, Sirotina recalls, her friends in the theater world began looking over their shoulders. One never knew who was next (Vaksberg, 1994: 80–102).

Though it is sometimes said that the purges of 1937–1938 targeted mostly well-known intellectuals and top party officials, Bertha Klimkovich remembers that a sense of growing urgency gripped her town as the Stalinist terror closed in. Born in 1924 in Borisov, Minsk, the red-haired, dark-eyed pediatrician recalled a slow but steady erosion of Jewish religious life throughout the 1930s:

When I was a little girl I remember my grandfather took me to synagogue. We made matzoh for Passover. There was still a Jewish school and a synagogue. My husband was two years older and he studied in a Jewish school for two years. But when I started school in 1932, the Jewish school closed. And then the synagogue. Then the Jewish people prayed in a small house. And at Passover we covered the windows with cloths. But the terrible years began in 1937–38 when we cannot sleep every night because we can feel that another neighbor has been taken. Another left every day, every night. Without any reason, somebody came knocking at the door and took someone away. This was Stalin's purges. This terrible time lasted until 1939. And then two years after, the Germans invaded.

Lyuba Halberstam was a 22-year-old student at the University in Kiev in 1939, when Stalin's foreign minister, Vyacheslav Molotov, signed a nonagression pact with Nazi Foreign Minister Joachim von Ribbentrop: "I remember reading about it in the newspapers. And I'll tell you something. At that time we were glad. We didn't understand about Hitler but we knew war was coming and we didn't want to have to fight. Only after 1939 when Jews started coming from Poland to Russia to escape the Nazis, then we began to know a little bit about Hitler."

Some Jewish members of the Communist Party, who criticized the alliance openly despite the potential consequences, questioned how the world's lead-ing socialist power could make peace with the Fascists, who had always been their enemies. Most, however, observed a stunned silence. Well-known test pilot Mark Gallai wrote later:

For my generation the 22 months between the signing of our nonaggression pact with Hitler and the outbreak of the war were strange and incomprehensible. . . . The Fascists were no longer called Fascists—it became impossible to find the word in the press and even in semi-official lectures and speeches. What we had been taught to abhor as hostile, evil and menacing . . . suddenly became, as it were, neutral. This was not stated in so many words, but the feeling stole into our souls as we looked at photographs of Molotov standing next to Hitler, or read reports of Soviet grain and oil flowing into Fascist Germany, or watched the Prussian goose step being introduced at that very time into our armed forces. Yes, it was very difficult to understand what was what! (Gallai cited in Ainsztein, 1978: 282–83)

The uncomfortable alliance was shattered in June 1941, when Nazi forces invaded the Soviet Union. Stalin adopted a scorched-earth policy, destroying tens of thousands of farms and villages to rob the German army of food. Millions of Soviet civilians were evacuated from the major cities to the Cen-tral Asian republics. Others were stranded far from their homes and spent the war on the run. Sixteen-year-old Bertha Klimkovich was studying in Leningrad when the Germans invaded her hometown of Borisov. Full of fear for her parents and siblings, she tried to return home, but her train was stopped at Smolensk by German bombs. She never saw her family again. Klimkovich headed back to live with relatives in Moscow, all of whom were later evacuated to the countryside. She continued to move throughout the war, always staying a few miles ahead of the German army.

Maya Shkolnikov, a sturdy blonde schoolteacher, was born in Gomel in 1930. She was just eleven when the Germans invaded. Like Klimkovich, Shkolnikov lost touch with her father early in the war, but her mother kept the rest of the family together:

When the war began in 1941, I was in the third grade. And we moved to Varonezh. We stayed just a couple of months because the German army came to Varonezh. So we moved to Kirghizstan. While we were in Kirghizstan my father came to us. But in 1942, January 1st, he went to the army. And he was killed in May. I cannot say whether he was fighting. We don't know what happened. My mother worked in the factory and we went to school. Mostly we were hungry so we just think about bread all the time.

While some found shelter during the war, half a million Jews joined the Red Army to fight against the Nazis. Many volunteered for service on the front lines. Victor Ourin ran away from his small Ukrainian town in 1939 at the age of 15 to become a poet in Moscow. The tall, gangly poet shakes his wild grey hair and gestures broadly as he tells his story in a rumbling baritone:

At 17, I was already in the war. I was in a small unit sent to fight against Fascism, against Hitler. We were sent off to defend the Motherland, Mother Russia. It was then that I wrote my first real poems. These were poems against Fascism, what it meant for people. My favorite of these was of a dream I had, of world brotherhood. I wanted to meet, as fast as I could, my American brothers, at the Oder River in Germany. I wanted to meet them in friendship, to celebrate the defeat of Fascism, and to begin the work of building peace in all the world.

But the romance of Ourin's dream mists the horror that Soviet soldiers, particularly Jews, encountered. Anxious about her family, wanting to do her part, Lyuba Halberstam joined the Red Army in 1942. Her recollections offer a rare glimpse into the lives of Russian women who served in combat roles more than half a century ago:

Still at that time we were patriots of the country. We didn't think the Russian government was against the people. So as a student I quickly volunteered and I became a soldier. The women had to replace the men who were killed. So we were in the same situation. We had to carry guns, just like the men, and we had to carry big packs. I also had to carry a big radio because I was in the radio battalion. It was all women and we would serve in the field to connect the different fighting units. We told them where to go, where the guns had to shoot. At the same time they expected us to do the things that women do. So we had to make bread and clean around camp.

Halberstam's first combat experience was at the 1942 battle of Stalingrad, the battle that changed the course of the war as the Soviet army delivered the first decisive defeat to the Germans. But the victory was won at terrible cost. "When they brought us to this battle," Halberstam recalls, "we were very raw."

So most of my friends were killed in the first few days. Those who lived, by the end, we were old, not girls any more. One time a lady lieutenant and six of our girls and I were surrounded. The lieutenant and I hid and we saw the Germans throw the other girls alive into a fire. With God's help the two of us survived. A peasant saw us hiding and he gave us clothes so that we could look like civilians.

She told this story sitting behind her desk at the tiny Brooklyn office of the Association of Soviet Jewish War Veterans and Invalids of World War II. By the time she was finished, quiet tears rolled down her cheeks.

Halberstam survived the war, but 1.5 million Soviet Jews, mostly civilians, did not. When the surviving Jews returned to their hometowns they found that, once again, much of southwestern Russia had been turned into a killing field. The Nazi *Einsatzgruppen*, the soldiers assigned the task of slaughtering Soviet Jewry, were far more systematic and efficient in their terrible task than even the White Army had been. Nazi occupiers murdered one in two Soviet Jews. Entire families were killed, entire towns erased. Halberstam was determined to find out what had happened to her family. She could find no information about her mother until she encountered a small group of survivors from her town near the end of the war. Later she found people who knew about her father and brothers:

On the day I had to take my final exams at Kiev University, the Germans occupied my parents' town. I had no news of my parents for months, no connection at all. Later people told me that my family tried to get out on horses. But they were stopped on the way by Hitler. My mother, my father, my brothers and all my relatives. They separated the men and women. The soldiers took all the Jewish men and at the city of Vinitsa they made them build an underground bunker. They used ten thousand men to build it and when they were done they shot them all. My father and brothers died that way. I don't even know where they are. . . .

My mother they took to a ghetto where she lived from 1941 to 1942. Then right before Yom Kippur, they took out all the Jewish people from that ghetto and they shot them. They were killed in a forest. I know where this place is now. They took them down into a valley which was so deep that no one standing outside it could hear the cries inside. And one by one they killed them all. . . .

How do I know this? Some young people just fell down. When the Germans shot them they fell down and pretended to be dead. And then when everything was finished they crawled out from that place. In this place now there is a monument. But because there is still anti-Semitism among the Ukrainian people, this monument was destroyed, two, three times. The Jewish people kept rebuilding it and again they would ruin it. So now it is just a small stone that doesn't say anything about Jews. It just says, "For the victims of Fascism." Under that stone my mother is buried.

Bertha Klimkovich did not get back to Borisov until 1946, but she too found that there was no one left: "From the Russian neighbors I learned what it was. It was a terrible time. The people told me the earth was still bleeding for several days after. They murdered many, many relatives. My father, my mother, my grandfather, my aunt, many, many cousins." Her voice shaking, she trails off into silence.

The Jews of Odessa were not formally evacuated but many tried to leave on their own. Sophie Spector's family decided that the one sister with children should be the one to try to escape before the Germans reached the city. She left with her mother and, like so many other survivors, she didn't find out until war's end what had happened to her loved ones. The stylishly dressed English teacher tells this story in her spartan office at the Brighton Beach Senior Center:

We were going to wait for the rest of the family at Novorossisyk. But very quickly the Germans came and occupied Odessa, and no more ships were allowed out. The rest of my family, all my aunts, uncles, cousins, they stayed in Odessa and they died there. We did not find out what happened to them until the end of the war and then we couldn't even go to the place where they were killed. The Germans took all the Jews from Odessa somewhere else to kill them. . . . We were hidden in a peasant woman's house on the road from Novorossisyk to Chikalov. It was dangerous for her to keep us there. But she would not let us move out. So we stayed there until the war was finished. I wanted to show you from this example that anti-Semitism does not start from the Russian people. It is the government that makes it.

Still, Spector is bitter about how little credit Jews got for their service in the Revolution and in the Red Army during World War II.

Jews were really patriots. They defended their country every step of the way. And after the war, after all the Jewish blood that was pouring out at the front and in the streets of the towns, and after Babi Yar and so many other valleys like that, not one word about the Jewish people buried in mass graves during the war. Not one word about the Jewish soldiers that were killed. These people were real heroes. Real Russian heroes. That's why for us it is so painful to be treated like this by the country we loved. That's why I love America so much. Here we came and we did nothing for this country and yet we're getting so much.

AFTER THE WAR: THE ANNIHILATION OF SOVIET JEWISH CULTURE, 1945–1954

After the horror of the war years, Soviet Jews tried to return to some semblance of normal life. Instead many encountered deep bitterness and outright hostility from those among whom they'd lived all their lives. Years of German occupation had left their imprint. Nazi ideology mixed with

Sophie Spector in her office at the Shorefront YM-YWHA, Brighton Beach.

native Russian anti-Semitism, creating an ugly atmosphere to which many Jews returned after the war's end. Despite serving in the military in numbers that far exceeded their representation in the nation's population, they were branded as cowards and draft dodgers. Though both Jewish and non-Jewish refugee families had been evacuated to unoccupied regions of Central Asia, there was a prevailing notion that Jews had fled there to avoid fighting in the war. A popular post-war joke had the "Jewish army" conquering Tashkent, a central Asian city where there were no Nazi invaders. Zvi Portnoi entered his apartment building in Kiev for the first time after the war to cold welcome from his neighbors. One girl with whom he had been raised, now a woman, shouted: "I'll go and tell the Germans that the *Zhids* [a derogatory term for Jews] are back."

Sophie Spector was devastated on her return to Odessa by revelations that people she grew up with had helped the German soldiers to murder their Jewish neighbors. She raps her desk rhythmically with a tightly balled fist as she recalls:

It is not written on a Jew that he is a Jew. Many times he could hide it. The Germans never knew for sure. But there were Ukrainians and Russians in Odessa who knew who was a Jew. And they would say to the Germans, "Don't let him go. This is a Jew." There were many traitors and some of these are still around. It was terrible to learn about them, to live with them after the war.

Bloody anti-Semitic outbreaks were recorded in Odessa after the war. In peace, as in war, Jews were afraid to venture out at night. It was not easy to return to normal. But Spector cautions against branding all Russians and Ukrainians as anti-Semitic collaborators. "To be fair," she says, "there were also many who helped. Especially Russian women, young women, who picked up wounded men in the streets and forests and took care of them and hid them. This is how many Jewish men married Russian women after the war. And there were many peasants who were very good to us. Like the woman we stayed with. It cost her a lot."

As was so often the case for Russian Jews, local anti-Semitism was fueled and recharged by government propaganda and persecutions. Shortly after the war, as Stalin entered his increasingly paranoid last years, a new wave of official anti-Jewish persecution was unleashed.

Irena Lunts, a blonde physician now practicing in Long Island, was born just before the war to an upper-middle-class Jewish family in Talin, Estonia. She was sent with her entire family into exile in Siberia for the crime of owning a downtown store: "They sent my father to the gulag as a capitalist. There was no court or anything. My mother and I were also sent to Siberia, to exile. My father was in a typical gulag like Solzhenitsyn describes, but he survived."

Stalin's worst enmity in the years after the war was reserved for Jewish writers. One of the first to receive censure was Boris Pasternak, most famous in the United States as the author of the sweeping novel of revolution and war, *Doctor Zhivago*. Pasternak had first come under attack during the 1930s purges for his criticism of Communist restrictions on artistic freedom. Most famous for his translations of Shakespeare's plays and poems, he believed that he survived the purge years by translating Stalin's favorite Georgian poets into Russian. But after the war, Pasternak was named an enemy of the Soviet people. His ability to publish and to travel was severely restricted.

Poet Victor Ourin, who studied with Pasternak for many years, is still amazed at how the change came about:

It was difficult to be a poet under Stalin. I remember during the time when the Germans were dropping bombs on Moscow, Pasternak had duty on the roof of his building. He watched the sky and it was burning and he was terrified. He wrote a poem about his fear, about the horror of war. It was a great poem. But the Writer's Union censored it because they said it was not good for the Soviet Union to appear before the world as if her people were scared. He said: "I was not writing about all of the people of the Soviet Union. I do not mean to say that all of the people of the Soviet Union are as scared of war as I. I was writing only about me, my feelings, my fear." They would not budge. "Poetry influences the people," they told him. "Poetry must instruct them how not to be afraid."

Pasternak survived, unable to publish or read his poetry, by translating Shakespeare, Goethe and Stalin's other favorite poets into Russian. Few of those who wrote or performed in Yiddish were as lucky. Between 1947 and his death in 1953, Stalin set out to destroy the remnants of the Jewish intelligentsia in the Soviet Union, and with them what was left of the culture of what was once more than 3 million Soviet Jews. Nechama Sirotina recalls:

Stalin started to kill the very best Jewish writers and actors in the Soviet Union. There were 14 Jewish theaters in the USSR before the war. In only two years after the war, they killed them all, all the greatest Jewish artists in Russia. First of all they went after Mikhoels. He was killed in 1948. They tried to discredit him by saying he was a spy but we all knew. He was a great Jewish leader not only in the theater but for the country.

Solomon Mikhoels, with Stalin's approval, had toured the United States during the war to raise money and collect clothing from American Jews. That provided the pretext for the spying accusation. In an interview conducted 32 years later, Nechama Sirotina—with the restraint and nuance of a great actress—described her beloved teacher's murder and funeral:

The American Jews gave to Mikhoels a gold cigarette case. He was very proud of it. When they arrested him and killed him, they ran his body over with a crane. The cigarette case was crushed right into his flesh. We were like made of iron when we carried him to the train. When we arrived in Moscow there were crowds, people from Minsk, and other cities, from every *shtetl* where we had played. They came to see him one last time. Everyone was scared to be seen there, scared of Stalin but

Nechama Sirotina recalls the final years of the Moscow Yiddish Theater after World War II.

they came anyway. This was the biggest funeral of that time except for when [Russian writer Maxim] Gorky died. The goodbyes seemed endless.

Three days and three nights there was an open house in our theater for people to come to see his body. There were horses and police around everywhere. And high up above the crowd was—you've heard of the *Fiddler on the Roof*? Believe it or not, there was a man with a violin. He played all night. He played *Kaddish* [the Hebrew prayer for the dead] and *Requiem* and all the music that you play to mourn. Out in the cold of a Moscow winter night he played. The tears were running down everyone's faces. We couldn't believe he could stand there playing with his white beard blowing and his shirt open and his chest bare.

After Mikhoels' death the government closed Moscow's world-famous Yiddish theater and ordered the actors to leave Moscow. Sirotina was allowed to stay because her husband was a military officer, but he was posted far from his family and she stayed on with her young son as the persecution intensified.

Restrictions on Jewish cultural expression were eased somewhat in the years immediately following the war. A few Yiddish schools were opened in the Baltic republics acquired during the war, and the Soviet government switched from opposition to neutrality in recognizing the state of Israel in 1948. It proved a brief respite. In September of 1948, under pressure from

Soviet censors, Ilya Ehrenburg, editor of the Yiddish newspaper *Aynikayt*, published articles calling Israel a tool of American capitalism and condemning Jewish nationalism. The government dissolved the Jewish Anti-Fascist Committee, on which prominent Jewish Communists had served throughout the war years. Despite Ehrenburg's kowtowing, *Aynikayt* was closed. The remaining Yiddish schools were closed and a round of arrests began of well-known Jewish writers and actors (Weinryb, 1978: 300–31).

On the heels of Mikhoels' arrest and murder came the arrests of Perets Markesh, Itsik Feffer, Dovid Bergelson, and many of the Soviet Union's leading Jewish writers. They were held in prison without trial for three years. In 1952 the KGB arrested Yiddish theater director Binyamin Zuskin, seizing him from his bed in a mental hospital, where he had been held since suffering a nervous breakdown after the murder of his friend and mentor Mikhoels. The sweep also picked up chemist Lina Shtern, an American Communist who had moved to the Soviet Union in the 1930s. On July 11–18, 1952, 25 arrested writers, actors and cultural activists were tried secretly for being enemies of the state, "agents of U.S. imperialism" and "bourgeois National Zionism," and for allegedly trying to sever the Crimea from the Soviet Union. All but Shtern were executed in the basement of Moscow's Lubyanka prison on August 12. Shtern was sentenced to life in prison. Jewish journalists and writers from the United States demanded that the Soviet ambassador provide some hard answers about the rumored murders of these leading Jewish cultural figures. Their requests for information were met with silence (Levin, 1988: 527–29).

That year a flood of false charges was unleashed against Jewish managers of factories, employees of banks, schools, ministries, cooperatives and theaters. They were accused of "swindling and embezzling," stealing state property, and accepting bribes. Newspapers and magazines were filled with "exposures" of criminals with conspicuously Jewish names. Echoing the Nazi charges that Jews had hoarded and profiteered while their neighbors faced starvation, Jews were now accused daily by the Soviet news media of siphoning off consumer goods at a time of shortages. Stalin cleaned his house of Jews. All high-ranking Jewish military officers were forced to retire. Military academies were barred to Jews. Jews lost their jobs at planning and industrial agencies, in trade unions, information agencies and newspapers. Jewish radio announcers were charged with insufficient knowledge of the Russian language, and there were mass dismissals of Jewish students from technical institutes. In the department of philology at the University of Moscow, where, before the war, Jews constituted 40 percent of students, by 1951 only three of 250 Jewish applicants were accepted (Levin, 1988: 531–33).

History was rewritten. Jews were virtually excised from the 1952 edition of *Bolshaya Sovietskaya Entsiklopediya* (the Great Soviet Encyclopedia), receiving an article of four columns as opposed to 108 in the 1932 edition. Stalin's essay, "Marxism and the Jewish Question," was cited in the short piece to prove that, unlike other legitimate Soviet minorities, Jews were not a real nationality but "different peoples having a common origin in the ancient Hebrews."

A flurry of conspiracy trials followed. There seemed to be innumerable ways to run afoul of the Stalinist authorities simply by being Jewish. Israel Emiot, imprisoned for writing poems about Jewish partisans during World War II, and for "implanting Jewish culture artificially" into the allegedly Jewish republic of Birobidjan, later wrote of his fellow inmates in prison. He found that Jews had been arrested for cheering Zionist Golda Meyerson (later Meier) when she came to Moscow in 1948. Jewish "nationalistic" writers has been imprisoned for Zionism, elderly Jewish Communists for Trotskyism. Bukharan Jews from Samarkand and Lyubavitcher Hasidim from the Ukraine had been sentenced to hard labor for praying in public. It was easy to displease Stalin in those tense final years, especially if one was Jewish (Levin, 1988: 540).

Nechama Sirotina was paralyzed with fear when one after another of her friends were arrested and murdered during the summer of 1952:

I was alone when the next terrifying time began. They took Mikhoels' successor, Binyamin Zuskin, to a hospital—"for a rest." He was really very anxious and nervous all of the time. They gave him drugs there to make sure that he would be like in a coma, sleeping all the time. Zuskin was still asleep when the the KGB dragged him from the hospital. He woke up in the KGB office. And when he woke he found himself among all the Jewish writers he knew. At first he thought he was still in the hospital and asked his friends, "How did you come to be here?" And then he saw the bars on the windows and he knew . . .

"They're taking me to my death," he was crying. He understood right away what was happening. He understood more than many who were less crazy than he. I think it was better that they killed him right there than for the ones they sent to the camps. They died many times. Although at least some of them lived longer than Stalin and they came back to tell their stories.

The year 1953 saw Stalin's final assault on Soviet Jewry, the "Doctors' Plot." On January 13, 1953, the Moscow daily paper *Pravda* published an account of the arrest of a group of "saboteur doctors" whose purpose, according to the government, was to assassinate Soviet leaders slowly by delivering lethal medical treatments. Bertha Klimkovich, who had graduated from one of Moscow's four medical schools in the late 1940s, watched from her small town as every one of her teachers were arrested. "They were killed, imprisoned, exiled," she recalls angrily. "And they were brilliant doctors." Lydia Timashuk, the physician who supposedly "exposed" the "Doctors' Plot" was awarded the Order of Lenin for service to her country and hailed in news accounts across the country. A frenzy of news and radio diatribes against "murderer-doctors" created mass panic. According to poet Yevgeny Yevtushenko, most Soviet citizens believed the reports of Jewish medical perfidy (Gilboa, 1971: 303–308).

The "Doctor's Plot," as many Soviet Jews recognized, was simply a modern version of the traditional "ritual murder" charges levied against them. Jews in Israel and the United States noted this parallel in their letters of protest to the Soviet government. Bertha Klimkovich, then a pediatrician in the Byelorussian town of Borisov, watched fearfully as similar accusations were made against groups of Byelorussian and Odessan physicians. In the end, no charges were leveled against her, she feels, because she was a low-level provincial doctor. Most of the venom was reserved for the leading Jewish doctors in the country, heads of major hospital departments, and renowned professors in the top medical schools. For her, the change was simply one of atmosphere as she went into work day after day while the media broadcast reports of "murderers in white gowns": "In 1952, with the 'Doctors' Plot,' nobody said anything. But I felt that something had changed. . . . I cannot say I lost my patients, though. I didn't have my own practice. I had a place with many doctors in one clinic. I worked in a clinic. The people could go only to me, not like here where you can change doctors."

Still, Klimkovich held her breath until Stalin's death, wondering if one of her patients would report her to the authorities. Perhaps, she says, they did not report her because she and her parents had lived in Borisov for so many years. Or maybe, because there was a shortage of doctors in her village, her patients needed her and so couldn't afford to believe anything negative about her. She carries the weight of a survivor on her shoulders, always wondering why she survived time and again when people close to her did not.

Following Stalin's death in 1953, there was a brief moment of national revelation in which many Soviet Jews found out what had happened to friends and family during the final years of Stalin's terror. Nechama Sirotina recalls meeting with Lina Shtern in 1954, after Shtern's 25-year sentence was commuted by Nikita Khrushchev. Shtern described to Sirotina what had happened to her friends, Zuskin, Markesh and the other Jewish writers. Shtern told Sirotina a chilling story about Perets Markesh's refusal to believe that his beloved Stalin could have had anything to do with his arrest or death sentence:

They took away the poet Perets Markesh. So sad. He was incredibly beautiful. I remember loving his beautiful head of curly hair. The first thing they did when they took him away was to shave off all of that hair . . . He continued to love Stalin even there, so that he stood in the prison screaming, "Wait until Stalin hears of this. Then you'll find out what trouble is." Even when they were taking him out to kill him, Perets still believed in Stalin. That is how strong Stalin's power over us was.

Despite Stalin's long history of anti-Semitic outbursts and persecutions, Jews were no less vulnerable to his cult of personality than were other citizens of the Soviet Union. Irena Lunts recalls growing up a devout Communist in the 1950s. Though her father had been imprisoned in a brutal gulag, and though she grew up nearby the gulag, in Siberia, her parents lived in too much fear to ever breathe a word of open opposition to Stalin. In the kitchen of her Long Island townhouse, Lunts recalls what she was taught in her Siberian school:

We were very brain-washed young. I was very active in *Komsomol*, the Communist youth in school. It added a lot to my appeal. I didn't know anything. My parents never told me. I didn't know what was going on with my family. We just knew my father was not here. When Stalin died, everyone cried. My parents never shed a tear. They were stone-faced when he died. In school the day when he died, they put us all in a line of children. And there was a huge portrait of Stalin in the middle with flowers. And the teachers were going crazy crying. And my mother had an absolutely stone face. And I couldn't believe. I said, "Mom, how can you?" And she said, "One day you will understand." And then everything gradually came out and we learned about it.

THE KHRUSHCHEV YEARS, 1953–1964:
SOME BREATHING ROOM AND A MORE
REFINED ANTI-SEMITISM

In the years following Stalin's death in 1953, there was a lightening of the general atmosphere for all Soviet Citizens, and violent assaults on Soviet Jews ended. When Premier Nikita Khrushchev made his famous speech at the Twentieth Party Congress in 1956 repudiating the excesses of Stalinism, Jews had reason to hope that the worst days were over. But, as Nechama Sirotina recalls, Khrushchev soon proved to be more repressive and anti-Semitic than he had seemed at first:

In the beginning it was a little easier under Khrushchev than it had been under Stalin. He let many people out from the camps and prisons. He admitted that Stalin was a criminal. But then he started his own monkey business. Instead of sending people to be killed like Stalin did, he said anyone who opposed him was crazy. Everybody was an enemy of the state and they were all crazy so he sent thousands to asylums. There they drugged them and made them sleep while Khrushchev lived a very good life. He got rich and the people got hungry.

Though Khrushchev condemned the "Doctors' Plot" persecutions and the most virulent forms of Russian anti-Semitism, he too harbored strong prejudices against Jews that were clearly rooted in historic European anti-Semitic stereotypes. Jews were "clannish," he commented in 1956, but also too individualistic: "They do not like collective work or group discipline" (1958) In his public commentaries Khrushchev also kept alive the notion of Jews as "rootless cosmopolitans," eternally alien to the mother country. He began to argue in the late 1950s that Jews were overrepresented in civil service positions, thus creating "jealousy and hostility toward Jews" among indigenous nationalities. (Indeed, Jews occupied almost one-fourth of such jobs in Byelorussia and the Ukraine, though they represented only one-sixteenth of the total population in those republics.) His solution was to establish occupational quotas based on the percentage of Jews in the total population of each republic (Low, 1990: 110–14).

Similar quotas were established in higher education, resulting in a sharp decline in Jewish representation in Soviet universities, from thirteen percent of all university students in 1935 to 2.5 percent by the late 1960s. Although the rationale for the policy was that the ethnic makeup of regional universities should reflect in exact proportions the ethnic makeup of each region, emigres and scholars of Soviet Jewry point out that the restrictions on Jewish admission to universities were unevenly applied. For example, medical schools remained relatively open to Jewish students. But Jews were excluded almost entirely from law schools, diplomatic and military academies, and had a very tough time getting into prestigious national universities like the University of Moscow. As a result, while the threat of imprisonment and death diminished under Khrushchev, Jews in civil service and professional positions suffered professional and financial losses. (Altshuler, 1987: 234–35; Low, 1990: 116).

And, though it was less widespread than Stalin's campaign of terror and arrests, Khrushchev did initiate a new form of legal persecution: arrest and trial for "parasitism," the legal designation for economic crimes. Between 1961 and 1964, 250 people were executed for so-called economic crimes, including bribery of state officials; 60 percent of these executed were Jewish. A great deal of media attention was focused on the Jewish cases, filling radio airwaves and newspaper front pages once again with images of Jews as money-hungry profiteers whose greed and lack of loyalty were a threat to domestic security. The situation for Soviet Jews was grave enough by 1963 that British philosopher Bertrand Russell issued a public appeal to Khrushchev on behalf of "those in the West who are dedicatedly working . . . to ease tension . . . and to end the Cold War" to cease the persecution of Soviet Jews. Yet, with all these subtle and not-so-subtle forms of persecution, possibilities for artistic expression opened up greatly under Khrushchev, and Soviet Jewish artists, particularly in the theater, tested the limits of their new freedom (Low, 1990: 117, 126–27).

THE THEATER AS A FONT OF JEWISH CULTURAL REVIVAL, 1955–1978

With the restraints on expression loosened a little bit in the late 1950s, the tattered remnants of the Soviet Jewish arts community nurtured a fragile spirit of resistance. There were a disproportionate number of Jews in the Soviet arts, even after their ranks were decimated by Hitler and Stalin. Jews made up approximately 8 percent of Soviet writers and journalists, and 7 percent of actors, musicians and visual artists into the 1960s (Low, 1990: 113). Many of these artists, now in the United States, recall a period of courageous activism in the two decades prior to emigration, when Jewish actors, writers and artists found ways to create a revival of Jewish literature, music and theater. Above all, theater became the font of Jewish creativity and culture in the Soviet Union, a forum for expressions of Jewish pride and identity that remained lively and popular through the 1970s. Soviet citizens hungry for Jewish culture could find its expression in a wide array of traditional and experimental performances that drew large crowds in Soviet cities, even in the grim period after 1967 when Soviet leader Leonid Brezhnev began once again cracking down on dissenters. Despite the climate of fear, Soviet Jews flocked by the thousands to fill both grand and small theaters and, curiously, the same authorities who refused to permit other forms of Jewish study allowed the theater to flourish relatively unmolested (Hirszowicz, 1978: 387; *Jewish Samizdat* 1975: 255–70).

Throughout the 1950s, Nehama Sirotina and other Jewish actors and actresses that she knew, unable to perform publicly, did hand sewing and whatever odd jobs they could find. Sirotina lived with other out-of-work actors in an old Moscow mansion paid for by an elderly Russian actress worried about the state of her Jewish colleagues in the aftermath of Stalin's devastating last years. In the early 1960s the remnants of the Yiddish theater gathered their nerve and established an ensemble, a group of 12 known as Moskoncert. They traveled and played in parks, on the street and occasionally in theaters. Sirotina excitedly recalls:

One night, oh, what a night, we got to play in our old theater in Moscow. The theater was jammed and people were standing on the street. It was buzzing from excitement so much that the floor shook. The Moscow Yiddish Art Theater had played in that building from 1921 until 1949, when they made us leave. We were so happy, so excited we could barely stand it. One elderly actress said, "I'm never going to leave it again." She hung a rope on the wall and she said she was going to hang herself there when the performance was over. Everyone was crying. We played our most famous play, "Tevye Der Milkhiger" [Tevye the Milkman, the classic Shalom Aleichem play on which the Broadway Musical, *Fiddler on the Roof,* was based], and the cast cried through the entire performance. It was 1966, 17 years since we had been allowed to play in our own theater.

Victor Ourin, age 21 when the war ended, also participated in a post-war arts revival. His first book of poems was published in 1946 and, as a result of Boris Pasternak's patronage, he was admitted to the Moscow Literary Institute and to the Soviet Union of Writers. But he received his degree at the peak of Stalin's assault on Jewish writers and decided to flee the city for Vladivostok, the easternmost Soviet city. Living in an old car for a decade, he survived on the generosity of his Central Asian countrymen and women and on a tiny remittance paid by the Writer's Union for his books of prose and poetry describing his journeys. His best-received work was what he calls "a book about heartbeats. Every living being must hold an ear to the other's beating breast." In one of his best-known poems he wrote:

> My travels are winds.
> Sometimes they stroke, sometimes they sting.
> The pulls of love are magnetic poles.
> I am battered by spite or dazzled by kindness
> As I wander through the hemispheres of the heart.

After many years of solitary running, Ourin began to feel a need to work with other poets and artists. On the 20th anniversary of the defeat of the Nazis, May 8, 1965, he founded the Poet's Theater. This began a decade of what Ourin calls "poetry activism" that would eventually force him to leave the Soviet Union. The Poet's Theater was a traveling ensemble of poets who

Victor Ourin at work in his Coney Island study.

recounted the great events in Soviet history in theaters across the country. From the beginning, the point of the theater was to involve ordinary people in the performance and reinterpretation of Soviet history. In a country where the contents of history books were carefully censored and the interpretation of history was rigidly controlled, such spontaneous reimaginings of historical events were bound to get the Poet's Theater principals into trouble.

Surprisingly, the Poet's Theater lasted for ten years, perhaps because its politics were implicitly rather than explicitly stated. Through the late 1960s and into the 1970s Ourin's troupe of poets traveled to different cities, settling in for short stints at regional Houses of Culture—community centers where local people could study acting, dance and other arts. Through the networks they met in each House of Culture, poets would locate elderly members of the community who remembered important dates in Soviet history. "Because the birth of the Soviet Union in the Russian Revolution had taken place only 48 years before the birth of our theater," Ourin recalls, "we could find heroes from the great events of our time to take part in our dramatization." It was wildly experimental theater intended to break down the distinction between professional actors and regular people, and to explore the intersections of history and myth. At each performance, Ourin included "a living hero from the time of the event being dramatized, a poet performing the poem he'd written about the event, pantomime actors miming the words of the ballad, and a chorus performing, speaking different parts of the ballad in tones high and low like an orchestra of instruments. This we called the Ensemble of Speeches and it gave to all our performances the richness of a symphony."

Ourin recalls one performance built around a rebellion of sailors during the Russian Revolution of 1917:

To dramatize this uprising we formed a group which was made up of sailors, not actors. We worked with them. While one group mimed the rebellion, other sailors worked on stage constructing a ship's deck where the next scene would take place. There was shooting, falling, fighting for life. In the midst of the action, an old man who had lived through the event appeared on stage dressed in a uniform of the time. He would say to the audience: "Fifty years ago it was really so. I participated in the rebellion. I remember." With tears in his eyes he confronted the audience, surprising whoever might disbelieve. Then the poet would leave his podium and begin a conversation with the old man. This was improvisation carried by the emotion of the moment. It never failed. The speech of the poet and of the hero were carried along on this wave of drama. . . .

To say that there was never another theater like this one is only true. The scenery moved with the rhythms of the drama, and we orchestrated a grand music of lights and sounds. The color of light, the tone of voice changed constantly according to the emotion of the moment, the level of the drama. I still have all the leaflets from the Poet's Theater, the posters, the stage plans. I smuggled them out with me when I left the Soviet Union. Some people smuggled gold. These leaflets and my books were more precious to me, more than gold, more than diamonds.

The intensifying restrictions of the Brezhnev era politicized Ourin. He says: "I found myself performing poems criticizing the bureaucrats, the thieves who got ahead in politics by bribery and other corrupt methods. How did I get away with it? I didn't." Ourin joined one of the first groups of Soviet Jews to apply for permission to leave the Soviet Union in the late 1960s. His application refused, he lived in a small Moscow apartment as a *refusenik* [a person denied an exit visa] for several years, unable to work, dependent once again on the kindness of others, this time fellow artists who gave him food.

Unbowed, he created an underground of young poets from around the world who had to come to study in Moscow.

At night they would gather at my house. From them, from their work and their words, I got the idea of beginning a library of world poets. I still have one of the constructions from the Poet's Theater, a mobile pipe and wire construction in which all of the arms radiated from a single center. There were 108 tubes, each tube representing a country. Inside each tube we placed a copy of a poem by one of the major poets of that country along with a translation in Russian. . . .

To honor this idea we convened a symposium of world poetry in Moscow. This worsened my troubles. Our exhibit was not well received because we did not judge poetry on the basis of its politics. We exhibited pieces by all of the world's best-known and loved poets even if they personally stood against Soviet policy. I made a statement: "I am a poet. I don't deal with politics. We are not here to represent the ideas of any government on earth, just those of poets and poetry." With statements such as those I knew that I could not remain in Russia much longer.

In 1979, Ourin was granted an exit visa. He emigrated to New York's Coney Island toward the end of that year. Once in the United States, he continued his correspondence with poets around the world, particularly those living under dictatorships—in Africa, in China—who will not stop writing though their lives are in danger. The Globe of World Poetry stands fully constructed in his kitchen. He continuously refills the tubes with scraps of paper containing the writings of today's persecuted poets.

Across the Soviet Union in the 1960s and '70s, many Jewish artists became involved in cultural activities that made them outlaws in the eyes of Soviet authorities. One center of Jewish cultural expression was Minsk, where poet Semyon Kommissar was one of the leaders of a movement that sought to interest the younger generation in Yiddish language and literature—the foundation of Jewish cultural nationalism in Eastern Europe. Much of the Jewish cultural explosion in the Soviet Union during the 1960s was focused on the Hebrew language as a symbol of the hopes that so many invested in the state of Israel. Kommissar was part of a smaller cultural revival movement whose participants, like Sirotina, sought to preserve the musical and literary heritage of Yiddish, the first language of Soviet Jews born before 1924.

Because it was no longer possible for Soviet Jews to publish in Yiddish by the late 1960s, Kommissar recalls, this Jewish *samizdat* (suppressed) literature had to be memorized and performed. Many of the performers were young men and women who reveled in a chance to flout the authorities. People of all ages gathered in apartments across Minsk, Kommissar recalls, sometimes at night, sometimes with blinds drawn, sometimes brazenly in the light of day, to listen to recitations and to write down the songs, poems and stories that they were hearing. Kommissar remembered with particular fondness "one young man who traveled around Byelorussia reciting. He knew hundreds of poems. And he spoke the most beautiful literary Yiddish. He was passionate about it and he moved people to tears. Sometimes it felt almost as if he was going to revive the language all by himself."

Kommissar performed his own Yiddish poetry at some of those illicit gatherings. Slowly, he set to memory everything he had ever written, for he had decided that, when the time came, he would leave the Soviet Union and he knew that he would never be allowed to take his writings with him. Like Ourin, Kommissar was denied permission to leave and so he lived for many years as a *refusenik*, unable to work, watched closely by the KGB. Before he left for the United States Kommissar buried 30 years of his Yiddish poetry and prose in a metal case under a tree in Minsk, harboring a faint hope that he might someday be able to return and dig them up. He arrived in the United States in 1978 and began the painstaking task of writing them down from memory.

Alexander Sirotin, 22 years old and living in Moscow in 1967, was one of those young people who found in Yiddish literature and theater a font of countercultural identity, a source of oxygen in the Brezhnev years when he says there was "not enough air to breathe." The kind of Yiddish cultural revival then blossoming in Minsk was not possible in Moscow, the capital of Russian culture and the epicenter of Soviet repression. Son of actress Nechama Sirotina, Sirotin was still a child when his mother's friends were being taken to their deaths in 1952. Growing up in the shadow of that terror Sirotin learned no Yiddish:

For the first four years of my life I was literally in the Yiddish theater every day. But, even when I saw my mother act I could not understand. This is our tragedy. This is our typical story. Young people, people in their middle ages among Russian Jews, most of us cannot understand Yiddish. This is what can happen in two generations. My grandfather and grandmother spoke only Yiddish. Even my mother's Yiddish was accented. Yiddish was her first language. But it is not mine. Whatever it meant to be a young Jew in the Soviet Union in the 1970s was thought and expressed in the Russian language.

And so Sirotin became involved in *samizdat* theater in Moscow in the 1960s with a variety of young people who wrote and performed in Russian. But for many of them, Jewish identity was central to their work because, although they thought, spoke and wrote in Russian, they were still seen by their Russian countrymen first and foremost as Jews. Now a Russian-language radio talk show host in New York City, Sirotin recalls the obstacles he faced as a Jewish actor in Moscow:

I was an actor for some time in the Russian theater but I saw quickly that this will be impossible. They would not let me act in Russian plays, play Russian characters

Alexander Sirotin in the studios of Radio Liberty, where he is a producer and on-air host.

because they said I had a Yiddish face. My directors would take me aside and say: "You can only play in plays from the West, not in Russian plays, because you have a special face, special nose, special eyes." It was like that for me also on Russian TV. It was impossible to be on TV with a Jewish face. TV there is dominated almost completely by white-haired, blond people with blue eyes. This is the "true" Russian who, of course, looks very different from most of the Russian minorities—the Armenians, the Central Asians, the Jews.

Unable to find serious work on the stage, Sirotin returned to school for a director's degree. From the late 1960s through the late 1970s he worked as a director in Moscow, but in the state-sponsored theater he was assigned only projects seen as suitable for a Jew—satirical and humorous sketches. "It was typical work for a Russian Jew," Sirotin muses, "because we are a very ironic people. We have a satiric mentality. After all, what could we do about the system of government under which we lived there? Nothing but laugh." By the early 1970s, Sirotin had gathered a multiethnic troupe of actors—Russians, Tatars, Ukrainians, Byelorussians, Poles and Jews—who performed theatrical sketches satirizing the Soviet government and the most difficult aspects of daily life under Brezhnev. Though political satire is a staple of American comedy, Sirotin comments, "you probably cannot imagine how difficult it was to get away with openly making fun of the government in Russia. I don't know how we did it but we did. I found quiet ways to poke fun. Russian Jews are very good at that, you see, because we had to live two lives all the time—a public life and an underground life."

It was only when I decided to leave Russia that I determined to be as public as I could. I thought that if the KGB will come to take me and jail me, maybe somebody in the West will know my name and print a story that in Russia they have jailed another Jewish writer. I don't know why I believed this. When I came here I realized that the press and politicians in the West pay attention only to the biggest names in Russia.

Though the West was uninterested in him, Sirotin soon developed a significant following at home. He was able to get many of his plays produced, and many of his short stories and monologues were published in local Russian papers. In 1976 a newspaper for young Communists honored him as the best author of satirical monologues in the nation. "It was very strange to get such an honor," he laughs, "but life was always strange in Russia."

Still he decided that he needed to leave the country because, he says,

for me it was impossible to be a Jew in Soviet Russia and to be intelligent, to think at all. Censorship was not only in our literature. It was in the air. They wanted to control our thoughts, our understanding of the world around us. And by making everyone scared to speak the truth they did succeed to a degree in changing our minds. We believed one thing and said another. Living like this day to day becomes a big problem, especially for an artist. Most people had no food, no housing, no money. I had a nice apartment. I had no problem with money. But without the life of the spirit there is no art. And, by the time I left in 1978, there was no spirit life left for Jews in Russia.

2

How and Why They Left: The Culture and Politics of Soviet Jewish Emigration, 1967–1997

After 1967, growing numbers of Soviet Jews demanded the right to emigrate. The loosening of social and cultural restraints during the Khrushchev era had raised many people's hopes and expectations that better times were coming. When Leonid Brezhnev consolidated power in 1967 and reimposed tight controls on freedom of expression, Soviet Jews were gripped by both depression and anger. Israel's military successes in the late 1960s and early '70s sparked unprecedented public demonstrations of religious pride and Zionism (support for a Jewish nation-state) in cities across the western Soviet Union. The Brezhnev government responded with a flood of anti-Semitic pronouncements and publications, equating Israel with the Nazi regime of Adolf Hitler. This campaign reignited deep-seated anti-Jewish feelings and created an increasingly ugly atmosphere for Jews in many parts of the Soviet Union. Energetic government enforcement of educational and occupational quotas in Moscow, Leningrad, Minsk, Odessa, and Kiev forced even successful and assimilated Soviet Jews to question what would become of their children if they remained in the Soviet Union.

AFTER 1967: ANTI-ZIONISM, QUOTAS, AND A NEW GOVERNMENT CRACKDOWN

When news of Israel's rapid and decisive victory in the Six-Day War of 1967 reached the Soviet Union, its Jewish citizens rejoiced. "The Six-Day War in 1967 was very important to Russian Jews," Alexander Sirotin recalls. "It really helped to revive hope after the long time of fear and terror." In

Moscow, Jewish students celebrated the Israeli victory in secret parties throughout the city. Foreign correspondents in Moscow reported that even non-Jewish Soviet citizens expressed admiration at the Israeli victory and questioned Moscow's decision to back the Arab states. Embarrassed and angered, the Brezhnev government cracked down on pro-Israeli sentiment and began arresting Jewish students along with older activists. The charge was simply "Zionism," which, like older accusations of Jewish "cosmopolitanism," encapsulated deep-seated Russian fears that all Jews were potential spies (Low, 1990; Levin, 1988).

In the months that followed, Zionism was identified as a crime in the eyes of the Soviet state, which equated Zionism with allegiance to a foreign government. The government response to the Israeli military victory was swift and furious. Soon after the war's end, the official press published accounts that accused Israel of atrocities on a scale comparable to those of Nazi forces during World War II. The Soviet Union's chief delegate to the United Nations, Nikolai Fedorenko, insisted publicly that Israel's troops were walking "in the bloody footsteps of Hitler's executioners." Premier Alexei Kosygin accused Israel of "heinous crimes" including the burning of hospitals and schools, and the execution of women, children and the elderly.

Though Israeli troops were not innocent of excesses during the Six-Day War, the use of distortions and outright falsifications by Soviet authorities in 1967 set the tone for a flood of official Soviet literature decrying Israel and Zionism that lasted through the 1970s. Embedded in these popular anti-Zionist tracts were traditional anti-Semitic images of Jews as conspiratorial and bent on the enslavement or murder of Christians (and now Muslims). Among the most famous of these tracts, Yevgeny Yevseev's *Fascism Under the Blue Star*, Vladimir Begun's *The Creeping Counterrevolution*, and Trofim Kichko's *Judaism Without Embellishment* were published in print runs of between 25,000 and 200,000 copies, anticipating a large audience already steeped in hostility toward Soviet Jews.

The common ideological thread in these books—and in most of the 1960s and '70s Soviet literature on Zionism—was the equating of Zionism with Nazism. Anti-Semitic Soviet authors argued throughout the Brezhnev years that Zionists and Nazis both believed in their own racial superiority and were willing to commit genocide to achieve their aims. New to this generation of anti-Semitic tracts was the charge that Jews had collaborated with the Germans during World War II—a charge that did not seem as outrageous to most Soviet citizens as to the rest of the world because Soviet censors had excised from history textbooks any discussion of the Nazi slaughter of European Jewry. It was in this context that the Soviet-sponsored 1975 U.N. resolution equating Zionism with racism was written.

Official hostility spilled over into the streets and the schools. Physician Khaya Resnikov recalls that her husband, whose dark eyes and hair distinguished him from his Slavic neighbors, experienced physical and verbal abuse almost daily: "On the street, on the bus, or in the train, other people always pushed him. They would say, 'Your place is in Israel. We don't need you here.' He felt it very badly." Sophia Shkolnikov, now a computer programmer living in Brooklyn, says that anti-Semitism was pervasive in Byelorussia during the 1960s and '70s. She recalls the chill of fear and embarrassment that she and other Jewish children felt at the beginning of each school year when asked to stand in class and identify their nationality. Admitting that they were Jews left them vulnerable to teasing and abuse by other children, she says, and frequently teachers joined in.

As she grew older, Shkolnikov says, and became a schoolteacher herself, she began to understand that state-sponsored and Byelorussian anti-Semitism were mutually reinforcing. "For example, on my way back home from the university where I was studying, I'd be waiting for a bus," Shkolnikov says. "The crowd would start pushing. I would say, 'You should be ashamed. There's an elderly woman. She should come first into the bus.' And somebody would turn around and say, 'Though you are Jewish, you seem to be a person with values.' That was said to me. And that incident happened in Minsk." As an adult, Shkolnikov says, such experiences "made me understand that if there is an opportunity to go someplace where I would experience less prejudice, then that's the place to go."

Popular hostility was also fueled by reports that Soviet Jews attended state-funded universities in numbers for out of proportion to their percentage of the Soviet population. By 1970 the percentage of employed Jews living in the major urban centers who had university degrees was 3.7 times that of the general population. The 1970 census also showed that more than 56% of Jewish wage-earners in urban centers were employed as professionals. The release of these statistics sparked public campaigns for university admissions quotas based on ethnicity. The late 1960s and early 1970s saw a sudden decrease in the percentages of Jewish students enrolled in Soviet universities. The numbers fell most sharply in the most prestigious schools (Altshuler, 1987: 125, 143–44).

The backlash against Jews attending universities was accompanied by a similar outcry against the "overrepresentation" of Jews in the professions and the arts. Edith Shvartsman, a pianist for the Soviet Olympic gymnastics team, and now director of a music and dance school for immigrant children in

Brooklyn, was very conscious of diminishing opportunities for Jews in music and Olympic-caliber sports during the 1960s and '70s. For example, she says, Jews were still being admitted to the music conservatories in the late 1960s and 1970s but they did not get good placements when they graduated. "In Russia when you graduated conservatory," she says, "it was a law they had to send you to work for three years. If you're Jewish, you'd go to a very small city very far away, someplace equivalent to Alaska. If you were not Jewish you could have a job maybe in Minsk" or another major city. "It definitely felt like it was getting worse." Shvartsman felt the discrimination, too, in the high-powered sports world that she was part of. "For example, I was working with the international team of Russia as a pianist. It was the Olympic Games in Toronto. I think it was 1976. And everybody knew who was Jewish; they would never go. It didn't matter how much work you had put in or how much talent you had. In the Olympic Games, they would send someone else. This was true for coaches, athletes, everyone." With opportunities diminishing, Shvartsman made plans to emigrate. "I had a small son," she says, "and I just began to wonder what he could look forward to." The vast majority of Jews who decided to leave the Soviet Union after 1976 were motivated by just such gnawing doubts about their future. When asked why they chose to come to the United States, the first response of most Soviet Jewish emigres is the same: "We left of course for the children."

1967–1975: THE DREAM OF ISRAEL REALIZED

Still, the doors of the Soviet Union might never have been opened for mass emigration were it not for an activist minority of Soviet Jews whose campaign for emigration rights made headlines around the world. Beginning in the mid-1960s, an upwelling of Jewish pride and a yearning for Israel moved tens of thousands of Soviet Jews to take on the Soviet Union directly in demonstrations, letter-writing campaigns, hunger strikes and individual acts of bravery. This impassioned group of Jewish political activists challenged Soviet repression at the same moment as a larger movement for human rights was sweeping Eastern Europe. Though they made up a fairly small percentage of the more than 1.25 million Jews who would leave the Soviet Union between 1967 and 1997, these dissidents played a crucial role in pushing the Soviet government to permit mass emigration for the first time in its history.

In 1966, novelist and Holocaust survivor Elie Wiesel returned to Moscow for the second time in a year to write a personal report on the state of Soviet Jewry. He was stunned by the change in atmosphere from his first visit in 1965. He wrote in 1966:

Young Jews in Russia have rejected the solution of assimilation altogether. Although they have had no education in Judaism—except what they have learned from anti-Semitic literature—they cling ferociously to their community. Although nonreligious, they celebrate Jewish holidays and sing Jewish songs. Under no circumstances will they allow their Jewishness to be degraded or killed. They learn Hebrew in secret, translate a Hebrew song into Russian, pass from hand to hand slips of paper with a few lines of Jewish history written on them. They listen to foreign broadcasts and circulate among themselves news of what is happening in world Jewry and in the Jewish state. Once awakened, Jewish conscience will not drift into slumber again. Nothing will ever be the same as before; either in Russia or outside Russia. (Wiesel, 1987: 91–93)

Wiesel was correct in marking a sea-change in the history of Soviet Jewry. His "Jews of Silence" had suddenly become some of the most vocal dissidents in the Communist bloc. Jewish holiday celebrations outside Moscow's Archipova Street synagogue attracted between 30,000 and 40,000 young Soviet Jews who danced in the streets and sang Yiddish and Hebrew songs. In open repudiation of the official Soviet history, which erased all mention of the mass murder of Jewish civilians during World War II, Soviet Jews began holding illegal memorial services for the victims of the Nazi occupation. Each year on Yom Kippur (the Day of Atonement) and Tisha B'Av (the anniversary of the destruction of the ancient temple in Jerusalem), thousands came to mourn at the site of the massacre of more than 30,000 Jews in the deep ravine outside of Kiev known as Babi Yar. At one such gathering, the story goes, a Kiev man asked an onlooker what was going on. She replied that it was a memorial for the 30,000 Jews killed here by the Nazis. "Too bad they didn't kill more," he replied. Whether the story is true or apocryphal, it conveys the sense of many Soviet Jews that they were still surrounded by people who wished them dead or gone (Orbach, 1979: 113).

The growing sense of nationhood among Soviet Jews was strengthened by Israeli military successes against Arab armies that vastly outnumbered them. In synagogue conversations, in small apartment study gatherings, at family holiday celebrations, the "miraculous" survival of Israel fueled hope that Soviet Jewry too could survive—but only if it relocated en masse to the Jewish homeland. By the late 1960s, tens of thousands of Soviet Jews had applied for permission to immigrate to Israel (Ro'i, 1991: 327).

This was a courageous act, for fewer than 750 Jews were permitted to leave between early 1963 and the end of 1964, and anyone denied permission was immediately fired and subjected to KGB scrutiny. In 1966, Premier Alexei Kosygin had promised to open the doors so that Soviet Jews could be reunited with their families in Israel. The Jewish State was the only destination that Soviet emigration officials would accept for Soviet Jews, and family reunification was the only rationale for emigration considered legitimate under Soviet law. Only 1,892 visas were granted that year and just 1,162 the next. For almost a year after the Six-Day War, Soviet authorities refused to give any exit visas at all. Having opened slightly and only for the shortest of times, the door seemed to have slammed shut once again (Ro'i, 1991: 328; Gilbert, 1985: 102–103).

After 1967, applying at all became increasingly dangerous. Almost all of those who applied lost their jobs and those who were refused permission to leave faced years of unemployment as well as prosecution under a Soviet law prohibiting "parasitism." Applicants for exit visas to Israel were sometimes jailed on charges of Zionism, which was construed by Soviet prosecutors as a treasonous allegiance to an enemy state. Their imprisonment galvanized further protests on behalf of those who came to be known as the "prisoners of Zion." Those not imprisoned but whose application for exit visas had been denied came to be known as *refuseniks*. Each year there were more of them. By the 1980s more than 22,000 Soviet Jews would find themselves living in economic, political and legal limbo for years at a time. Ironically, the vulnerability of their position made many *refuseniks* bolder than ever. Sit-ins, hunger strikes, and open street demonstrations soon gave international visibility to "the plight of Soviet Jewry" (*Macleans*, January 19, 1987: 99).

These protests were strengthened by the human rights campaign that swept Eastern Europe after the Soviet invasion of Czechoslovakia in 1968. The Red Army's brutal suppression of the Czech movement for "Communism with a human face" sparked a rebellion by Soviet bloc intellectuals of many ethnic backgrounds, the first of its kind since World War II. This new democracy movement was embraced enthusiastically by Soviet Jews, who constituted more than a third of its leadership. The Christian majority among the dissidents took up the fate of Soviet Jewry as a central concern of their human rights struggle. One of the most powerful defenses of Soviet Jewish rights was penned by a non-Jew, celebrated dissident physicist Andrei Sakharov. In his 1968 essay, "Progress, Co-Existence and Intellectual Freedom," Sakharov charged Stalin with an "unenlightened zoological kind of anti-Semitism," and vigorously condemned the Brezhnev government for "backsliding into anti-Semitism" since the Six-Day War (Lewis, 1978: 333–48). *Khronika*, the leading Soviet human rights journal, offered detailed coverage of the arrest and trial of Jewish activists, published protest letters from Jews seeking the right to emigrate and, in 1971, began publishing a regular section titled "The Jewish Movement for Emigration to Israel" (Kochan, 1978: 349–65).

Though they took solace from this support, many Soviet Jewish activists felt that they needed to bring their message to the West if they hoped to bring international pressure to bear. Beginning in 1968, they began to smuggle protest letters out of the Soviet Union. Some of these found their way to major newspapers and magazines in the United States and Western Europe. These accounts of Soviet government harassment provided fuel for fledgling Jewish organizations in the United States and England, among them the Student Struggle for Soviet Jewry, the Academic Committee on Soviet Jewry, and the Universities Committee for Soviet Jewry. By the end of the 1960s, there were demonstrations on behalf of Soviet Jewry in major European capitals and at the United Nations in New York (Orbach, 1979: 28–34).

At the same time, activism continued to heat up in the Soviet Union. The heart of the new movement was in the Baltic regions—most notably Lithuania—which had only become part of the Soviet Union after World War II. Lithuania's Jewish population was less assimilated and less Russified than those of the central republics. "In deep Russia," Lithuanian emigre builder Izak Sperling says, "Jewish people gave Russian names to their children, like Alexander and Vladimir. "But in Lithuania we all got Jewish names. I was named after my grandfather. This was a tradition so everyone always knew who you were. Even if your face wasn't very Jewish then the name was Jewish. This is how it was for us."

Before World War II, the Lithuanian capital of Vilna had been the center of Jewish culture and learning in Eastern Europe. Proud of their continued observance of Jewish traditions in the face of Soviet occupation, Lithuanian Jews felt it appropriate that they assume a leading role in the new emigration movement. In February 1968, 26 Jewish intellectuals from Vilna wrote a letter to the head of the Lithuanian Communist Party protesting discrimination against Jews, repression of Jewish cultural expression and pervasive anti-Semitism. The letter also demanded that the Lithuanian party grant them the right to emigrate: "If the borders were opened up for emigration today, some 80 percent of the entire Jewish population would leave Soviet Lithuania and go to Israel. . . . We face a paradoxical attitude. We are not wanted here, we are forcibly denationalized, oppressed and even publicly insulted in the press—and at the same time we are forcibly detained" (Cited in Lewis, 1978: 351–52).

That letter was published in the West at the end of 1968 and, over the next three years, hundreds of protest letters from Soviet Jews appeared in the U.S. and Western European press. In many of them individual Jews publicly renounced their Soviet citizenship and demanded the right to emigrate. Meanwhile, inside the Soviet Union, militant Jewish activists engaged in a level of protest unprecedented in the Soviet Union since the era of the Revolution. Once again, Vilna was a hotbed. On June 14, 1971, the city's Jewish leaders sat in at the Interior Ministry. In July and again in December they went on hunger strike (Orbach, 1979: 113). Sitting in his New Jersey townhouse, Izak Sperling remembers a keen sense of exhilaration and fear among the Jews of Vilna as the emigration movement gathered steam:

When immigration started and people became more brave and demanded freedom to leave, they went to the Vilna synagogue because that was a natural place to meet. And when people came there, the KGB would intimidate people. Their presence is intimidation already. But they would also take pictures of people. It would go into your file. And people had to ask themselves what it would make of their lives if they were not able to leave.

The brooding presence of KGB operatives at Jewish gatherings and at synagogues across the country, the brutality of Moscow police who broke up demonstrations with clubs and shouts of "dirty Jew," and the continued arrest, trial and imprisonment of key Jewish activists represented one strand of an official and familiar response by Soviet authorities. Soviet officials sought to dissuade prospective emigres through intimidation, repression and an intensification of the media campaign against Israel. But something had clearly changed in the Soviet exercise of power. For suddenly and without explanation—except to say that family reunification had always been a priority in the workers' state—the Soviet government began to open the doors. Between March 1971 and March 1972, an estimated 20,000 exit visas were granted, more than 10 times the number of even the best year in the 1960s (Lewis, 1978: 356).

There were two major reasons for this stunning turnaround by the Soviets. The first was a fear that the Jewish emigration movement would spread to other ethnic minorities, and that the democracy movement might "infect" the larger population. Emigration was one effective way to get rid of the troublemakers. The radical Jewish poet Joseph Brodsky was forced to emigrate to Israel in 1972. (He later moved to the United States.) The second pressure came from without: Appeals by Soviet Jews had resulted not only in political pressure from the United States and Western Europe but also from Western Communist parties.

Once the doors began to open, hundreds of thousands of Jews applied to leave. In 1972 alone, recall Bela and Izak Sperling, it seemed as though all

Izak and Bela Sperling in their Edgewater, New Jersey townhouse.

of Lithuanian Jewry began packing. Izak Sperling says that his parents, who remembered Lithuania before Soviet domination, had talked about emigrating from the time that he was a child: "Somehow I always knew that the moment the gates will be opened a little bit out of the Soviet Union that I must leave. This was how I was brought up." Bela, in her early 20s and a newly licensed physician when the emigration began, says that most people felt they had to move quickly, before the authorities changed their minds: "I have two sisters and they both left. It was like a mass immigration, a panic. Every day we heard that one of our friends had gotten permission. And I was in a panic. 'We will be the last. Everyone will leave and we will be the last!' "

Bela Sperling's sense that Jews were abandoning Vilna en masse is borne out by the statistics. Nearly half the Jewish population of Vilna left between 1972 and 1975. Indeed, most of the early Jewish emigres from the Soviet

Union came from the Baltic Republics—Lithuania, Estonia and Latvia—with smaller numbers from Georgia and Central Asia (Hirszowicz, 1978: 372–73). In the Baltic Republics, many Jews still claimed Yiddish as their mother tongue, and Zionism had taken a strong hold. People like Bela and Izak Sperling focused with passion and hope on the dream of making a new life in Israel.

Bela Sperling recalls the glowing vision that she had of Israel when she immigrated there in 1972. "We were really quite idealistic," she says now, having left Israel and moved to the United States. "At least I was. The idea that everybody there was Jewish fascinated me. Everybody's a Jew. And everybody's together. It must be a great place." Elie Wiesel noted that Soviet Jews to whom he spoke in the mid-1960s generally reflected this sort of naivete about what life in Israel would be like, this failure to recognize the complexities of raging ethnic conflict in the Middle East. The idea of Israel had become confused with Soviet Jewish hopes for a life free of anti-Semitism, with the determination of Soviet Jews to survive as a people. Between 1968 and 1981 nearly 650,000 Soviet Jews asked Israeli family and friends for invitations to move to Israel. According to Soviet rules, Jews could apply to emigrate only after such an invitation had been received. Approximately 260,000 were granted permission to go (Gilbert, 1985: 74–76).

TOWARD A DIFFERENT PROMISED LAND, 1975–1981

Until 1975, almost all Soviet Jews granted exit visas emigrated to Israel. These early emigrants were the most religious, the least assimilated of Soviet Jews. Many of them were from Georgia, Bukhara, Uzbekistan and Kirghizstan. Others were Zionist activists, some of whom were leaders in the early emigration struggle. Only one-third of Soviet Jewish immigrants to Israel in the early 1970s were from the Russian or Ukrainian republics, fewer still from the big cities of Moscow, Leningrad, Kiev or Minsk. When emigration from those regions of began in earnest in 1975, the desired destination of most emigres changed. Between 1975 and 1979, an increasing number of Jewish emigres from the Soviet Union chose to settle not in Israel but in the United States. During the second half of the 1970s, nearly 110,000 Soviet Jews emigrated to the United States, representing the largest Jewish migration to the United States since World War II. Unlike the earlier wave of Soviet emigres to Israel, 85 percent of these were from the large cities of Russia and the Ukraine—Odessa, Moscow, Leningrad and Kiev. Most of them were well educated and few had strong attachments to the Jewish religion or to Israel.

This new emigration was made up of assimilated, successful urban professionals who were more interested in escaping the anti-Semitism of the Soviet Union, the limitations placed on their professional development and their children's educations, and the increasingly severe food shortages plaguing all Soviet citizens than in "making *aliyah*" (moving permanently) to the Jewish homeland. A decade of anti-Israeli propaganda by the Soviet government had also had its effect on later Jewish emigres. Though they recognized that official portrayals were biased, many had nonetheless come to believe that life in Israel was difficult and dangerous. Without a keen Zionist commitment, few wished to trade the hardships of Soviet life for the insecurities and dangers of life in the war-torn Middle East. They saw a brighter future in America.

Leningrad natives Marya Frumkin, Tamara Katyn and Igor Katyn exemplified the early Soviet Jewish immigration to the United States. Marya, a teacher of English and a fierce devotee of Russian literature, music and art, was born in Leningrad in 1917, when only a handful of Jewish families were allowed to live there. Raised to speak both Russian and French, and schooled to speak English with the clipped precision of a BBC broadcaster, Marya saw herself first as a citizen of her beloved "Petersburg" (she refused to accept its Soviet name, Leningrad) and second as a European. She had never lived among Jews or attended Jewish functions. "In other parts of Russia there were Jewish schools, even synagogues," Marya remembers, "but not where I lived. I never heard Yiddish on the streets, among our friends or in our house." Her cultural life was based on affection and appreciation for the art and architecture of St. Petersburg, and the writings of the Russian masters: Leo Tolstoi, Aleksandr Pushkin and Anton Chekov.

The Katyns too were more Russian than Jewish. They lived in a comfortable apartment building in a new district of Leningrad with only one Jewish neighbor that they knew of. "We lived like Christians," Igor Katyn recalls. "We don't know how to speak Jewish. Everyone could tell me, 'You are Jewish,' but I don't know what it means to be Jewish. I am not religious. My parents were. But they didn't have a chance to be religious. They lived in Byelorussia. It was very difficult." More typical than Marya Frumkin in the sense that their families emigrated to Leningrad after World War II, the Katyns were still far from having any sense of Jewish roots. Says Igor: "In Leningrad there were 250,000 Jewish people living. And there was one synagogue. And everybody cannot go because special people were looking to see who was in the synagogue. If you had a good job, especially, you could never go into a synagogue." Igor worked as a coach for the Soviet Olympic weightlifting team. Tamara was the head of financial research at the University of

Leningrad. Neither could risk public expressions of Jewishness without fear of being fired. But that alone did not stop them from entering synagogue. They were genuinely nonreligious, and wished simply to live as Russians.

Still, as Alexander Sirotin points out, even the most Russified Jew was constantly reminded of his ethnicity. All Soviet citizens had to carry a domestic passport, to be presented when traveling, applying for jobs, or enrolling in school. On the fifth line of that passport, every Soviet citizen was required to state his or her nationality. And whether they were deeply religious or never attended synagogue, political or apolitical, Yiddish scholars or Russian-only speakers, they were identified officially as Jews. "In the USSR," Sirotin said, "Jewishness had nothing to do with religion. Jewishness was a nationality." And the letter J emblazoned in their domestic passports subjected Jews like Frumkin and the Katyns to all kinds of petty harassment. "I fought very hard all of the time to keep my position," says Tamara Katyn. "They knew everything about a person, his grandmother, his grandfather. Even if someone's nationality was listed as Russian, they would try to find out if there was a Jew hiding in her background. There was no protection."

Marya Frumkin had always thought of herself as a rebel. But her blows for freedom in the 1960s and '70s were not to smuggle Jewish literature or news of Israel into the Soviet Union. Instead, with her fellow English teachers in Leningrad, Marya illicitly consumed American popular culture. She and her friends traded American records, magazines and movies. One dog-eared copy of Jacqueline Susann's *Once Is Not Enough* passed from hand to hand among the English teachers of Leningrad. "Inside ourselves we knew it was a distorted picture of American life," says Marya. "But it offered up everything forbidden by Soviet censors—drugs, homosexuality, rich living. In a way we wanted to believe that was America—pure abandon."

For many who were born after World War II, the Russian equivalent of baby boomers, 1960s rebellion took the form of dancing to American rock music, reading American literature and dressing in jeans and styles imitative of American young people. The majority of young Jews in Moscow and Leningrad did not participate in the explicitly Jewish counterculture, but many of them did partake of the forbidden fruits of American pop culture, prized in the Russian urban underground. For people like Marya and her friends, and their younger counterparts, when the Soviet government began allowing Jews from the major cities to emigrate in the mid- to late 1970s, there was no question that they would go to their own promised land— America.

As conditions for Jews deteriorated in the late 1970s and the economic climate worsened, the yearning for America grew more intense. Indeed, just as Israel came to symbolize survival of Soviet Jews as a people, America came to symbolize a degree of material comfort that contrasted sharply with the deepening poverty of the Soviet people in a time of severe shortages. There was an eery ghostliness in the great department stores of Leningrad in the 1970s, recalls Marya. These were very grand buildings, marble clad with crystal chandeliers and winding staircases and grand balconies. They were so empty, she says, that her every footstep echoed: "There was nothing at all left to buy."

Marya Frumkin, Ira Lunts, Khaya Resnikov, Victor Ourin, Sophia Shkol-nikov, and Edith Shvartsman all sought a brighter future for themselves and their children. All were drawn by the intangible lure of freedom and they began to see America as the realization of that dream. Marya grows wistful when explaining why she chose to leave Petersburg: "It's hard to explain in English but really it is very simple. I wanted to finish my life in freedom." By the mid-1970s, Soviet authorities were flooded with hundreds of thousands of requests to emigrate.

Even those whose reasons for leaving were not ideological were politicized by the experience of applying for visas. Tamara Katyn was fired immediately from her position at the university. "They didn't want her talking to students," her husband Igor explains. Also the application to leave had to include permissions from former employers, building superintendents, even parents: "When I applied for immigration, I had to get tons of signatures from everywhere," says Sophia Shkolnikov. She left her teaching job as soon as she applied for a visa because she did not want to create problems for the friend who had gotten her the job. Even so, she had to attend a meeting at the school where her colleagues tried to talk her out of going or, at least, if she insisted on emigrating, to leave her four-year-old daughter behind.

Marya Frumkin recalls the exhaustion and frustration of trying to leave: "You would go from line to line and they wouldn't give you the papers. And all the time you couldn't work, maybe you couldn't eat, and you never knew if they were going to let you go. I didn't believe that it was real, even after the plane was off the ground. I was afraid to get off the plane in Vienna."

Emigrants determined to go to the United States found a new set of problems facing them in Vienna, the first way-station for Jews leaving the Soviet Union. Though some were more culturally Jewish or religious than others, the majority of Soviet Jews seeking exit from 1975 to 1981 were not drawn to Israel. When the Soviet authorities loosened immigration restrictions yet again, responding in part to trade incentives offered by the U.S. Congress in 1974, greater numbers than ever before began to leave. But, says emigre scholar Igor Birman, it was the possibility of going to America, more

than any significant changes in Soviet policy, that caused the dramatic increase in the numbers of immigrants from 1976 to 1979. There were, Birman
says, hundreds of thousands who wanted to go to the United States and not
to Israel. This shift in destination caused increasing tension between Israeli
immigration officials and representatives of American Jewish charitable agencies stationed in Vienna. It is important to note here that the Soviet government was not the only obstacle for those who wished to emigrate to the
United States. Israel wanted immigrants, and until 1976, U.S.-based Jewish
organizations accepted the Israeli government's demand that all emigrating
Jews be settled in Israel (Birman, 1979: 46–63).

From the beginning of the Soviet emigration, the U.S.-based Hebrew
Immigrant Aid Society (HIAS)—which had helped more than 2.5 million
Jews leave Eastern Europe for the United States since the 1880s—allowed
Israeli officials to control the processing of new emigres from the Soviet
Union. This meant that immigrants were given no choice but Israel. By
1974–1975, as greater numbers of assimilated urban immigrants from Russia
and the Ukraine poured into Vienna, the demand for assistance to emigrate
to the United States grew stronger. Simultaneously, growing numbers of
Soviet Jews who had emigrated to Israel and were unhappy with what they
found there were pouring into Brussels and Rome, where they applied for
permission to enter the United States.

By 1976 increased immigration to the United States had so angered the
Israeli government—which badly needed the skills and technical expertise
that those highly educated Soviet emigres had to offer—that it convened a
committee of four Israeli officials and four representatives of American Jewish
charitable agencies to study what Israelis called the "dropout" problem. Israeli officials proposed that American charitable groups cut off assistance to
Soviet Jews who wished to go anywhere but Israel (Sawyer 1979: 207–12).
Summing up the response of the American Jewish charities, Lewis Weinstein
of the American Jewish Committee recalls his outrage: "I was shocked . . .
and I stated that such action would be the first time in Jewish history, to my
knowledge, when Jews declined to help other Jews escape from tyranny to
freedom merely because the escaping Jews chose to go to one area of freedom
[the United States] and not another [Israel]" (Weinstein, 1988: 610).

In 1976, HIAS announced that it would begin assisting Soviet Jews who
wished to emigrate to the United States, but the process was convoluted and
risky. Because Soviet authorities would grant exit visas only for Israel, even
those who had no intention of emigrating there had to at least pretend that
they did. In addition, they still had to receive written invitations from relatives in Israel before the Soviet authorities would give them permission to

emigrate. Although a tiny handful received permission to emigrate directly to the United States, the vast majority of emigres could not reveal their desire to go to the United States until reaching Vienna.

Irena Lunts' family did change their minds during the process: "From Israel our relatives sent us invitations. It took about five or six months to get out. But in the process of waiting, my husband thought, what is he going to do in Israel? He was very exposed to American literature. He had connections in his field. He had studied English for years. America just made more sense." After dealing with Soviets who were hostile to Jews wishing to go to Israel, Irena was surprised to encounter hostility in Vienna against those who wished to go anyplace other than Israel: "We thought we must simply say that we want to go to America. But several times they sent us to another Israeli who would try to change our minds. They were very rude. They practically insulted us for wanting to go to America; they made us feel like we were not Jews."

Though now committed to providing emigres interested in the United States with whatever aid they needed, HIAS allowed representatives of the Israeli government to try twice more to convince Soviet Jews that Israel should become their new home. First a Russian-speaking representative met them in Vienna and then, even after the family was flown to Rome to take English classes and await permission to enter the United States, an Israeli official would urge them to reconsider. Exhausted and anxious, having given up certain entry to Israel in favor of uncertain status as refugees applying for admission to the United States, nearly 100,000 Soviet Jews settled temporarily into residential neighborhoods on the outskirts of Rome.

Marya Frumkin's first evenings in Rome were suffused with a sense of elation, tinged with disbelief. "In Rome we got our first taste of the West," she recalls emotionally. "It was beautiful, not only the history, which was of course interesting to us, but the clothes, the food. We went crazy walking those streets, looking in those windows." But elation at being outside the Soviet Union melted quickly into fear of the unknown as emigres tried to make their tiny cash allotments last until U.S. authorities decided their fates. It was a particularly hard time for the elderly, who suffered physically and emotionally from the travel and uncertainty, and for children who found themselves suddenly in a strange land. "We were so anxious to get to New York," Marya says, "to begin our new lives, that we could hardly stand the waiting." During the second half of the 1970s, according to HIAS, 110,000 Soviet Jews received permission from the U.S. government to leave home and enter the United States with full refugee status. Some New York-based

Soviet immigrant groups believe that nearly twice that many came to the United States during those years.

BEHIND CLOSED DOORS ONCE AGAIN, 1982–1987

In 1982, Soviet authorities once again slammed shut the doors to further emigration. A handful of Jews were still granted exit visas each year, but after a high of 51,320 in 1979, numbers plummeted to just 522 in 1984 and rose to just 914 in 1986. This dramatic decline in Jewish emigration from the Soviet Union was accompanied by a renewed government campaign against the study and promotion of Jewish culture, and by official condemnations of Zionism that sounded eerily similar to the rhetoric of the post-1967 era. The arrests and show trials, too, began again. Some Jewish activists were sentenced to long prison terms in labor camps that, while not as lethal as those of Stalin's day, were nevertheless shockingly similar to the conditions described in the works of Alexander Solzhenitsyn. Soviet Jews living in the United States and Israel feared for the safety of relatives left behind (Freedman, 1989; Gilbert, 1985; Drinan, *The Christian Century,* 1983).

All Jews who wished to go to Israel had already emigrated, Soviet authorities insisted when questioned by the Western press. The others had heard from friends and relatives that life was hard in Israel and had chosen to stay in the Soviet Union. As for those who said that they were being held against their will, Soviet authorities claimed these were people whose work had exposed them to state secrets. The Soviet state reserved the right to keep an eye on them. While not discounting these arguments entirely, there were other, more pressing reasons for what was clearly a shift in policy directed from the top echelon of Soviet government.

During the final years of Brezhnev's regime, his closest advisers grew increasingly worried that, if they allowed Jewish emigration to continue, they would receive a flood of visa applications from the most educated Soviet citizens. For a short time in the early 1970s, the government tried to levy a diploma tax on emigres, requiring that they pay back a portion of the cost of their educations. This was seen by critics as a way to discourage the most highly educated Jews from emigrating and to dissuade young Jews from applying to prestigious universities and graduate schools. The tax was rescinded after a barrage of international criticism, but the sentiments that fueled it remained and played a part in the debate among high-level Soviet officials about whether to allow continued Jewish emigration (Sawyer, 1979: 194–97; Cullen, 1986–87:258; Freedman, 1989: 3–25).

Brezhnev's intransigence on the emigration issue was strengthened by his anger at the Reagan administration's harsh line toward the Soviet Union. He declared the president's concern for the rights of Soviet Jews insincere, citing the U.S. decision to grant China most-favored nation trading status despite its abysmal human rights record, and Reagan's policy of "constructive engagement" with the internationally condemned apartheid government of South Africa. Despite the decision to allow 250,000 Jews out in the 1970s, the Soviet Union had received no trade concessions from the United States, and Brezhnev saw no reason to continue (Drinan 1983; Cullen, 1986–87: 258–259; Goldman, 1989: 141–59).

There were serious foreign policy concerns surrounding immigration to Israel that made Brezhnev's successors, Yuri Andropov and Mikhail Gorbachev, loath to reopen the emigration question. The arrival of more than a 100,000 Soviet Jews in Israel had created tensions with the Soviet Union's Arab allies. They rightly saw Soviet emigres as a boon to Israel's economic and military prospects. But there was an even more direct challenge to Arab interests. The Israeli government seemed to be taunting Palestinians by building thousands of new units of housing for Soviet emigres on the hotly contested West Bank (Cullen, 1986–87; World Jewish Congress, 1997).

For all of these reasons, the doors remained closed for five years. The suddenness of the Soviet government's reversal on emigration created a crisis for hundreds of thousands of Jewish families who found themselves in political and economic limbo. Nearly 400,000 Soviet Jews had asked for and received the "invitations" from relatives in Israel that were the required first step in the process of applying for exit visas. When the doors closed suddenly in 1982, they were stuck in the Soviet Union for the forseeable future. They were not technically *refuseniks* because the application process had halted before they were denied permission to emigrate, but this huge pool of people experienced many of the same economic, personal and legal difficulties that made the lives of official *refuseniks* so precarious.

As soon as aspiring emigres began to gather the permission signatures that emigration authorities demanded from employers, teachers and building superintendents, they put themselves at risk. Many lost their jobs soon after they announced their intention to emigrate. Enduring months or even years of unemployment while they awaited permission to leave, tens of thousands of Soviet Jews were subject to legal prosecution for the crime of "parasitism." More commonly, Jews were targets of verbal abuse and physical harassment in their workplaces, neighborhoods and schools. The sense of omnipresent discomfort was palpable even to small children. Eugene G, who grew up in Minsk in the 1980s, remembers feeling in kindergarten that "being Jewish in Russia wasn't very easy. . . . I remember being little and being teased about, insulted about being Jewish. *Zhid*, a nasty word for Jew in Russian, was a common word to me. Little kids used it all the time."

The uncertain position of Soviet Jews was made more fraught by the launch in 1983 of yet another government-instigated anti-Zionist and anti-Semitic media campaign, in response to the widely condemned Israeli invasion of Lebanon the year before. On the first anniversary of the invasion, the newly created Soviet Public Anti-Zionist Committee held a heavily publicized press conference open to the international media. The stated purpose of the committee—which included some carefully vetted Jewish writers and academics—was to "educate" the public about the brutalities perpetrated by Israel and its Zionist allies in the United States and Europe. However, the committee's first press conference in June 1983 revealed a more concrete purpose: to deflect political pressure from the Kremlin by insisting that the decline in Jewish emigration after 1982 was completely voluntary (Korey, 1989:26–50).

There was almost no discussion at the press conference of the Israeli invasion. Instead, law professor Samuel Zivs held forth on why his fellow Jews no longer wished to leave the Soviet Union. It is unlikely that the press conference convinced anyone concerned with the fate of Soviet Jewry, for Soviet Jews were no longer cut off from the rest of the world. By the 1980s they were in regular contact with more than a quarter million of their friends and relatives living in the United States and Israel. Those who had emigrated in the 1970s provided political and material support. Perhaps more important, emigres' letters home ended the state's monopoly on news from abroad, providing Jews still living in the Soviet Union with reliable information about the realities of life in the West, and the political efforts being made by American, Israeli and European Jews on their behalf.

This steady flow of mostly good news from abroad sustained Jewish religious, cultural and emigration activists even in a time of increasing anti-Semitism and deteriorating material conditions. As food and fuel shortages worsened during the brief ineffectual tenure of former KGB chief Yuri Andropov (1982–1984), many believed that it was only a matter of time before the Soviet leadership, desperate for aid from the West, would have to reopen the doors and allow free emigration. That hope enabled Soviet Jews to live through the trying final years of the Soviet regime.

The rhetoric of the Public Anti-Zionist Committee—the voice of the Kremlin on Jewish matters—became nakedly and crudely anti-Semitic, shielding itself by using Jews as spokespeople. In 1983, the committee issued a bizarre novel by Jewish writer Yuri Kolesnikov in serial form and translated it into several foreign languages (including English). The novel revolved around the "revelation" that Nazi officer Adolf Eichmann had been a Zionist agent sent to infiltrate the Nazi movement in 1932, to create a crisis that would force Jews to emigrate to Palestine. The point of the book, which was widely touted in *Pravda's* weekly magazine, was that Zionists had invented and promoted Nazi anti-Semitism and the ensuing genocide.

Over the next two years, as the Soviet government prepared for a huge 40th anniversary commemoration of the defeat of the Nazis in 1945, the committee paraded "experts," one after another, to "document" their contention that a "criminal alliance of the Zionists and Nazis" had led directly to the Holocaust and that Israel was continuing the bloody work that its founders had begun during World War II. In 1985, the committee and the Association of Soviet Lawyers (the equivalent of the American Bar Association) gathered their "facts," figures and photos in the *White Book*, which was to be the ultimate answer to anyone inside or outside the Soviet Union who questioned Soviet treatment of Jews.

The book, published in a run of 200,000, purported to prove three major points, each clearly intended to deflate critics of Soviet emigration policy. First, the authors picked up on that perennially popular theme in Soviet literature: the supposed secret relationship between Nazis and Zionists. Second, the book produced testimony from Soviet Jews who had emigrated to and returned from Israel to prove that the immigrant experience in Israel was an "odyssey of torment and suffering." And finally, the authors exposed what they called the growing problem of anti-Semitism in the United States. A barrage of radio broadcasts and mass distribution of smaller booklets explaining "the foul role of Zionists as accomplices of the Nazis in exterminating millions of working Jews" contributed to an atmosphere in the Soviet Union that by 1985 could only be described as profoundly hostile to Jews.

Throughout this period, authorities continued to arrest *refusenik* emigration activists and teachers of Hebrew. They were charged with the generic crime of "anti-Soviet activities," and received harsh sentences that seemed calculated to quash any hopes that Jews might have of getting out. Almost all of those arrested were *refuseniks* who had lost their professions after applying to leave and had then become teachers in underground Hebrew academies. Former engineer and Hebrew teacher Iosef Begun was sentenced in 1983. After a year in prison awaiting trial and having already served five years in exile, he was given an additional sentence of 12 years hard labor in a "strict regime" labor camp. Chemistry professor Yuri Tarnapolsky was sentenced that year to three years at hard labor after staging a hunger strike to protest the authorities' repeated refusals to permit his family to leave the Soviet Union. Hebrew teachers Leonid Volvovsky and Alec Zelichenok and cellist

Alexei Margarik were sentenced as late as 1985 and 1986 to three years hard labor. The mid-1980s were as bleak a time for Soviet Jews as any period since the Six-Day War. Then, suddenly, political winds began to shift (Gilbert, 1984; Wiesel, 1987; Friedgut, 1989:13–15).

THE FOURTH WAVE BEGINS, 1987–1991

In 1985, Mikhail Gorbachev came to power, replacing the aged Andropov. At first, the government of this lifelong Communist Party politician did not seem to promise an improvement of conditions for the Soviet Union's Jews. His first year was business as usual. But his reformist tendencies soon became apparent. In the summer of 1986, world-renowned *refusenik* Anatoly Shcharansky was released from prison after nine years and allowed to emigrate to Israel. In December of that year, the most famous of Soviet dissidents, physicist Andrei Sakharov and his wife, Elena Bonner, were permitted to return from exile to their home in Moscow. Ida Nudel, the exiled Muscovite activist, who had led a 15-year campaign to alert the world to the situation facing her fellow *refuseniks*, was allowed to return to Moscow for the first time since 1978. In October 1987, without explanation, she was granted the exit visa for which she had first applied in 1971. Vladimir Slepak, another of the country's most famous *refuseniks*, was granted an exit visa after waiting 17 years. Iosef Begun was freed from prison that year, too, as were several other well-known "prisoners of Zion" (Nudel, 1990; Friedgut, 1989:20–21).

Simultaneous with these high-profile releases, which were calculated to capture the attention of the West, Gorbachev took steps that year to make emigration less difficult. In January 1987, he announced a new emigration law that was intended to shorten the time from first application to receipt of a visa. The full effects of the law were not yet clear by year's end. Indeed, its critics noted that while it made it easier for those with close relatives abroad to emigrate, the law tightened restrictions on the large and amorphous group of Soviet citizens who had been "exposed to state secrets" in the course of their work. Still, as Soviet and American diplomats prepared for a summit between Presidents Reagan and Gorbachev, the mood seemed right for a substantive change in Soviet emigration policy (Jacoby, *Newsweek* 1987).

The renewal of emigration from the Soviet Union had become international news. Beginning in March 1987, not only Jews but ethnic Germans and Armenians—the two other ethnic groups whose members had sought exit visas in large numbers—were being given permission to leave. In May, 871 Jews and over 1,000 Germans were allowed out, almost as many in one month as had been granted permission to leave during all of 1986. The focus on Jews and Germans seemed to be tied to Gorbachev's desire for better relations with the United States and West Germany. It was an exciting time for Soviet Jews. Virtually everyone allowed out during the spring and summer of 1987 had been waiting for years. But the new emigration also meant the break-up of families. Computer programmer Victor Hatutsky, his wife, mother, grandmother and child were allowed out that year. But his wife's father, Yuri Zieman, who was denied a visa because he allegedly knew "state secrets," was forced to stay behind. A *refusenik* for more than a decade, Zieman found Gorbachev to be no more sympathetic to his case than Brezhnev or Andropov had been (Stranglin, Trimble and Fenyvesi, *U.S. News & World Report* 1987:37–38).

Gorbachev soon announced his new policies of *glasnost* (openness) and *perestroika* (restructuring), causing widespread celebration in the Eastern bloc and cautious optimism in the West. But the results for Soviet Jews were mixed. While the democratization of speech and press in the Soviet Union allowed Jews to speak openly about their desire to emigrate and about the condition of imprisoned activists, freedom of communications also created space for old-fashioned Russian anti-Semitism to surface anew. This time it bubbled up from the bottom, rather than being sponsored by the government. The most influential of the new Russian nationalist groups was Pamyat (Memory), an organization formed in 1980 to preserve Moscow's crumbling monuments. On May 6, 1987, 400 Pamyat demonstrators marched on the Moscow city government, demanding and receiving a meeting with Moscow party head Boris Yeltsin. They falsely blamed Jews for the destruction of important historical and cultural monuments in Russia, for the terrible problem of alcoholism that was sapping the strenth of the Russian people, and for hoarding meat at a time of severe shortages (Spier, 1989:51–57).

The official Soviet press condemned Pamyat, not because of its anti-Semitism but because it was a genuine grass-roots phenomenon and thus hard to control. But Pamyat-affiliated writers, speakers and musicians did a brisk trade in underground tape cassettes (Low, 1990:187). The visceral anti-Semitism that Pamyat stirred was given violent expression in the fall of 1987 when 70-year-old Naum Nechenko, a Jewish cultural activist from Leningrad, was murdered shortly after he announced his intention to travel to a conference on *glasnost* and anti-Semitism in Moscow. His friends and neighbors said that he had been executed by a paramilitary offshoot of Pamyat. Moscow police stated simply that the murder had taken place in the course of a robbery and there were no suspects. Though the anti-Semitic attacks were not emanating from the government this time, few Soviet Jews felt confident that the government would protect them. The Nechenko investigation seemed proof of that (Friedgut, 1989:21–22).

In 1989, on the 1,000-year anniversary of the Russian Orthodox Church, a Jewish woman writer, who was soon to emigrate, sat barricaded in her Moscow apartment, fearing pogroms that had been threatened for that day. Across the city, Jews found violently hostile leaflets in their mailboxes and crosses painted on their apartment doors. The writer, afraid to use her name, published an account of her experiences in *Ogonyok*, a Moscow weekly: "I come home after shopping. . . . [M]y path is blocked. 'Hey, you Jew swine, show me what you have in your shopping bag! It's you who are consuming all our meat.' At the editorial office of a progressive newspaper, two sweet women of my age approach me, hissing into my face, 'Leave amicably before we slaughter the lot of you' " (*Harper's* 1991:18, reprinted from *Ogonyok*).

This anonymous article captures the fear that gripped many Soviet Jews when Gorbachev began to reopen the doors of the Soviet Union to those who wished to leave. The response, says sociologist Robert Brym, was a "panic emigration." Soviet Jews rushed the American Embassy. The author of the *Ogonyok* article was 36,124th on a waiting list for visas to enter the United States. "The reason I am leaving is not because there is no meat, sugar, boots, soap, cigarettes, almost nothing in the country," she wrote. "And not even because the reward for any work is unimaginably small." She did not hope for miracles of personal prosperity or career development in the United States. Neither, she believed, did the others who waited with her outside the American Embassy that day: "What's driving them into exile? They share one disadvantage that makes them unfit to live in the country in which they were born. They are Jews. I too am Jewish."

The outside world continued to place the plight of Soviet Jews within the context of the Cold War, but even as the Soviet Union continued to liberalize, even after the Berlin Wall fell in 1989, hundreds of thousands of Jews applied for exit visas. Suddenly the United States was faced with a political problem. Despite the defeat of Communism, Soviet Jews continued to apply for refugee status, citing anti-Semitic persecution. In 1989, 38,395 were helped by HIAS to enter the United States. Another 22,000 emigrated to Israel. In January 1989, as one of his final acts, President Reagan ended automatic refugee status for Soviet Jews. From that time on they would be subjected to the same case-by-case assessment as applicants from other countries. Undaunted, Soviet Jews continued to seek asylum (*Congressional Quarterly Weekly Report*, 1989:2389–390; HIAS, 1995).

The Bush administration foresaw political trouble as skyrocketing numbers of Soviet Jewish refugees threatened to crowd out applicants from more

dangerous areas of strife-torn Africa, Latin America and Asia. Deputy Sec-
retary of State Lawrence Eagleburger told reporters that the United States
had never agreed to take everyone that the Soviet Union released. As it
became clear to the Bush administration that Gorbachev planned to release
as many Soviet Jews as wished to go, the Republican president began to spar
with a Democratic Congress over the thorny issue of placing limits on the
number of people that the United States would accept from the Soviet Union.
At the time of the House debate, in the spring 1989, 27,000 Soviet Jews had
applications pending for U.S. refugee status—20,000 were waiting in Moscow, and 7,000 had already left and were living in temporary housing in
Rome.

Unwilling to compromise with Bush, both houses of Congress passed bills
that granted "presumptive refugee status" to Soviet Jews as well as to Vietnamese, Cambodians and Laotians fearful of retribution. The bill was extremely unpopular with Latino organizations, which argued that, by giving
preferential treatment to refugees from Communist countries, Congress was
effectively eliminating desperately needed refugee slots to those fleeing political repression in Central and Latin America. Also, various versions of the
bill raised in conference committee proposed to pay for this increased number
of refugees by taking money from health care and educational programs that
were intended for the general immigrant population and that particularly
benefited poor Latino immigrants (*World Press Review*, November 1989:16–
17; Lee, *Los Angeles Times*, April 27, 1989; *Congressional Quarterly*, 1989).

The situation reached a crisis in the fall of 1989, when 14,000 Soviet Jews
living in intensely crowded conditions in Rome refused relocation to any
country but the United States. Early in September, the U.S. State Department announced that it expected 100,000 Soviet Jews to apply for refugee
status in 1990, meaning that there would be only 12,000 refugee slots for
all other applicants worldwide. A battle royale ensued between Congress and
the president as the administration sought to limit the number of Soviet Jews
who could enter the United States as refugees (Goshko, *Washington Post*,
1989).

Then in the spring of 1990, President Bush made an abrupt about-face.
In an attempt to shore up support among conservatives and American Jews,
he sought to position himself as an advocate of Soviet citizens seeking to
emigrate, and as a tough adversary of Gorbachev. In May 1990, he announced that plans to grant most-favored nation trading status to the Soviet
Union would be put on hold because the Soviet Union had not passed a law
guaranteeing free emigration. Although Soviet practice was certainly what
the United States had been asking for, with more than 60,000 Jews permitted

to emigrate in 1989 and projections of twice that many before 1990 was out, Bush refused to waive long-standing congressional trade restrictions until the Soviet Union codified its free emigration policy. In September of that year, Bush raised the ceiling for refugee admissions to 131,000. He also met Congress' demand that he reserve 50,000 slots for Soviet Jews, twice the number allotted for 1988 (*Congressional Quarterly Weekly Report*, 1990; *Chicago Tribune*, October 16, 1990).

Although the annual influx of Soviet Jews to the United States never reached that number, the flow of immigrants was very heavy over the next few years. Between January 1989 and December 1991, 106,677 Soviet Jews emigrated to the United States. Despite the elimination of automatic refugee status after the collapse of the Soviet Union in 1991, by 1996, another 156,901 had come, well over a quarter of a million people in six and a half years. These numbers count only legal immigrants. Activists in the Soviet immigrant community in the United States estimate that illegal immigration in the United States now adds another 10 percent to 30 percent to the official count. Soviet illegal immigrants, like the illegal immigrants from Poland in the 1980s and so many others from across Europe, Asia and Latin America, have come on tourist or student visas and stayed on when their visas expired. From an American perspective, schooled as we have been to believe that the Communist government was the source of all problems in the Soviet Union, these numbers are a little perplexing. If the fall of Communism was what the United States had been striving for since the end of World War II, why have so many Jews (along with hundreds of thousands of non-Jewish Soviet citizens) departed as quickly as they could after the dissolution of the Soviet Union?

The mass immigration to the United States would most likely have been even higher had the federal government continued to provide each immigrant with the financial assistance guaranteed to refugees. From 1987 to the present more than 700,000 Soviet Jews immigrated to Israel, where there is settlement assistance for all new arrivals. More than 860,000 Soviet Jews departed in the first half of the 1990s, with mass emigration likely to continue beyond the millennium. Add approximately 100,000 more who have moved to Germany, Australia and Canada and the total exceeds 1 million Jewish emigrants in the first six years since the dissolution of the Soviet Union (HIAS, 1995, 1997).

WHY THEY CONTINUE TO LEAVE, 1991
TO THE PRESENT

The reasons for the continued migration of Jews from the republics of the former Soviet Union are both complex and simple. For the majority of Fourth Wave immigrants there are three answers: family reunification, resurgent anti-Semitism and the aftermath of the 1986 Chernobyl nuclear reactor explosion. For the rest there are many and varied reasons that affect not only Jews. Jews who emigrated for these reasons are part of a flood of former Soviet citizens who have headed for the West in the past decade, driven out by intensified food and housing shortages; spiraling inflation that has placed basic foods almost out of the reach of the average family; ethnic strife that has escalated into warfare in some former republics and created millions of refugees; an astonishing explosion of violent crime, particularly in Moscow; and the predations of a range of new, regional, authoritarian regimes that have replaced the old Soviet state (*New York Times*, January 11, 1997: A1).

The desire to see and live close to loved ones once again was perhaps the most important force propelling a million Jews out of the former Soviet Union during the most recent wave of emigration. Earlier, during the 1970s and early '80s, when a quarter-million Soviet Jews received exit visas, many left family members behind. Some were denied visas because their work supposedly exposed them to state secrets. Others, including the elderly, who simply could not imagine giving up the only life that they had ever known, did not wish to go. Many young and middle-aged Jews who had done well professionally in the Soviet Union feared, not without reason, that they would have to give up their careers if they left. Some had non-Jewish spouses who refused to leave their own families behind; many faced this cruel choice because few non-Jews could get exit visas in the 1970s. Still others believed that they would follow soon and so urged loved ones not to risk waiting but to go as soon as they were granted permission. Many of those who sent children or parents off to lay the groundwork abroad were still waiting when the doors slammed shut again in 1981. By the time the doors opened again in 1987 the separation from children, parents, siblings and other loved ones had become so unbearable that hundreds of thousands lined up to leave as soon as there was a chance.

Writer and English teacher Natalie Zundelevich, who left Leningrad with her husband and daughter in 1976, did not see her mother again until 1988. She wrote and called regularly. Her mother wrote but was afraid to call, afraid to have a California phone number recorded on her monthly bills. The longing to see each other grew more intense with the years. Some immigrants Zundelevich knew became so desperate to see or bury their loved ones that they tried to sneak into Russia from European cruise boats. They were stopped by armed soldiers, sometimes in sight of their relatives waiting below at the port. "For years," she wrote in 1989, "the efforts of emigres to meet again with their relatives had been as useless as trying to bring someone back from the dead; the doors of the netherworld remained closed. Then mighty jolts began to come from there, and, to our disbelief, one dear shadow emerged after another." Zundelevich's mother was able to emigrate to the United States after 12 years of separation from her daughter and granddaughter. Watching her elderly mother walk toward her at a California airport, Zundelevich wept: "My heart breaks loose, rips the cobweb of veins tying it to the rest of my body and starts beating wildly against my chest, as if asking out. Out to her who is walking alone, all alone toward me—my mother" (Zundelevich, *New York Times Magazine,* 1989).

Across the United States, that scene has been repeated endlessly. Almost nightly since the late 1980s, New York's Kennedy Airport has been the scene of tearful reunions as children, parents, sisters and brothers greet each other for the first time in years. Unlike the immigrants of the 1970s, who were usually met by caseworkers from the New York Association for New Americans (NYANA) or by representatives from whatever Jewish community was preparing to welcome them, most of the immigrants who have arrived since 1987 have had family to meet them and help them find housing and work. They are, in a real sense, coming home as much as they are leaving home, and the presence of family has made their resettlement experiences far easier emotionally. But on a practical level, the lack of refugee status—which had provided so many Soviet emigres with housing subsidies, English classes, cash assistance and a clear path to citizenship—made the first years of many post-1989 immigrants much more difficult.

The powerful pull of family is not the only reason that Jews have continued to pour out of the former Soviet Union. The revival of populist anti-Semitism that began with Pamyat in the late 1980s has grown and intensified, particularly in Boris Yeltsin's Russia, where more than 150 newspapers are published daily that blame Jews for myriad problems facing that nation. For more than a decade, there have been anti-Semitic demonstrations in the capital. And throughout the country there are at least 80 ultra-nationalist and fascist organizations, many of which use violently anti-Semitic rhetoric as an organizing tool. Blaming Jews has become increasingly popular as food shortages, unemployment and violent crime have worsened during the 1990s. And populist anti-Semitism is often reinforced by the intransigence of local government officials. When members of a paramilitary organization wearing swastikas broke up a 1996 Jewish community meeting in the town of Orel and threatened to murder local Jewish leaders, town officials refused to prosecute the perpetrators or to provide security for the community. Several synagogues were bombed in 1996, including one in Moscow. Jewish cemeteries were vandalized in a number of cities and a Jewish center in Smolensk was robbed and covered with anti-Semitic graffitti. Once again the greatest concern of Jews in these communities was the resistance of local authorities to investigating or prosecuting these crimes. No suspects were even identified, except in the Smolensk case. And in Moscow, members of Russian National Unity, the same organization that broke up the meeting in Orel, regularly patrolled public parks in 1996, reportedly at the request of police in that district (Union of Councils for Soviet Jews Action Reports; U.S. Department of State 1997).

Concerns about institutionalized anti-Semitism in Russia have grown more urgent through the 1990s. Candidates representing anti-Semitic organizations have had a good deal of success in Russia since the collapse of the Soviet Union. With each election, extremists have won more seats in the national parliament and have exerted greater influence in regional and local governments. The June 1996 election was a particularly uncomfortable time for Russian Jews as a number of presidential candidates—most notably ultranationalist Vladimir Zhirinovsky—made anti-Semitism a part of their campaigns. Although Zhirinovsky was painted as an extremist by the Russian and the U.S. media, there was almost no discussion of the fact that both leading opposition candidates, Alexander Lebed and Gennady Zyuganov, had strong historic ties to nationalist anti-Semitic movements. Yeltsin's invitation to Lebed to join his government did nothing to calm the fears of Russian Jews.

One of the most remarkable developments of the post-Soviet era has been a resurgence of the libelous and inflammatory charge that religious Jews murder Christian children and clergy each year and use their blood to make matzoh (unleavened bread) for the spring festival of Passover. In the early 1990s, a Russian publisher reprinted an 1844 study commissioned by Tsar Nicholas I that purported to prove Jewish involvement in numerous ritual murders. To enhance the book's credibility, the publisher attributed the text not to the obscure royal adviser who wrote it but to Vladimir Dal, a venerated figure in Russian letters. The book sold well, and continues to do so. So does a 1990s reprint of that most famous of anti-Semitic texts, *The Protocols of the Elders of Zion*, a faked account of a meeting by Jewish leaders that has been used for a century by anti-Semitic organizations the world over as "proof" of Jewish plans to enslave the rest of the human race.

The blood libel accusations were given greater exposure in December 1991 when *Molodaya Guardia,* a publication with a circulation of over half a million, published a lurid account of the unsolved murders of several children in Central Asia. The author concluded: "The suspicions came to my mind. The incidents had all occurred before Passover. . . . Perhaps they were ritual murders." The author concluded with a call to Christian Russians to stand up and fight these crimes or be accomplices to "the tormentors of children."

Perhaps the most dangerous of these accusations was leveled in May 1993, after the Easter murder of two monks and a priest by a deranged veteran of the 1980s Afghan war. Although this vet had displayed extremely violent behavior several times since his return from Afghanistan, no less venerable a newspaper than *Pravda,* Moscow's leading daily, published an article by Dmitry Gerasimov charging that the arrest of the suspect, a non-Jew was just a cover-up for Jewish ritual murder.

Gerasimov pointed the finger at the Lyubavitch Hasidim (a Jewish religious sect of Russian origin), who were then suing for the return of a library of Lyubavitch religious books that had been confiscated by the Soviet government in the 1920s. Although hundreds of religious groups in the former Soviet Union were then engaged in similar battles to win back confiscated churches, mosques, synagogues, books and cemetery land, Gerasimov insisted that the motivation behind the Lyubavitch campaign to reclaim their deceased rebbe's library was the desire to hide historic Jewish texts explaining how to perform ritual murder. "According to many scholars," Gerasimov asserted without citing any of them, "these ritual murders have survived until now, for example, among the Hasidim." He concluded his *Pravda* article by claiming that there were 45 to 50 unsolved murders each year in Russia that bore signs of blood rituals. The editors of *Pravda* added a note at the end of the article to remind readers that the Lyubavitch Hasidim were preparing again to celebrate Passover. (This was untrue as Passover had already passed for that year.) When the U.S. State Department protested the publication of this article, the Russian government replied that *Pravda* was not an official publication (Reznik, 1996: Chap. 9).

Acting on such inflammatory literature, Tashkent police in 1995 moved to prosecute the first Jewish ritual murder case since the world-famous trial of Mendel Beilis in 1911. Iosif Koenov, a 72-year-old elder of the Bukharan Jewish congregation of Tashkent, was charged with murdering his tenant, a young Muslim man, and draining his blood to use for religious rites. Koenov was traveling at the time of the murder and had a cancelled train ticket to prove his whereabouts. Nevertheless, he was arrested and imprisoned amid hysterical media coverage. It took a months-long international campaign by the Union of Councils of Soviet Jews and the Caucasus Network, and 25,000 letters of protest to the Uzbek government, to win Koenov's release from prison.

The Koenov case was soon followed by the arrest of a young Jewish man, 23-year-old Dmitrii Fattakhov, who was beaten "almost to the point of insanity" according to a U.S. State Department report, to make him confess to a murder that he did not commit. Again it took an international campaign by emigres, advocates of Soviet Jewry, human rights organizations, 15,000 letters and feverish negotiations by Western diplomats before he was released and allowed to leave for Israel with his mother in February 1996 ("Union of Councils for Soviet Jews Action Reports," 1997).

In Uzbekistan, as in Russia and many other republics of the former Soviet Union, the post-Soviet revival of ethnic nationalism has left longtime Jewish residents feeling vulnerable and fearful. Once targeted as counter-revolutionaries by the Bolsheviks for clinging to their ethnic identity, Jews now found themselves painted as Communist Party faithful and anti-religious zealots. In Russia and Ukraine (since the collapse of the Soviet Union, the Ukraine has become the independent nation of "Ukraine"), anti-Semites paint Jews as enemies of the Orthodox Church; in Uzbekistan and other Central Asian republics like Azerbaijan they are seen as agents of Russian imperialism, linked to Soviet attempts to stamp out Islamic nationalism. Although the general climate in Uzbekistan has been friendlier to Jews than that in Russia or Ukraine, continued fear of nationalist excesses and—in Georgia and Azerbaijan—bloody ethnic strife not directly involving Jews have driven a steady stream of Central Asian Jews to Israel and the United States. Since 1989, 24,650 Azeri Jews and 62,169 Uzbek Jews have immigrated to Israel. Most of the latter group are Ashkenazim (Jews of European origin). But there is also an ancient indigenous community of Bukharan Jews in this region who speak a dialect of Tajik, eat Middle Eastern food, play Arabic music and engage in religious practices that are completely distinct from those of European Jews. In the 1970s most of these Jews emigrated to Israel as well, but in the last two decades many have left Israel for the United States. Between 40,000 and 50,000 now live in the United States, most of them in New York.

CHILDHOOD'S END: THE FALLOUT FROM CHERNOBYL

There is an even more potent fear driving continued emigration from Byelorussia and Ukraine, and it has gripped Jews and non-Jews alike. Citizens throughout those republics have been devastated by lingering effects from the 1986 accident at the nuclear power plant in Chernobyl, a small city in northern Ukraine. Seventeen million people, including 2.5 million children under the age of five, were exposed to radiation from the accident. The exploding nuclear reactor poisoned 260,000 square kilometers of land, releasing as much radioactive fallout as a medium-size nuclear strike. Because Chernobyl is close to several cities with large Jewish populations, among them Gomel and Kiev, between 600,000 and 1 million Jews were among those exposed. Fully 53 percent of post-1987 Soviet Jewish immigrants to the United States were from regions contaminated by Chernobyl.

The long- and short-term effects of the accident were terrifying. Contamination of grazing lands caused massive numbers of livestock deaths in Byelorussia, Ukraine and Russia and as far away as Finland, Sweden and Norway. Crops and milk in Poland, Germany, Austria and Hungary were so heavily irradiated that they had to be destroyed. It is difficult to measure the initial impact on nearby populations because Soviet authorities moved quickly to cover up the evidence of major disaster. But interviews with Soviet emigres in the United States and Israel have revealed widespread death and suffering, especially among children. Emigre physicians Grigory and Celia Chernov, who now live in Cleveland, saw patients in their home city of Gomel immediately following the accident. Both recall with bitterness that they were forced by Soviet military authorities to lie about what they saw. Celia Chernov rejects U.N. reports that have found no discernable health effects in Ukraine or Byelorussia. Every month she receives letters from former colleagues in Gomel reporting their battles with leukemia and lung cancer. Sometimes, she says, it seems as though every communication from home is about "somebody dead or dying of cancer" (Discovery Channel Online, "Chernobyl: The Survivors," 1996; Weinberg, Kripalani, McCarthy and Schuli, 1995: 408–12).

On the 10th anniversary of the reactor explosion, in April 1996, Yuri Scherbak, a physician, outspoken critic of the post-Chernobyl cover-up and now Ukraine's ambassador to the United States, cited Greenpeace Ukraine's estimate that 32,000 people have died of illnesses related to the accident. The hardest hit have been the children. Thirteen thousand children received radiation doses to the thyroid of at least twice the maximum recommended for nuclear industry workers for an entire year. Four thousand children received 20 times that dose. The result has been a tenfold increase in the rates of thyroid cancer among Ukrainian children. In Byelorussia the numbers are higher still. And even analysts for the pro-nuclear International Atomic Energy Commission predict a continued increase in thyroid cancer rates that could last for decades (Scherbak, 1996: 44–49; International Conference One Decade After Chernobyl, 1996).

Thyroid cancer is the most dire of parents' worries but not the only one in the regions affected by the Chernobyl explosion. In 1993, the Ukrainian government reported that 77 percent of children in the country were chronically sick, a dramatic shift from pre-1986 statistics indicating that the majority of the country's children suffered from no serious chronic disease. The Republic of Belarus studied tens of thousands of children evacuated from their homes after the accident. Two-thirds suffer from chronic digestive disorders. Almost half have diseases of the thyroid, and more than one third are afflicted with blood disease. This is triple the rate for Byelorussian children living in uncontaminated regions. Most important in determining thousands of families' decision to emigrate is the fact that staying in the region seemed to make children sicker. Forty percent of Byelorussian children still living in the contaminated zone in 1992 showed signs of heart and circulatory system malfunction, and even those young people who were unafflicted faced frightening prospects for their children. Infant mortality in Ukraine has been twice that of the rest of Europe since the accident. Birth defects are twice as common as they were prior to 1986, and there has been a 50 percent increase in miscarriages (Discovery Channel Online, 1996).

If Jews in other regions of the former Soviet Union continued to leave because they feared for the future of their children, those who lived in areas affected by the explosion had far more urgent worries about their children. Those worries were made worse by the Soviet government's attempt to cover up the truth about what had happened. Thousands of Kiev schoolchildren attended outdoor May Day festivities in 1986 as if nothing had happened. Their parents were not told that they were standing in a cloud of radioactive fallout from the Chernobyl accident six days earlier. Neither were Kiev families warned that their children should no longer drink milk from regional farms. Soviet authorities allowed hundreds of thousands of children to drink milk contaminated by heavy concentrations of radioiodine, which collects in the thyroid gland. One thousand cases of juvenile thyroid cancer have been diagnosed since 1990; as noted above, myriad other chronic illnesses afflict tens if not hundreds of thousands. There has also been an epidemic of neuropsychiatric disorders among Ukrainian and Byelorussian children and elders since the mid-1980s. Depression, anxiety, nightmares and headaches were commonplace; so was a desperate desire to leave the region far behind. Physical and psychological ills were intensified by an economic collapse in the region since 1986, as the Ukrainian government has had to spend 5 percent of its annual budget dealing with the aftermath of Chernobyl.

Ukrainian and Byelorussian Jews were not the only ones to suffer from the Chernobyl accident, but they represent the vast majority of Chernobyl survivors who were able to leave the region in search of uncontaminated food and water, and better medical treatment in the West. There are now more than 100,000 people living in the United States who were potentially exposed to radiation as a result of Chernobyl. Some showed signs of radiation-related illness at the time of emigration, including tumors or suppressed immune systems. Many others are expected to develop symptoms in the coming years (Baylor College of Medicine, 1997; Weinberg et al., 1995).

Because the latency period for radiation-related cancers lasts years or even decades, immigrants from these regions also show the signs of tremendous stress, according to researchers at Baylor Medical School in Texas. These researchers have begun a nationwide study of immigrants from Ukraine and Byelorussia now living in the United States who believe that they were exposed to radiation after Chernobyl. Physicians find that these patients interpret even the most benign illnesses as signs of the onset of cancer resulting from their radiation exposure, And, says the Baylor team, there's no way of knowing for many years whether or not they will develop cancer. Researchers predict that American health care providers may need to prepare for an epidemic of radiation-related cancers in regions of the United States with large populations of Soviet immigrants (Weinberg et al., 1995).

As U.S. immigration regulations have tightened, it has become increasingly difficult for those afflicted by Chernobyl-related diseases to come to the United States for medical care and even more difficult for them to stay. The case of 12-year-old Vova Malofienko, a New Jersey sixth-grader, made many Americans aware for the first time of the desperate straits of children with cancer in cash-starved Ukrainian and Byelorussian hospitals. Vova's mother explains: "We have a lot of hospitals in Ukraine but they do not have the proper medication to treat people. Even simple antibiotics are not available for the treatment, not to speak of expensive chemotherapy, which was never available in needed amounts for kids. Besides that, our doctors don't have needed experience in the treatment of leukemia because of the lack of money for research" ("Children, Chernobyl and the Internet," 1997).

In 1995, Malofienko and 10 other Chernobyl survivors were brought to Connecticut to attend Paul Newman's Hole in the Wall Camp for children with cancer. The following year, Malofienko became a *cause celebre* in New Jersey when immigration authorities moved to deport him and his parents when their visas ran out. After a resolution by the New Jersey state legislature and personal action by Sen. Frank Lautenberg, the Malofienko family's visas were extended. Still, no special status has been conferred on Chernobyl survivors wishing to emigrate to the United States or to seek medical attention here. Most still languish in Ukraine. An increasing minority are staying in the United States illegally, as desperate not to be sent back as any refugee fleeing lethal political persecution ("Children, Chernobyl and the Internet," 1997).

For the remainder of the more than 1 million Jews who left the Soviet Union and its successor states in the 1980s and '90s, their reasons for doing so were complex and varied. Rampant unemployment across the republics of the former Soviet Union has forced out many who would have preferred to stay. Says Roma Rosenberg, an unemployed factory worker who did not leave the former "autonomous" Jewish region of Birobidzan until 1997: "It's 100 percent for economic reasons. I've been unemployed for six months, my wife's been unemployed for a year and a half. My son can't find work. Every second person in this city is out of work. The factories are closed. What else are we supposed to do?" Even for many who are employed, particularly those trained in technical fields, the lure of work abroad is strong. A computer programmer, a chemist, an electrical engineer simply cannot make the kind of money in Minsk or Odessa or even Moscow or St. Petersburg that she or he could in New York or California. Those are the "economic" immigrants, looked at askance by some earlier Soviet emigres who believe that seeking higher pay is an illegitimate reason for immigrating.

In truth, it is impossible to clearly separate economic motivations for emigration from political ones. Many so-called "economic" immigrants have also experienced anti-Semitism, or were genuinely fearful that they might become caught up in the fratricidal ethnic strife that has taken so many lives and left so many homeless in Georgia, Azerbaijan and Chechnya since the dissolution of the Soviet Union. Other "economic" immigrants were victims of the stunning rise in violent crime, particularly in Moscow and its outskirts. State Department human rights reports for 1996 note that violent assaults on women and children are rampant across the former Soviet Union, particularly in Russia. In the first half of 1996, 46,000 rapes were reported in Moscow. That year there were 22,000 murders, a statistic that makes the murder rate in even the most violent U.S. cities seem low. During that same year, New York City reported 2,332 rapes and 983 murders. Emigres from the Soviet Union during the 1970s were shocked by the crime that they encountered in cities like New York. In 1980, Igor Katyn said of his new neighborhood of Brighton Beach that "American democracy was unworkable unless the government could protect its citizens from terror in the streets." His 1990s counterparts from Moscow, like Ilya Radin, see relatively safe urban U.S. neighborhoods as havens from the violence in post-Communist Russia (U.S. Department of State, 1997; FBI, 1996:101).

With conditions in the former Soviet Union deteriorating steadily, and with more than 400,000 Soviet Jews now living in the United States, many more immigrants are sure to come. Annual numbers have dropped since the federal government ceased granting Soviet Jews automatic refugee status in 1991, but even with legal entry restricted to parents, children, spouses and siblings, that still leaves tens of thousands of families able to bring their loved ones to the United States. And, as hard as it may be to resettle in the United States without government assistance, all facets of life are far easier here than in the former Soviet Union. No doubt, there are some Russian, Ukrainian, Byelorussian, Azeri and Uzbek Jews who are doing well financially and who will choose to remain there. But for each of them, there are many others still anxious to leave. Twenty-five years after it began, Jewish immigration from the former Soviet Union to the United States shows no signs of ending.

PART II

WHAT THEY FOUND AND WHAT THEY CREATED IN THE UNITED STATES

3

Settling Soviet Jewish America: New York and Beyond

THE RUSSIFICATION OF NEW YORK

In the mid-1970s, Soviet Jewish emigres began to arrive in the United States. From that time to the present, more than half of each year's new arrivals have chosen to stay in the New York metropolitan area. The social, cultural and economic roots put down in New York by this 50-plus percent of the Soviet emigre population—more than a quarter of a million people—are deep and permanent. Energetic entrepreneurial immigrants have transformed street life in much of Brooklyn and Queens, while young computer wizards and commercial artists have left a lasting imprint on the city's financial and design worlds. Soviet emigre painters, sculptors, playwrights and dancers have made New York one of the world's most important centers of Soviet Jewish culture. The immigration has both revitalized and transformed the flavor of New York Jewish life.[1]

Most Soviet emigres to New York have gotten their first taste of "America" in communities that were ethnic enclaves long before they arrived. From 1976 on, the vast majority have settled—at least for a while—in crowded Brooklyn and Queens neighborhoods among tens of thousands of elderly East European Jews who were themselves once immigrants to the United States. Each group developed quick and strong impressions of the other as

---

[1]Undocumented portions of this chapter are based on 17 years of observation of Soviet-Jewish immigrant life in New York City, particularly in Brighton Beach, Brooklyn. The two most intensive periods of observation and interviewing were 1980–1987 and 1996–1997. See bibliography for full citations of author's interviews.

they interacted on the streets, in the hallways of apartment buildings, in senior centers, shops and synagogues. These new neighbors fell into a strained sort of intimacy, like estranged cousins bound to one another by bloodlines in the distant past, related but uncomfortable. They had high expectations, for each had nurtured idealized images of the other during the long years of struggle to "free Soviet Jewry." And so there were inevitable disappointments, turf wars and misunderstandings over the new immigrants' relationship to Jewish religion and culture; over the traditionally left-wing politics of the old immigrant Jews and the "New Americans' " conservatism; over the newcomers' flashy style of dress and the non-kosher foods they lined up to buy; over the oldtimers' jealousy of the financial subsidies that the new immigrants received; over the perceived gruffness, unfriendliness and aggressiveness of the new immigrants; and over the small numbers of gangsters and racketeers who slipped in among the masses of honest emigres, bringing extortion, prostitution and gangland-style killings to neighborhoods that had not been visited by these plagues before.

Battles between old and new East European immigrant cultures strained Jewish life in New York during the late 1970s and early '80s, as Soviet refugees began to settle in large numbers in many of New York's historically Jewish communities: Brighton Beach, Kings Highway, Boro Park and Midwood, in Brooklyn; Rego Park and Forest Hills in Queens; and Washington Heights in Manhattan. These neighborhoods were already changing. As their longtime residents—elderly immigrants who had fled tsarist armies, peasant violence and Nazi death camps—died or moved to Florida, they left increasing numbers of residential and commercial vacancies. Soviet Jewish families began to move into the apartment buildings, rowhouses and bungalows they left behind. Hallways long redolent of chicken soup and potato pancakes now harbored the sharp aromas of Ukrainian *borscht* (a stew of meat and tomatoes as well as beets) and *kharcho* (lamb and rice soup). The sounds of opera and minor key melodies of Yiddish songs now competed with the complex rhythms of popular Russian and Central Asian music.

The Soviet Jews breathed new life into the withering economies of these old neighborhoods and enlivened fading commercial streets that had been built during the 1910s, '20s and '30s. They added neon exteriors to storefronts housed in three-story walkups. They opened black and silver-accented nightclubs, Georgian restaurants and sushi bars, state-of-the-art electronics stores, "international" groceries, and boutiques selling fur coats, European designer clothes and Italian leather. These flash and glass establishments quickly replaced the kosher delicatessens and dairy restaurants, tailoring and shoemaking, glazier and furrier shops that had been run there for decades by earlier waves of Jewish immigrants from Russia, Poland, Czechoslovakia and Hungary. For a while in the late 1970s and early 1980s you could still see the outlines of the old signs against the red brick. But by the 1990s, most remnants of the old world were gone. The last kosher delicatessens, the last dairy restaurants, disappeared.

The new Russian emigres reinforced the Jewish character of these communities by creating cultural institutions to replace those abandoned as earlier immigrants died or moved away. But their expressions of Jewish identity were often unrecognizable to the elderly East Europeans who had been raised speaking Yiddish and reading Hebrew religious texts. The heritage that these new immigrants sought to pass on to their children was often neither expressly religious nor explicitly Jewish. It was the culture of Jews raised in an anti-religious country where publications in Yiddish or Hebrew were virtually outlawed from the 1930s through the late 1980s. During these long years, many Jews in the Soviet Union had defined themselves by their disproportionate representation in Russian theater, music and literature. And so, as immigrants, they opened Russian schools of music, art, dance and gymnastics in the mildewing shells of old Hebrew schools, Yiddish cultural centers, and once-grand synagogues with dwindling congregations.

Initially, Soviet immigrant settlement was concentrated in a few areas of the city. The first and most famous enclave of this new immigration was a tiny Brooklyn neighborhood called Brighton Beach. The crowded strip of land by the Atlantic seashore soon became known as "Little Odessa," in recognition of the Ukrainian origins of most of the new arrivals. By 1980 it was the largest Soviet emigre outpost in the world. By the time the fourth wave of immigration began in 1987, Brighton apartments were difficult to obtain, but for some Soviet newcomers, the neighborhood held little allure. Class condescension and regional snobbery among well-educated emigres from Moscow and Leningrad had long generated cracks about "the Odessan riffraff" washing up on the shores of Brooklyn. Intentionally or not, the image of a rough and ready gangster-ridden ghetto was reinforced by sensational media coverage of "the Russian mob," and semi-regular stories in the local and national press about the area's "exotic, foreign" flavor. Brighton's ghetto image repelled many new immigrants. To them Brighton had become what the Lower East Side was to earlier generations of American Jews and their immigrant forebears: an ambivalent symbol of the immigration's early years, a place to shop, to gather for family parties, to visit one's elderly parents, maybe to indulge in a bit of nostalgia for home, but not a place for ambitious new Americans to live. Whenever they could, Fourth-Wave immigrants settled elsewhere.

Reading "The New Russian Word"—New York's Russian language daily newspaper—on the Brighton Beach Boardwalk.

By the 1990s, Jews from many regions of the former Soviet Union had created new communities across Brooklyn, giving much of the borough's southern tier a decidedly Russian flavor. Soviet emigres spread across the New York metropolitan area, revitalizing fading neighborhoods, making demands on educational, health and social services, and riding the subways to work each day like millions of other New Yorkers, with briefcases and newspapers folded under their arms. As we near the end of the millennium, a complex and highly diverse mix of Jewish immigrants from Moscow, Petersburg, Minsk, Kishinev, Kiev and Tashkent has transformed large areas of

Brooklyn, Queens, Manhattan and, more recently, parts of the Bronx, New Jersey and Long Island into a vast patchwork of Soviet emigre communities. And despite more restrictive immigration laws, the flood is likely to continue.

THE CREATION OF NEW ETHNIC ENCLAVES:
SETTLING AN EXODUS IN THE 1970s

Soviet immigrants to the United States were not, like so many immigrants before them, farmers or small-town craftspeople suddenly thrown into the confusing roar of highly urbanized American cities. Since World War II, most Soviet Jews had become big city dwellers, accustomed to subways and buses, the jostling and speed of urban life. And they came with skills to offer. An astonishing 55.7 percent described themselves as academics, scientists, professional or technical workers. Some were able to find work almost immediately. The youngest, strongest, and most adaptable were quickly absorbed into the booming economy of New York in the early 1980s and 1990s. But many of these immigrants experienced rather dramatic downward mobility, at least initially. That downward slide was more common for immigrants in New York than in many other cities (Tress, 1996:263–79).

There were several reasons why many new immigrants to New York had a harder time getting started than did their counterparts in other cities. The first problem was simple competition. The 1980s and '90s saw the largest influx of foreign-born adults to New York City since the 1920s. This meant that Soviet Jews were competing with hundreds of thousands of other new arrivals. And, in contrast to earlier waves of immigration, many of these newcomers were, like the Soviet Jews, well educated in technical and scientific fields. This glut of engineers, computer experts and health professionals drove wages down throughout the city, and in other immigrant centers as well, particularly Los Angeles. Studies have shown that, in cities with large numbers of immigrants, wages tend to be lower than in cities where the work force is stable and largely native born. This meant that even those Soviet Jews in New York who were able to find employment quickly often earned less for the same kinds of work than did their fellow emigres in other cities. And for those who arrived after 1987, the job situation was even more difficult. New York's continued loss of manufacturing jobs further limited opportunities for new immigrants seeking well-paid work (Dugger, *New York Times*, 1997).

But competition and a changing economic base were not the only reasons that some Soviet Jews struggled financially in New York. The slower adjustment and lower rate of employment also reflected three demographic trends particular to the New York Soviet Jewish immigration: greater numbers of elderly, of people without college degrees, and of those with no family in America. For them the vast numbers of Soviet Jews in New York represented not just competition but comfort, a cultural and economic safety net. It is these immigrants who created and sustained new ethnic enclaves in Brooklyn and Queens (HIAS, 1996).

Most Soviet immigrants found their way to these enclaves through the intercession of private Jewish resettlement agencies, the most important of which was the New York Association for New Americans (NYANA). Founded after World War II to offer counseling, job-placement and housing assistance for Jewish Holocaust survivors, NYANA has since that time aided many other Jewish refugees: Romanians, Greeks, Hungarians and Egyptians in the 1950s; and Cubans, Czechs and Poles in the 1960s. In the 1970s and '80s, NYANA worked with Jewish and non-Jewish refugees from 39 countries, including Haiti, Vietnam and Ethiopia. But the largest project in its history was begun in 1972 when Soviet Jewish immigrants began to arrive in New York City at the rate of 300 per week. By the late 1970s, the flow had increased to more than 100 per day and NYANA caseworkers could afford to do little else (HIAS Annual Reports, 1972–1997).

In 1969 NYANA began meeting every new arrival at John F. Kennedy Airport, offering a bilingual packet of information about New York City and the United States. These were not simply tourist brochures but practical tips on housing, transportation, the public schools, medical facilities and the like. The caseworker would immediately set up an appointment for the immigrant at NYANA headquarters and offer cash to sustain the new arrival until that meeting. Especially in the beginning, there were many who stepped off the plane knowing not a soul in the United States. NYANA workers took them by bus to whatever temporary lodgings the agency had been able to arrange at the time—hotels, rooming houses, student dormitories. Working with a network of Jewish agencies—neighborhood YM-YWHAs (Young Men's and Young Women's Hebrew Associations), Jewish Community Centers and the Metropolitan Jewish Coordinating Council on Jewish Poverty—NYANA social workers faced the daunting task of finding permanent housing for tens of thousands of new immigrants every year.

They decided on a strategy of settling as many of these immigrants as they could in historically Jewish neighborhoods where, they assumed, the local populations would be most welcoming, and where there was already a social service system in place to care for the Jewish elderly. Since affordability was a pressing concern (immigrants were not allowed to bring cash with them from the Soviet Union), NYANA looked for apartments in aging, inner-city

Jewish communities with good housing stock and high vacancy rates. The first settlement sites chosen for Soviet emigres were Washington Heights in Manhattan, Rego Park and Forest Hills in Queens, and Williamsburg, Boro Park and Brighton Beach in Brooklyn (Fisher, 1975: 267–69; Jacobson, 1975: 190–94).

Once new immigrants had found permanent housing, NYANA assigned vocational counselors to each working-age adult, tested them for English proficiency and enrolled them in English as a Second Language courses. The NYANA method of teaching English enabled many new arrivals to grasp basic conversational English in a few weeks. The agency then offered newcomers vocational training in business and accounting, industrial trades, carpentry, building maintenance and food service. It also provided retraining programs for engineers, computer scientists and health care professionals (NYANA, 1996).

Unfortunately, only a small percentage were able to take full advantage of these programs. NYANA simply did not have the resources to reach such a large immigrant population. The vast majority of immigrants had to fend for themselves, or try to make use of networks established by friends and family members who had been in New York longer. How successful immigrants were at making the transition to the American work world depended a great deal on their gender, age, and class. Women were able to find jobs more quickly, but men earned more, even for the same jobs. Most young adults with strong educational backgrounds were able to find work and move to comfortable homes. For elderly immigrants, for those without higher education, and for the middle-aged who could not find work in their fields, it was easiest to remain in one of the new Soviet immigrant enclaves in Brooklyn and Queens.

Ethnic enclaves are plentiful and extraordinarily varied in New York, which vies with Los Angeles as the nation's immigrant capital. These insular demi-worlds give their residents (whether they are Chinese, Dominican or Soviet Jews) an adapted but still familiar atmosphere of "home." Though immigrants who choose to live in ethnic enclaves often do not learn English well, even after years in the United States, and don't learn a great deal about American life or culture, they are able to function effectively in their day-to-day lives. Speaking only Russian, perhaps mixed with a smattering of Yiddish, Hebrew and English, residents of Soviet ethnic enclaves in New York have been able to find employment, purchase food and clothing, seek medical care, enjoy restaurants, attend movies and live performances. These ethnic enclaves also create a lucrative market for Soviet immigrant entrepreneurs, who hire and cater to their fellow immigrants, often through an underground cash economy that requires no tax statements or Social Security numbers. There are many Soviet outposts strung across Brooklyn and Queens, but the first remains the most visible—a crowded stretch of seafront called Brighton Beach.

A CASE STUDY OF BRIGHTON BEACH: THE MOST FAMOUS "RUSSIAN" NEIGHBORHOOD IN AMERICA

The first Soviet Jews were settled in Brighton Beach in the mid-1970s by NYANA caseworkers. Soon the neighborhood was a mecca for Russian and Ukrainian immigrants. The housing stock—mostly 1920s Art Deco apartment buildings—was inexpensive and in excellent condition. Commercial space was plentiful. And there were well-established social services geared to elderly Jews. With nearly one-third of the first immigrants over the age of 60, that last fact was important. Brighton was also emotionally appealing. Its residents were almost all Eastern European Jews, many of whom spoke Yiddish as their first language. This meant that the Soviet elderly could begin to communicate with their neighbors immediately. Unlike many other Jewish neighborhoods in New York, Brighton was culturally Jewish but not overwhelmingly religious. Finally, it was located on a narrow strip of land facing the Atlantic Ocean. A four-mile-long boardwalk stretched along the sea, perfect for walking, for meeting neighbors, for breathing in the fresh salt air. Thousands of Odessans and other Ukrainians, pining for the Black Sea, found in Brighton Beach a little of the feel of home. By 1980, more than 30,000 Soviet Jews had crowded into the mile-long neighborhood.

These emigres found a community that seemed almost stuck in time. With its fruit stands and street peddlers, pickle barrels and crowds of haggling shoppers, Brighton Beach Avenue in the early 1970s felt like an early 20th-century East European ghetto. Indeed, it had been a vibrant East European Jewish immigrant community since World War I. The neighborhood had first become popular among East European Jewish immigrants as a summer resort, where bungalows and boarding houses offered respite from the heat and unhealthy conditions in crowded inner-city neighborhoods. When the first apartment buildings were constructed there in 1919, thousands of emigres from Russia, Poland and Hungary moved their families to Brighton-by-the-Sea for a bit of peace and "a year-round resort lifestyle." The neighborhood was particularly alluring to sufferers of asthma and other respiratory illnesses. Family physicians promised that the sea air would make it easier for them to breathe. No doubt this was true for those who fled the stench

For elderly Ukrainian Jews, the Brighton Beach Boardwalk, with its wide open views of the sea, helps to assuage pangs of nostalgia for the Black Sea vistas they remember from home.

Younger Soviet immigrants enjoy a chance to relax on summer weekends on Brighton's long sandy beach.

of rotting garbage and inadequate sewers on the old tenement blocks of the Lower East Side, Brownsville and Williamsburg.

A building boom in the 1920s brought thousands of young garment union families to Brighton, suddenly urbanizing this sleepy, seaside village. Within five years, thirty six-story apartment houses were built on a lattice of short streets running from the boardwalk to the elevated subway on Brighton Beach Avenue. By the end of the 1920s Brighton was a thriving and diverse community of Jewish immigrants, their children and grandchildren. It supported four synagogues—a ritual bathhouse, a variety of Yiddish-language afternoon schools with competing ideologies, myriad charitable and cultural organizations, and branches of the Jewish Labor *Bund*, the Zionist *Farband*, and the Democratic, Republican, Socialist and Communist parties.

During the Depression, Brighton lost the last traces of its resort air as residents invited struggling family members from across the city to live with them. Three and four generations crowded into each of the bungalows, the walk-ups, the airy six-room apartments, pooling their scant funds to pay rent. Desperation fueled neighborhood politics. Fiery radical speeches could be heard on every street corner. "Brighton in the 1930s was the most Communist neighborhood in New York," recalled Russian emigre and Communist Party activist Jack Freedman, "maybe the most Communist neighborhood in America. These people didn't take setbacks sitting down." Determined to protect their families from the worst ravages of the Depression, immigrant housewives formed the Emma Lazarus Tenant Council, named for the woman whose poem was enshrined on the base of the Statue of Liberty: "Give me your tired, your poor, your huddled masses yearning to breathe free." The "Emmas" boasted that no Brighton family would be forced into homelessness for inability to pay rent. When city marshals carried an evicted family's furniture out onto the street, angry women jumped atop the displaced couches and chairs before they could be placed in waiting trucks. The women sang, made impromptu speeches and brandished tea kettles filled with scalding water, daring the marshals to challenge them. In the evenings, victorious Brightonites gathered on the boardwalk to sing songs from the Russian Revolution. "We all believed the Revolution was coming," one Polish immigrant recalled.

World War II brought another immigrant wave to Brighton—Eastern and Central European survivors of the Holocaust. Having spent years in displaced persons' camps, survivors from Poland, Czechoslovakia, Romania and Hungary began to appear in Brighton hoping to find relatives or at least to find work, affordable housing and a supportive Jewish community. Like many immigrants seeking help from those who came before—and like the Soviets who would come a quarter-century later—the Holocaust survivors found an ambivalent welcome in America.

For Brighton Jews to fully embrace these survivors meant acknowledging what had happened to their own relatives in the Nazi ghettos and concentration camps, and there was a great deal of denial among American Jews in the early post-war years. The war had also taken a toll on the children of the immigrants who called Brighton home: The neighborhood lost a staggering number of the sons it had sent to fight.

Tensions soon developed between the two waves of immigrants. These haunted newcomers came with different experiences of Jewish life in Europe than the older immigrants. They had grown up not in the Russian Pale but in the towns and cities of East Central Europe. While some were quite religious, others were secular, modern Jews. Urbane denizens of Warsaw and Berlin, some of them found Brighton clannish and provincial, while many older Brighton residents thought the newcomers aloof and ungrateful. It was a foreshadowing of the tensions to come 30 years later.

In time, these second wave immigrants adjusted to and changed Brighton. They opened new businesses, often employing out-of-work refugees. The

Brighton Dairy Restaurant, owned and staffed entirely by concentration camp survivors, became a neighborhood landmark for the next 50 years. The new immigrants celebrated their Jewishness and mourned their unimaginable losses, bringing new meaning to the daily mourning prayers said in local synagogues. And they created a new kind of bonding ritual, a new rite of memory—a commemoration that was also an expression of fierce pride. Instead of focusing on death and suffering in the camps, the survivors chose as their day of communal mourning the anniversary of the April 1943 Warsaw Ghetto Uprising. In that rebellion, Jewish men, women and children kept the Nazi army at bay for three weeks, armed only with stones and bottles stuffed with flaming, kerosene-soaked rags. Every year, Brighton's survivors have gathered to sing Yiddish songs of the Jewish anti-Nazi resistance, the fierce anthem of their survival, after saying *Kaddish*, the prayer for the dead.

In the late 1960s, Brighton was the destination of an equally large internal migration of Jewish elderly from other parts of New York City. In 1967, the Amalgamated Clothing Workers' Union completed construction of a massive apartment complex on the border of Brighton, built to provide reasonably priced housing for current and former garment workers and their families. From 1967 through the early 1970s, thousands of retirees poured into the neighborhood from East New York, Brownsville and other increasingly dangerous and decaying inner-city neighborhoods. This last migration made Brighton Beach one of the two largest senior citizen communities in the country; only Miami Beach had more. This was the world that the Soviet Jews found. With its intensely crowded shopping streets, open-air fruit markets, street vendors, kosher dairy restaurants and delicatessens, and street-corner proselytizers, Brighton Beach was far more Jewish and European in flavor than it was American. That should have made for an easy and comfortable transition, except that the Soviet Jews who began arriving in Brighton Beach in the 1970s did not look, act or think like their Jewish immigrant predecessors.

WELCOME, CONFLICT AND NEGOTIATION: NEW IMMIGRANTS MEET THE OLD

As is so often the case, when new immigrants to the United States come to live alongside earlier immigrants of the same ethnic or national origin, the initial encounters are testy. The first contacts between Brighton's Soviet Jews, Holocaust survivors and pre-1924 Russian Jewish immigrants were not at all smooth or easy. The issue of Jewish identity among the Soviet Jews was perhaps the greatest bone of contention in the early years of the immigration, and it remains an issue today. In the 1970s, observant Jews throughout Brooklyn reached out to the newcomers, hoping to school them in the fundamentals of a religious practice that Jews in the Soviet Union had been prevented from observing for half a century. Brooklyn synagogues and Yeshivas launched outreach programs to attract and teach the new immigrants. They leafleted apartment buildings with invitations in Russian to attend special Russian-language holiday services. Of the 11 synagogues in Brighton, only five were able to attract Soviet immigrants to join, and these were almost all people over 60, much closer in age and upbringing to the majority of Brighton's religious Jews than to their children and grandchildren.

With such a lukewarm response from the Soviets, tempers flared among older Brighton immigrants. Many felt that the Soviets were pushy and unfriendly, unwilling to return greetings or wait their turn on line. With less justification, they also railed against the generous federal and private subsidies that the newcomers received, perhaps forgetting that they too had been aided by Jewish charitable groups when they arrived decades earlier. Their resentment was openly expressed. You could hear it on the streets, on the boardwalk, in the synagogues, in the stores: "Why did we fight to bring them here? Why did they want to come here? They're not even Jews. They don't want to be Jews." The Soviets irked Brighton residents for a host of reasons, but the oldtimers' anger often took the form of a single rebuff: The newcomers were not really Jews.

Some strongly Jewish-identified members of the immigrant community tried to mediate. Alexander Sirotin formed the Jewish Union of Russian Immigrants to sponsor activities with a Jewish theme among the new arrivals. Through the 1980s he was host of "Gorizont" (Horizon), a Russian-language radio show on the Lyubavitch Hasidic radio network. The message of Sirotin and other Jewish-identified community leaders in Brighton was: Let the Soviet immigrants nourish their Jewish identities in their own ways, in their own time. As examples, he pointed to an emigre Yiddish theater troupe and to gatherings of senior citizens at which Yiddish songs and poems were sung and recited by recent Soviet immigrants.

By contrast, many American Jewish attempts at outreach were perceived by newcomers as somehow threatening, no matter how well intentioned. Several days after he arrived from Moscow in 1974, Victor Rashkovsky awoke to find two young men whom he did not know, and who spoke no Russian, praying and nailing a *mezuzah* (decorated case containing a holy scroll) to his doorpost: "All I understood was that they wanted to proceed with some ritual they considered to be important." He thought that he recognized them from a local synagogue and so he let them proceed but he had no idea what they were doing. "Only later did I learn this custom" (Sawyer, 1995).

Though most Soviet emigres have not embraced Judaism in the United States, more than one-third have sent their children, at least for a while, to yeshivas (religious academies) run by Orthodox Jewish congregations. Years of sensationalized reports in the Soviet press about the lawlessness and violence of American schools had left immigrant parents terrified of putting their children into the public system. Though few immigrants had money to pay for private school, many New York yeshivas offered one year of free tuition to the new arrivals. Schooled in a Soviet system that placed heavy emphasis on values as well as academics, many parents found the thought of their children attending these yeshivas appealing, at first. But soon most placed their children in public schools. Sometimes parents pulled them out of the yeshivas because they were angered by what they saw as the brainwashing of their children. More than a few cited the requirement that emigre parents circumcise their sons. At least several thousand Soviet Jewish families in New York submitted to voluntary circumcision for sons and fathers. But many other parents and children felt coerced by the religious school authorities, and withdrew not only from the yeshivas but from further contact of any kind with religious American Jews (Howells, 1985).

Alexander Sirotin sums up the cultural tension that divided Soviet immigrants from other immigrant and native-born American Jews: "Here in America the first concern of the Russian Jew was not religion. Being Jewish had kept them from getting many good things in Russia. They want those things first: good apartments, good jobs, respect, education for their children. But the American Jews offered prayer books, candlesticks, prayer shawls." When Soviet emigres chose not to accept them, their American neighbors were insulted and often lashed out. "In Russia," Sirotin says sadly, "I was told I cannot be Russian because I have a Jewish face. Here, the Jews say, 'Can these be Jews? They're so Russian!' What does it mean to be a Jew without feeling for the religion that is a whole national-spiritual-ethical way of living? I can't explain it. But I feel Jewishness in my essence, under my thoughts. I feel it in my heart. So now we are trying to find a way to be. It was very difficult to be a Jew in Russia. But it is not easy to be a Russian Jew in America."

A 1990s emigre, Irene Vershinin, echoes Sirotin's comments. Formerly a teacher of French and Italian, Vershinin made a living cleaning houses after arriving in New York in 1993. She believes that the loss of self-esteem resulting from a dramatic drop in professional status is the primary concern for many Soviet immigrants. "When we come here we feel dependent [on

A 60-year-old Brighton synagogue seeks to attract new Soviet immigrants with a
Chanukah concert and special programs for children.

American Jews], obligated to show we are good Jews," she says. "Yet many
of us don't feel it. It's a painful process to become religious after a lifetime
of no religion."

Why did Jews in the United States find that so hard to grasp? One reason
was that decades of struggle by Jews in the United States to "Free Soviet

Jewry" lent a Biblical tinge to many Americans' perceptions of the immigration. The campaigns by the United Jewish Appeal, HIAS and others likened the emigration of Soviet Jews to the exodus from Egypt. Some American communities added new sections to the liturgy said at Passover (the spring holiday commemorating the exodus of the ancient Hebrews from Egypt), praying for the release and safe passage of Soviet Jewry. Perhaps it was inevitable that accusations of worshiping the golden calf would follow. In an era when American Jews are becoming increasingly less observant and the rate of intermarriage has climbed to nearly 50 percent, many Jews in the country looked to Soviet emigres to create a Jewish spiritual revival. When the newcomers seemed more interested in partaking of the fruits of capitalism than the rites of Judaism, some disappointed Americans angrily labeled them heretics, traitors to their Jewish heritage.

In truth, just like American-born Jews and earlier waves of East European immigrants, Soviet Jews embrace a wide range of Jewish identities: Among the new immigrants are some who are very religious and others who identify strongly with Yiddish language and culture but not with religion. Some began attending synagogue and studying Hebrew in the 1960s and 1970s as an act of resistance; some identify themselves as both Russian and Jewish; others claim Russian language and culture as their own. Still, all of them are clear that they are Jews. How could they not be?

Elie Wiesel has written:

Think a minute. Who were the first, the principal victims of the pogroms? They were. The first to be eliminated in the Communist purges of the thirties. And the first to be murdered by the invading Germans. These first, hundreds of thousands of Jews, old men, women and children, in the Ukraine and White Russia, from Minsk to Kiev, from Lvov to Vilna. . . . And in Stalin's last years, who were the victims of his mad liquidation programs? They were. The first to be victimized, the last to be redeemed. (Wiesel, 1966: 21)

More than a few of the new immigrants were outraged that those who had lived comfortably in the United States for much of this time would dare to tell them that they were not Jews. Indeed, surveys of Soviet immigrants in the United States show that a large majority strongly identify as Jews, far more strongly than do most American-born Jews. As a group, they are only slightly less rigorous in their religious observance than most American Jews. Thirty-percent to 40 percent enroll their children in Jewish afternoon or Sunday schools, even if they themselves are not observant. And, like many American-born Jewish families, they celebrate the more popular and less religious holidays like Passover and Chanukah with family gatherings and ritual meals at home.

After decades of repression, finding comfortable ways to express Jewishness has taken time for Soviet Jewish immigrants. Brighton storekeepers who at first offended the sensibilities of observant Jews by staying open on the Jewish High Holy Days—Rosh Hashanah and Yom Kippur—soon began to close their businesses on Jewish holidays and post signs wishing their customers *mazl* (luck) and *shalom* (peace). Hearing the language again on the streets of Brighton after a half-century, many elderly and middle-aged Soviet immigrants have revived the Yiddish phrases of their youths. The *mamaloshn* (mother tongue) once again peppers the repartee in crowded groceries, bakeries and butcher shops. One even finds relatively young shopkeepers here and there whose Yiddish seems surprisingly good. "Many years ago I used to hear my grandparents speak," one storeowner explained in the mid-1980s. "But I forgot it all until I moved here. Suddenly it came pouring back."

BONDING ACROSS THE IMMIGRANT WAVES THROUGH COMMUNAL MOURNING

Community in Brighton Beach, as in other Soviet emigre settlements across the country, is rooted not only in a celebration of Jewish identity but as much in an ever-present memory of shared losses. Although many Soviet Jews resisted invitations to join American Jews and earlier waves of immigrants in various Jewish religious observances, they responded wholeheartedly when invited to share in communal commemorations of the Holocaust. Through such events, they began to forge bonds across the cultural divides that separated older immigrants from the new.

The Warsaw Ghetto Memorial, held each April at the Shorefront YM-YWHA, is a community ritual established by Brighton Holocaust survivors in the 1960s. By the time that Soviet immigrants began moving to the neighborhood, the commemoration had become a major event attracting 500 to 600 people annually, along with politicians, reporters, and the children and grandchildren of survivors. Each year, just before the first night of Passover, participants would crowd into the Y's simple gymnasium to testify to the experience of loss and survival, to read poetry, to sing Yiddish songs of the partisans, to light memorial candles and to say *Kaddish*. One could feel a different sort of sadness and electricity after the Soviet emigres began attending. In the first years especially, their faces trembled with a mixture of anxiety and relief, letting go at last after decades of suppressed emotion.

For some elderly Soviet emigres, a vitally important part of the process of adjustment to Brighton (and to other parts of the United States) has been a recognition that they are not only refugees of authoritarian Communism but also Holocaust survivors, with all of the psychological and physical scars that survivors of that terrible trauma carry. Accepting that identity has meant not only a re-examination of themselves but a recasting of the way that they represent themselves to other people. Until recently, scholars of the Holocaust have focused mainly on the death camps in Poland and Germany. Too little has been said about the Soviet Holocaust, though the wounds were as deep, the losses as vast as in other parts of Europe.

The repression of facts and destruction of sources by the Soviet regime were partly responsible for this. For nearly half a century, Soviet Jewish survivors of World War II have carried their memories with them as the only documentation of the murder of hundreds of thousands of their friends, family and loved ones. Until the most recent wave of Soviet emigration, most Holocaust scholars believed that 1.25 million Soviet Jews had been killed by Nazi troops between 1941 and 1945. Now, with the testimonies of immigrants finally being recorded, and long-hidden archives being opened in the former Soviet Union, experts estimate that the death toll was closer to 1.5 million. Since 1989, 80,000 pages of documents have been uncovered and released. And in New York, Los Angeles, Chicago, Detroit and Jerusalem, elderly survivors are at last able to tell their stories. They are determined that evidence of murdered loved ones be recorded for posterity. "Hundreds are coming in with documents," says Latvian emigre Bella Kirshner, a researcher for Israel's Yad Vashem Holocaust memorial, "people who have never told anyone until now" (Pevtzow, *Detroit News*, 1996).

One of every two Soviet Jews died during the Nazi occupation, victims of slave labor camps and execution squads. And yet Soviet Jewish survivors of slave labor camps of ghettos where thousands were slowly starved, and those who crawled wounded from mass graves hidden deep in Ukrainian forests, were excluded when the West German government began paying reparations to Jewish victims of the Nazi terror after World War II. The West German government simply refused to send money behind the Iron Curtain. Only after the emigration began were elderly Soviet Jews finally able to apply for the reparations that they should have been receiving for decades. In cities across the United States, and Israel they lined up to do so.

Survivors can also finally gather in public to memorialize murdered loved ones. In 1980, Soviet emigres added a new commemoration to Brighton's communal calendar of mourning, a day of remembrance for the victims of the Nazi slaughter at Babi Yar in Kiev. As on the day of mourning for the victims of the Warsaw Ghetto, the commitment to remember, to memorialize the millions of lost Jews of Eastern Europe binds the different waves of immigrants into one community. East European Jewish immigrants from all three waves join at the Y to sing, pray and cry together, marking the losses not in millions but in memories of individual loved ones: mothers, husbands, wives, children, friends. And a few blocks from the Y, old men play chess and old women in colorful, gold-flecked headscarves chat on benches in a tiny vest-pocket park, the Babi Yar Triangle. It is very small, and there's not much in it besides the tarred ground, wood benches and a few stone tables with inlaid chess boards over which old men in berets bend low in concentration. But it is a public marker of the kind that one could not find in Kiev, Riga, Vinnitsa or Borisov. It represents freedom to mourn, freedom finally to name the dead aloud without fear of reprisal, freedom to cry in public or even to laugh and tell stories of the good times—a small thing, like breathing.

HOW BRIGHTON BEACH BECAME "LITTLE ODESSA"

The Soviet immigration has unquestionably preserved the Jewish immigrant character of Brighton Beach, as it has that of West Rogers Park in Chicago and West Hollywood in Los Angeles. On Brighton Beach Avenue you can still buy pickles from a barrel; freshly baked kasha (buckwheat), potato and cheese knishes (soft pastry pockets); and wet-smoked whitefish, sturgeon and salmon with the skin still on. Old-fashioned caps with small brims are still the most common form of headwear for men over 40, and elderly women still cover their hair with the brightly colored scarves that American-born Brighton children call *babushkas*, applying the diminutive Russian word for "grandmother." The streets are as jammed with slow-moving elderly people as ever. And small business owners still compete fiercely with enterprising sidewalk vendors who set up carts and displays across what little walking room there is.

Entrepreneurship is the lifeblood of all sorts of new immigrant enclaves, and Brighton Beach hums with the business of buying and selling. From the beginning of the Soviet Jewish immigration, small businesses have been a major source of income for new arrivals—both those who already had some experience with retail sales in the former Soviet Union and professionals who felt they needed a new way to make a living in the United States. One early study of New York immigrants indicated that nearly three-quarters of Soviet emigres to the United States dreamed of opening their own businesses. Partly this was an idealized vision of American capitalism. To own one's business was to have no boss, no restrictions on where one could settle and no limitations on what one could earn. It was also a recognition that, with limited

Crowded Brighton Beach Avenue on an average winter shopping day.

English, it might be difficult to find other work. Many new arrivals believed that they could run a successful business in a Russian immigrant neighborhood without becoming fluent in English. Brighton Beach Avenue is testimony to that (Author's interviews, Brighton Beach, 1983–1997; Lubin, 1985; Taylor, 1986).

The first of the Soviet immigrant-owned stores to appear on "the Avenue" were groceries, clean, bright and quite modern-looking compared with the old-fashioned corner stores that they replaced. These stores occupy a special place in the life of each immigrant family for they offer daily reminders of the difference between the former Soviet Union and the land where they now live. Here every day is testimony to the miracle of abundance that was at the core of so many dreams of America. For shoppers from Moscow, Leningrad, Minsk, keeping a family fed meant standing in line for hours each day just to purchase the essentials, bribing truckers, farmers and grocery store workers, and keeping abreast of the latest news about where black-market shipments were soon to arrive. In Brighton, immigrants can choose between at least a dozen groceries offering Polish, Hungarian, German, Russian and American meats, cheeses, juices, chocolates. Bakeries, butcher shops,

Older women shoppers bring home familiar foods from Eastern Europe to prepare for their families.

Street vendors sell everything from baggage to Russian-language books.

fish stores and fruit stands compete with the groceries and each other to create increasingly eye-catching displays of delectables. These stores have become informal community centers: news is exchanged, and congratulations or condolences are offered as the largely elderly clientele rubs shoulders and jostles elbows on lines that snake back from each counter to the humming store center. For some immigrants who now live in other parts of the city or the country, these stores have also become places to assuage pangs of nostalgia by shopping in familiar surroundings for foods they know from home.

Like the communal societies of earlier Jewish immigrants, Brighton's Russian restaurants and nightclubs also serve as important public gathering spaces where a sense of group identity is forged and reinforced. Brighton's restaurants and nightclubs reflect the geographic and cultural diversity of the immigrants. Increasingly, restaurants serve a smorgasbord of cuisines from different areas of the former Soviet Union, reflecting both a growing sense of pan-Soviet identity among the immigrants and the popularity of certain dishes across the former Soviet Union. However, many cater to specific regional tastes. Ukrainian food, not surprisingly, is the most commonly served, along with traditional Jewish specialties and an odd amalgam known as Odessan-style continental. But Georgian restaurants are also popular, as are restaurants serving Uzbek and other Central Asian cuisines.

Two generations of Odessan immigrants behind their Brighton meat counter.

Meat, cheese and potato-filled dumplings are variously called *pirogi* (Ukrainian), *pelmeni* (Central Asian) and *vareniki* (Russian), but they can be found almost everywhere. So can *shashlyk* (shish kebab, made with lamb, chicken or sturgeon and served on a sword-like skewer) and Chicken Kiev (fried with butter and mushrooms at the center). Emigres organizing a party often choose the restaurants for regional specialties like Odessan shrimp in garlic sauce, *lavash* (a crusty round Georgian bread eaten hot and sliced like a pie), *chakhokhbili* (a Caucasian chicken stew with tomatoes) and *baklazhan* (eggplant) with pomegranate sauce or *satsivi* (walnut sauce). Whatever the restaurateurs' region of origin, groaning banquet tables are the norm in these establishments, covered with *zakuski* (appetizers), flowers and elaborate place settings. Plates of smoked fish, pickled vegetables, and cold vegetable salads greet arriving guests, with bottles of vodka, water, wine and soda rising like islands in the sea of food.

The restaurants in Brighton vary greatly in size and grandeur. On the most casual end of the spectrum are small luncheonettes with counters and the Russian equivalent of fast food. In the middle are cafes and boardwalk restaurants with umbrellas and tables overlooking the sea. At the top end are vast gilded nightclubs like The National and Rasputin, which can hold up to 500 people for a full-blown evening "affair." Common to all but the most

A shopkeeper jokes with customers outside his store.

casual of the Russian restaurants is an extravagant taste in interior design that makes even the smallest of them feel more like a stage set than a dining room. From the red walls of the Primorski restaurant, with its small colored lights and stained-glass sailing ships, to the marble bathrooms, crystal chandeliers, chrome and black enamel banquettes, gilt-edged balconies and strobe-lighted dance floors of the big nightclubs, these restaurants reek of indulgent fantasy. Every detail is intended to enhance the air of surreality. Blonde Russian torch singers in skin-tight, low-cut Spandex, a perfect Stevie Wonder impersonator at the Primorski, big bands with congas and horns, even full-scale floor shows like the pistol-packing gangster dance number at the Rasputin, complete with fedoras and double-breasted pinstripes, are a throwback to the dinner theater clubs of an earlier era. They also suggest a sense of irony and a capacity for self-parody in the owners and patrons of these clubs. The fantasy, the irony, the food, the music and the vodka all work together to create moments of shared emotional release that build intimacy and group feeling. They also make for great parties.

These restaurants have their roots in Soviet Jewish culture, where for half a century, from the 1930s to the '80s, it was not only difficult but dangerous for Jews to gather in groups. With the KGB on the steps of many synagogues, and gatherings in private homes subject to sudden police raids, restaurants were among the only places where Jews could gather in a relaxed atmosphere. In the Soviet Union, these communal spaces had to be camouflaged to deflect the attention of the authorities. That custom has been carried here. Although this is now beginning to change, for years Russian restaurants in Brighton hid their fabulous interiors with blank fronts, heavy curtains and blackened street-facing windows. This custom, which reflects both a lingering distrust of strangers and a desire to discourage casual browsing by outsiders, marks these restaurants as off-limits for tourists. Some of the fanciest of the clubs have been most extreme in their attempts to keep strangers out. The National, which replaced a two-floor furniture store that had been there for decades, removed a large plate-glass window and replaced it with a black metal wall broken only by a windowless wooden door. There is no way to imagine the strobe-lighted dance floor, the shows or the balcony tables inside unless you know what's there.

The owners of the Sadko, a two-floor, black and silver discotheque built on the site of an abandoned pizzeria, were even more intent on camouflage. For years, the Sadko preserved the pizzeria storefront, left exactly as it was on the day that it closed, complete with white counter and pizza ovens. Most casual shoppers on the avenue probably did not notice that over the faded letters of the sign for Mama Mia Pizzeria, was the word Sadko. The door to the pizzeria was double padlocked. A bare light bulb burned in the vestibule behind the store. There was absolutely no indication of the sleek discotheque within. But each weekend night, dark cars and limousines pulled up at the side entrance to the former pizzeria, where a signless wooden door admitted those in the know. In the mid-1980s, perhaps reflecting a greater sense of ease, the owners erected a nautical facade, but the port holes were high above the eye-level of passersby.

Such precautions have effectively kept strangers from venturing into most of the Russian restaurants in Brighton, and when they do they are often made to feel as though they have intruded on a family celebration. Still, in recent years, the signage has become more conventional: neon and gold lettering beckons from still-opaque windows, and enticing photographs of food and entertainers are often posted by the entrances. The *Village Voice*, the *New York Times* and other newspapers have begun to review the restaurants

Shuttered and unwelcoming during daylight hours, Russian restaurants in Brighton Beach come to life on weekend and summer nights as immigrant families gather for birthdays, anniversaries and *bar mitzvahs*.

in Brighton—even the infamous Rasputin—encouraging adventurous New Yorkers to make the trip. As a result both restaurateurs and patrons have grown somewhat more accustomed to outsiders entering their sanctuaries. For newcomers this may still be a bit daunting, but for emigres who have been living in New York for 20 years or more, fear and mistrust of strangers have abated and they have learned that tourism in ethnic enclaves is a time-honored part of American pluralism.

THE *BAR MITZVAH* AS A RITE OF AMERICANIZATION

Soviet Jewish emigres have shown other signs that they are absorbing American pluralist traditions. Soon after their arrival, parents began to make large parties to celebrate their children's *bar* and *bat mitzvahs*, the traditional Jewish initiation of 13-year-olds into full status in the religious community. Although some of the foods served, the music played and the settings where these ceremonies are performed seem shockingly irreligious to observant Jews, the same can be said of many *bar* and *bat mitzvah* parties thrown by American-born Jews. For Soviet immigrants, however, who were once afraid to observe Jewish rituals even in the privacy of their homes, this new freedom to express their Jewishness openly, with music and dance, reminds them how far they have come from the Soviet Union. It is also a sign that they are becoming acculturated to American Jewish ways. In this country, the *bar mitzvah*—traditionally just a proud day in the life of a boy and his parents— has been transformed into a rite through which the family displays to the larger community how well it has done in America. Living almost exclusively among other Jews, Soviet Jewish immigrants have become not just more American in their thoughts, dress and rituals of collective identity but more American-Jewish.

The Odessa restaurant on Brighton Beach Avenue has been for the past 20 years a favorite spot for Soviet immigrant *bar mitzvahs*. At one such celebration in the 1980s, poet Semyon Kommissar summed up the emotional meaning of the ritual for emigres like himself. "You don't know what it means that we can just get together like this in public to celebrate a *bar mitzvah*," he said with emotion, standing by the Odessa's centerpiece, a plaster Cupid fountain with delicate sprays of colored water. "Now I know I am in America. In Minsk I had to circumcise my grandson secretly, hiding, afraid all the time that someone would report me and I would be arrested. In Minsk, if this many Jews were gathered together for any reason the KGB would already be knocking at the windows." He laughed. "It couldn't happen."

I had come to the Odessa that night with several American-born Jews, two Polish Jewish immigrants and a non-Jew knowledgeable about Jewish religious culture. Everything about this *bar mitzvah* baffled them. "But this is Friday night," one said, "after sundown. It's already Sabbath. How can they hold a party on Friday night?" The others pointed aghast at the band, and literally gasped when electric guitars accompanied the *bar mitzvah* boy's blessings over the food and wine. As the father of the boy blessed his son, praying through the microphone that he become a source of pride to the Jewish people and to his new country, one of the American Jews noticed that waiters were serving shrimp appetizers to the guests. (Shrimp is strictly forbidden according to the laws of *kashrut* that govern the diets of religious Jews.) "Amazing," my friend whispered. The room was filled with the white light of cameras flashing. The guests heartily applauded the boy and sat down to eat their shrimp.

Between the shrimp and the main course the guests got up to dance. Crowding onto the dance floor they formed three circles, one inside the other. Then, with arms across each other's shoulders, they whirled in controlled glee to the electrified Russian and Yiddish disco songs that the Odessa band specialized in.

"It is possible," Kommissar said, explaining the seemingly irreligious ceremony, "that we have forgotten everything about the Jewish religion. But we have not forgotten that we are Jews. Can you understand what it is to these parents, and even more to the grandparents, to hear their boy recite Hebrew prayers in front of the community, their friends and neighbors? This is a wonderful thing for everyone here, not just friends and family. This is something that we did not even dream of. This is something that we are only just learning here in America."

Dinner too suggested that there were strong memories of Ashkenazi (European) Jewish tradition in this family. Brisket of beef, gefilte fish (ground carp and whiting with onions), and stuffed derma (bread stuffing in beef intestines) were served during dinner, a meal that would be familiar to most American Jews of East European descent. Afterward the guests rose to dance again. The band launched into a medley of Yiddish show tunes from the once-flourishing immigrant theater on Second Avenue in New York. The melodies and lyrics had somehow made their way to Odessa and now back to Little Odessa. At midnight the band struck up its theme song, "Oy Odyess." All the dancers kicked off their shoes and began to sing. Even outsiders were drawn into the party, invited to drink to the boy, then to his grandparents, to Odessa and finally to America. Soon nearly everyone was on the dance floor with arms around each other, dancing in raucous circles. The party did not break up until 2 A.M.

Since that evening the Odessa has changed its colors several times. The mirrors on the wall are gone, as are the gold sparkles and the plaster Cupid. A street-level storefront selling seafood and crepes has come and gone, as have several noted names in Russian-American organized crime. Brighton's Russian restaurants seem to be toning down. Women diners wear less purple chiffon and pink satin. Fewer men wear shirts open at the chest. Circle dancing seems largely to have disappeared, giving way to spirited dancing in pairs. By the summer of 1997, the band members at Primorski insisted that they did not know any circle dances, though they had played them enthusiastically only a few months earlier. A strain of highbrow snobbism has crept into the Russian restaurants of Brighton Beach. Still, they pulse with activity every Friday and Saturday night, as newly arrived immigrants join those who have been in the United States more than 20 years to eat, drink and dance. The arrival of tens of thousands of immigrants each year has kept alive the newcomers' hunger for safe places where they can relax and show off their recently acquired American wealth and style. But there is clearly an emotional

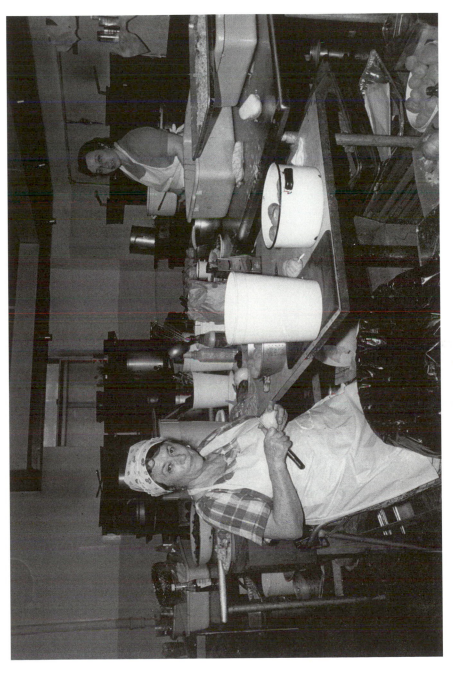

Preparing Ukrainian Jewish delicacies in the kitchen of the Odessa restaurant.

The hostess at the Odessa restaurant before the banquets begin.

need among Soviet immigrants old and new for a sense of community that these gathering places satisfy. For that reason the restaurants and nightclubs that line Brighton Beach will likely continue to play a central role in Soviet Jewish America for years to come.

FROM LITTLE ODESSA TO *VOROVSKOY MIR*
(THIEVES' WORLD)

During the 1980s and '90s, restaurants like the Odessa have also been the scene of some less than friendly "family" gatherings. Since the 1970s, several violent organized crime syndicates have made their headquarters in Brighton and have frequented these restaurants both to toast their friends and assassinate their enemies. The "Odessa mob" has made the name of Brighton Beach infamous among law enforcement agents from New York to Moscow. This trend began in the mid-1970s with the arrival of a small group of primarily Ukrainian Jewish gangsters who had learned their trade in the wide-open port city of Odessa. Released from prison by the Soviet government, they were granted exit visas in time to accompany the tens of thousands of honest citizens departing for Israel and the United States. They slipped into this country unnoticed by the FBI or local law enforcement. Some were non-Jews who used the identification papers and visas of deceased Jews. Typical of these early gangster immigrants was Evsei Agron, a short, Josef Stalin look-alike who listed his occupation as jeweler when he arrived at Kennedy Airport in 1975. He neglected to mention the seven years he had served in a Soviet prison camp for murder or the gambling and prostitution rings that he had been running in West Germany for the previous four years. Agron became the first boss of a Brighton-based Soviet mob operation profiting from extortion, prostitution and drug sales. A far more sophisticated organized crime syndicate was established in the late 1970s by Odessan black marketeer Marat Balagula, who masterminded multimillion-dollar gasoline frauds and created a crime network that stretched from Brighton to San Francisco. Though Balagula was convicted of fraud in 1994, his organization continues to run a network of corporations that invest illegally obtained cash in oil refineries, tankers, gas stations and truck stops (Friedman, *New York*: 1994; Friedman, *New York*: 1996; Burstein, *New York*: 1986).

On arrival in New York, Soviet criminals, like so many other Soviet Jewish emigres, headed straight for Brighton Beach. Brighton was a good spot for Russian mobsters for a variety of reasons. It was just a short drive from Kennedy Airport, an air link to fellow gang members in Europe and the former Soviet Union. Its teeming streets gave perfect cover; it was easy to hide among the 30,000 to 40,000 Soviet immigrants already living in Brighton. When immigrants first started arriving in the mid-1970s, there were plenty of vacant apartments, some of which were bought up in large blocks by gang bosses and rented to street soldiers as needed. One immigrant who moved to Brighton in the early 1980s recalls that there were entire buildings in one part of the neighborhood—huge Art Deco edifices with turrets, mosaics and long, dark hallways—that belonged to criminal families (Rosner 1986: 106).

Like most criminals, the Russian mob preyed first on their own: fellow Soviet refugees. The Odessa Mafia, as it was called by the FBI, first appeared in U.S. newspapers as "the Potato Bag Gang" for a fraud scheme in which it bilked Soviet emigre storekeepers in different parts of the United States out of thousands of dollars each by promising to sell them bags of gold coins that turned out to be filled with rocks and potatoes. In Brighton, as in so many immigrant communities, gang members also began extorting storekeepers for "protection" money; of course the "protectors" were those whom shopkeepers most feared. Evsei Agron ran protection rackets in Brighton that, by 1980, averaged $50,000 per week, extorted from local emigre shopkeepers with threats of violence. Loan sharks lent money at astronomical interest rates to naive aspiring entrepreneurs, new immigrants wary of any sort of official paperwork. Car-theft rings began to prowl the streets as well, sometimes recruiting children under the age of 16—who could not be sentenced to long prison terms—to commit the actual crime (California Office of the Attorney General, 1996).

For those who had known Brighton in earlier years as a community with little violence, the transformation was a shock. Suddenly people were being gunned down on the streets, sometimes in broad daylight. One October day in the early 1980s there was a particularly flagrant crime. On Yom Kippur, the Jewish Day of Atonement, one man was shot to death at close range in front of the Gastronom Odessa, a boardwalk cafe and social club. The gunman disappeared into the crowds on the boardwalk. It is always busy on the boardwalk on Yom Kippur because observant Jews fast on that day to atone for their sins and many pass the hours walking with friends and family, taking in the sea air. Stunned elderly Jews dressed in somber Holy Day attire gathered around the scene of the crime. One angry old man's voice could be heard above the crowd: "There is something very sick happening in this neighborhood. They shoot each other on the holiest day of the year. These cannot be Jews."

Since the collapse of the Soviet Union in 1991, many Soviet emigres most active in the U.S.-based underworld are in fact not Jewish. The most powerful competitor to Balagula is a *gory* (Moscow crime boss) named Vyacheslav Ivankov who moved to Brighton in 1992, masquerading as an ordinary Jewish immigrant. Sent by a consortium of crime syndicates that believed the U.S. market was too profitable to be left to Jewish gangsters alone, Ivankov established bases for more than 200 Russian crime families in U.S. cities, the majority of whose members are non-Jews who have emigrated since 1992. In 1995, Ivankov was arrested in Brighton Beach for extorting $3.5 million from two Soviet emigre investment bankers whom he had kidnapped at gunpoint from the bar at the New York Hilton. As with Balagula, Ivankov's imprisonment has not stopped the activity of the families he controls (*U.S. News & World Report*, 1995).

The reputation of Soviet Jewish immigrants, particularly those who live in Brighton, has suffered as a result of the adverse publicity generated by these criminals. By the mid-1990s, new Soviet immigrants shuddered angrily when asked if they lived or wanted to live in Brighton Beach. "I am not like the people there," one elderly woman said vehemently. "I work. Everyone in my family works. We are not like *that*."

Many Soviet emigres are deeply ambivalent about Brighton Beach, which they feel has created a distorted picture of them. The 1994 film *Little Odessa*, by Tim Roth, exemplified the media stereotyping that makes Russian emigres leery of association with Brighton Beach. In this grim portrayal, Brighton Beach is populated almost exclusively by leather-jacketed, gun-toting thugs. Though most Russian emigres reject that depiction, they fear that it still reflects badly upon them, and so they are quick to distance themselves from the area.

What they don't talk about are the ways in which Brighton Beach still serves as an emotional and cultural home base for Soviet Jews across the New York area—a place to shop, to visit relatives, and to celebrate birthdays, weddings, and anniversaries at Russian restaurants. It is the symbolic portal of immigration through which many, if not most, Soviet immigrants pass, but like most immigrant ghettoes, it has become a revolving door.

OTHER SOVIET JEWISH ENCLAVES IN NEW YORK

Brighton Beach has been overcrowded for years now. Apartments are hard to come by and rents are higher than in neighborhoods where housing is less in demand. With a flood of immigrants pouring into the city throughout the 1990s, what was once a fairly well-contained ethnic enclave in Brighton has become a citywide phenomenon. More recent immigrants have moved to Bay Ridge, Bensonhurst and Boro Park, among other parts of Brooklyn. And when apartments there became scarce in the 1990s, Jewish resettlement agencies began to look toward another neighborhood whose Jewish residents were dying or moving to Florida: Co-op City, a massive 35-building apartment complex in the Bronx built by the Amalgamated Clothing Workers Union.

All of the areas settled by the most recent emigres are working-class communities, solid neighborhoods with blocks of row houses, substantial 1930s Art Deco buildings or airy modern apartment towers. The more urban, the better for many of the emigres, who were almost all big-city dwellers in the Soviet Union. Many people would be put off, for example, by Co-op City, a 300-acre island in the South Bronx jammed with towering high-rise dwellings, but the Moscow, Kiev and St. Petersburg expatriates who have flocked there since 1987 seemed content with their urban aeries (Bryant-Friedland, *Bronx Beat Online*, 1995).

Many of the new emigres are proud of not living in Brighton, and speak glowingly of the friendships they have made with non-Russian neighbors. In Bensonhurst, tough-talking Russian emigre shopkeepers develop strong white-ethnic urban identities, enhanced by their sense of kinship with Italian-American and Italian immigrant neighbors. Similar bonds have been formed in Boro Park and Williamsburg, where Soviet Jews live in varying degrees of comfort with their intensely religious Hasidic neighbors. Among the older generation, friendships are often made in the stores and markets along the main avenues where Russian and Hasidic women sometimes speak to each other in their shared language, Yiddish. While many of the Hasidic customs bemuse and bewilder the Russians, some have proven quite helpful. On occasion, Hasidic women, in keeping with their religious mandate to care for the sick, have brought food and medicine to elderly Russian Jews living alone. While the Russians, raised in a state profoundly hostile to religion, find it difficult to relate to the Hasidim's religiosity, they express pleasure that religious Jews can practice their faith openly in America.

In fact, Russian emigres are comfortable enough with their Hasidic neighbors that they have taken to sharing the same summer retreats. Overwhelmed by the summer heat and humidity, both groups spend as much time as they can each summer in the old Jewish Catskills. The more successful Soviet emigres vacation at renovated, "Borscht Belt" resort hotels well known to an earlier generation of American Jews and children of immigrants. These hotels, which had their heyday in the 1950s and '60s, are once again enjoying sell-out crowds. But even those emigres who cannot afford these resorts leave the city for ramshackle 1920s-era bungalow colonies in neighboring Catskill towns.

They are reviving an even older Jewish-American vacation tradition of renting the decaying summer cottages in White Lake and Monticello, New York, that were the summer refuge of Jewish immigrants in the 1920s, '30s

This mother and son are two of the recent Ukrainian Jewish immigrants who have rented out this summer bungalow colony in White Lake, New York. Founded in the 1920s, this and other nearby colonies were then vacation rentals for pre–World War I Jewish immigrants from Eastern Europe.

and '40s. These white-and-green summer cottages are once again filled with children and grandparents on weekdays. Working parents join them on weekends. They share these summer communities with the Satmar Hasidim—the most insular Hasidic sect—who stroll along White Lake in black caftans and wide-brimmed hats. Together, they have given new life to these resort ghost towns, as they have to so many fading Jewish institutions of an earlier era.

Soviet emigres have also revitalized other early 20th-century Jewish immigrant landmarks in New York, Boston and Chicago. One of the loveliest is the Ocean Parkway Jewish Center in Brooklyn, built in the 1920s, with

This woman came from Minsk to Bensonhurst, Brooklyn, in 1995 because she needed heart surgery. During the summers she cares for her grandchildren at this bungalow colony in White Lake, New York. The children's parents come up for weekends.

wide curving wooden stairways on either side of the lobby and an intricate stained-glass dome atop the sanctuary. Long the pride of an earlier immigrant community, the Jewish Center had been losing members for years as elderly congregants died or moved to Florida. There were too few members left by 1984 to pay for the upkeep of the once grand building. That year, Minsk immigrants Edith and Alex Shvartsman came to the officers of the congregation with a proposal. They wished to rent space inside the synagogue to run a school for the children of Soviet Jews and any other child who wished to attend. Leasing the space would enable the cash-strapped synagogue to survive, and the school, the Shvartsmans promised, would emphasize Jewish cultural heritage, even though it would not offer religious instructions.

That year, they opened the International Children's Center for the Performing Arts, a music, dance and gymnastics conservatory. The Shvartsmans had three purposes in creating the Children's Center. Edith says that she "wanted to help other immigrants who were musicians, performers, dancers. It is not easy in America to find jobs in the arts." Second, she and Alex wished to ease the trauma of relocating by creating a friendly after-school space for Soviet immigrant children to develop social skills and self-confidence, not easy in a strange culture. Finally, they wanted to teach children of immigrants about Jewish culture and heritage. Although they do not teach religion, children learn music pieces in Yiddish and Hebrew as well as Russian and English. They learn Israeli and Ashkenazi as well as Russian dance. Interestingly, as word has gotten out about the quality of the arts training there, the student body has diversified. The school has met that challenge by training students in Italian and Latin music, song and dance as well.

For the dwindling congregation of this synagogue, many of whom attend the annual Spring concert given by the school, there is mixed sadness and joy as they crowd into the sanctuary to hear the children sing Yiddish songs that date back a half century or more. The International Children's School and other new immigrant institutions like it mark the passing of an earlier Jewish way of life even as they affirm a Russian-Jewish identity in a new generation. Scores of similar schools have appeared in fading synagogues, religious schools or Yiddish socialist meeting halls. Like other immigrant parents, Soviet emigres push their children to attend, hoping to ensure that they will hang on to the language and culture into which they were born, but many of these schools, unlike the International Children's Center, have failed fairly quickly. Like most children, young Soviet emigres resent having to attend yet another school at the end of their regular school day. In that, they have something in common with children of every religion and race.

BUKHARAN AND GEORGIAN JEWS IN REGO PARK AND FOREST HILLS, QUEENS

Far removed from Brighton Beach culturally but similarly insulated and close knit are two ethnic enclaves created by Soviet Jewish immigrants from Georgia and Uzbekistan. Both have established islands within the larger Russian Jewish communities of Forest Hills and Rego Park, Queens, where they keep mostly to themselves, praying in separate synagogues, celebrating in their own restaurants. The larger of the two groups consists of Bukharan Jews from Uzbekistan, Tadjikistan and Kazakhstan in Central Asia. Since the 1970s, more than 35,000 Bukharan emigres have created a bustling ethnic enclave in Forest Hills, with Central Asian restaurants, barber shops, specialty food stores and five Bukharan synagogues giving 108th Street the nickname "Bukharan Broadway" (Gorin, *Newsday*, 1995).

Culturally, linguistically and religiously distinct from their Western Soviet counterparts, Bukharan emigres believe themselves to be descendants of an ancient Persian Jewish community, and trace their origins in Uzbekistan as far back as the fifth century. Bukharan Jews have never spoken Yiddish. Their language is a dialect of the Tadjik variety of Persian, but like Yiddish, it contains many words in Hebrew and is written in Hebrew characters. During the early Stalin years, when writing in Hebrew was banned, many Bukharan Jews started writing in Arabic characters; during the purges of the 1930s, to further deflect attention, they switched to Cyrillic characters. Nevertheless, having lived for centuries in a land bordered by Iran, Afghanistan, Pakistan and China, Bukharan Jews consider themselves Asian and Middle Eastern, and share in the cultural identity of Tadjiks and Iranians—just as Western Soviet Jews identify with Russian culture and with Europe more generally (Carr, 1997; Federation of Jewish Philanthropies of New York, 1982).

Since the fall of the Soviet Union, three major factors have driven more than 60,000 Uzbek Jews to emigrate: a strong nationalist revival, the rise of an anti-Semitic Uzbek government, and an increase in grass-roots violence against Jews. Most Ashkenazi Jews who had been living in Tashkent, the capital of Uzbekistan, emigrated to Israel. But the majority of immigrant Jews of Bukharan origin from Tashkent, Bukhara and Samarkand have moved to the United States. It is difficult to get exact numbers for this immigration but, based on HIAS and federal government statistics, there are close to 50,000 legal Bukharan immigrants in this country. There are small Bukharan communities in Chicago, Los Angeles, Seattle and Denver. But just as Brighton has become the symbolic center of the immigrant community for Russian, Ukrainian and Byelorussian Jews, so the ethnic enclave that spans Rego Park and Forest Hills, Queens, is the heart of Bukharan Jewish life in the United States. The largest outmigration of Bukharans occurred in the 1990s. With only a small community left in Uzbekistan, it may be said that Queens is now one of the most important centers of Bukharan Jewish life in the world (*World Jewish Congress on line* 1995–1996; Halberstadt and Nikolsky, 1996).

From the ancient domed and pinnacled cities of Bukhara, Tashkent and Samarkand, which were already weathered one thousand years ago, it is a vast geographic and cultural leap to the 20-story apartment buildings and sprawling grid of numbered streets that dominate the landscape of Queens.

Rego Park got its name in the 1920s from a real estate developer who advertised his buildings as "a real good place to live." Forest Hills is greener than Rego Park and the streets are curvier, but the neighborhood's main artery, Queens Boulevard, is a freeway-like monster that discourages all but the most fearless pedestrians. An unlikely setting for an ethnic enclave, this section of Queens is the largest area of Soviet Jewish settlement in New York after Brighton and one of the most diverse Jewish communities in the country ("Our Story," *Newsday*, 1998).

Relations among these different groups of immigrant Jews are not always smooth. Elderly Polish Jews complain that the Bukharans are noisy and lawless. "They don't live by any rules," says one longtime Forest Hills resident. "If someone gets married, the band and wedding reception are in my hallway. The men drink and keep the women in their place." Recent Russian and Ukrainian immigrants complain that the Bukharans reflect badly on them. "They're not real Russians," says David, a 13-year-old immigrant who attends a Queens junior high school with Bukharan children. "We get offended when you call them Russians." Children of other Soviet Jewish immigrants are quick to reject Bukharan classmates who try to befriend them, says Susan Sokirko, who runs a program for Russian-speaking students at Forest Hills High School. The Bukharans "feel like outcasts because of their accents and backgrounds. They get made fun of and that keeps them from trying again" (Gorin, *Newsday*, 1995).

Such conflicts have reinforced the Bukharans' tendency to form a close-knit, insular community. The problems that their children have encountered in Queens public schools have convinced some Bukharan parents that the best route to success is not through education but through the family business. As in the largely Ukrainian Jewish community in Brighton, immigrant entrepreneurship has played a key role in Bukharan acculturation to New York life. Children are expected to play a full part in those businesses as soon as they hit their mid-teens. With a long heritage as merchants and artisans, Bukharan Jews were allowed to own their own property and engage in business well into the Soviet era. Their long-established commercial ties allowed them to become adept commodities traders during periods of shortages in the major cities of the Soviet West.

Although they eventually were barred from owning businesses, like everyone else in the Soviet Union, Jews in Uzbekistan gravitated to retail or service occupations; they worked as retail sales clerks, cab drivers, cooks, restaurant managers, barbers and hairdressers. Many Bukharan families built on their experience in those trades to open similar businesses in Queens. Some of the more successful businessmen moved their shops to Manhattan. A number of

Rakhmin Pinkasov, an elder of the Bukharan
Jewish community in Rego Park.

furniture stores on Lower Broadway and jewelry stores on 47th Street—
where Hasidic immigrant diamond cutters practice their trade—are owned
and run by Bukharan immigrants. In comparison with many Soviet emigres
from the West, the economic adjustment of Bukharan Jews has been rapid
and successful. Family businesses, which rely on the combined labor of children, parents and grandparents, are flourishing. As in many immigrant families, the long hours of working together reinforce traditional family structures
and the close-knit nature of the community. They also pave the way for
teenage rebellion by those who wish to blaze their own paths in this country
(Halberstadt, 1996: 246).

 With relatively few Bukharan Jews left in the former Soviet Union, emigres
are conscious of re-creating a nation in exile in their Queens, Brooklyn and
Jerusalem neighborhoods. In stark contrast to Jews in the Western Soviet

Revekka Pinkasov and her sister in the living room of their Queens apartment.

republics, Bukharan Jews were deeply religious prior to emigrating—and they have retained that devotion. While Jews from the western Soviet Union have, in the main, rejected attempts to make them religious (stressing instead preservation of the language, literature and music of Soviet Jewry), Bukharan Jews have embraced Orthodox religious practice. That religiosity has generated close ties between Bukharan immigrants and New York City's fast-growing community of Lyubavitch Hasidim (an Orthodox sect founded in Russia that has made a mission of bringing non-observant Jews back to the fold). One in three Bukharan children attends yeshiva rather than public school. And one well-known community member, Rabbi Yitzhak Yehoshua, became a practicing Lyubavitch and developed a large following among his fellow Bukharan emigres (Gorin, *Newsday*, 1995).

But the Lyubavitch-affiliated Bukharans are still a minority. Most continue

The Pinkasov's granddaughter, dressed for a family celebration.

to practice their ancient traditions. They celebrate Jewish holidays in the Persian style that they have followed for more than a thousand years, observe the Sabbath and strictly follow the laws of *kashrut* (dietary restrictions.) Keeping kosher was easier in Central Asia than in the Soviet West because the majority of the population was Muslim. Muslim ritual slaughtering is very similar to kosher slaughtering and, like Jews, Muslims abstain from eating pork. Up to and through the time of emigration, Bukharan Jewish families continued to make *bar mitzvah* ceremonies for their 13-year-old sons and to throw lavish weddings for their children. Weddings were the most important celebrations for Muslim and Jewish families in Uzbekistan and many saved throughout their lives to marry their children off in proper fashion (Halberstadt, 1996; Carr, 1997).

Bukharan traditions have changed very little in the United States. Many parents still arrange marriages for their children, and *toys* (weddings) remain one of the central rituals in the life of the community. Like their Russian and Ukrainian counterparts in Brighton, Bukharan Jews celebrate weddings in grand style, often in the Central Asian restaurants of Forest Hills and Rego Park. Interestingly, the vogue locale for Bukharan Jewish weddings is Leonard's of Great Neck. Thirty years ago Leonard's was the sine qua non for extravagant Jewish *bar mitzvahs* and weddings. With its ice sculpture swans holding beds of chopped liver on their backs, a two-story crystal chandelier and a plexiglass grand piano, Leonard's was the pinnacle of excess (read success) for an earlier generation of Jewish immigrants and their children. Now it has become so for the least assimilated of all Soviet Jewish immigrants, who act out visions of the "American Dream" at Leonard's that are as fantastic as the fabled cities from which they have come. Whatever the path of migration—from Samarkand to Queens or from Minsk to Brooklyn to Long Island—the rites of Americanization for immigrant Jews seem to take place on the same gaudy grounds.

Much of the substance of the immigrant *toy* is imported from home, but the rest is an amalgam of Russian, European, Israeli and American influences. As in many Soviet weddings, there is a *vedushchii* (master of ceremonies) who introduces the members of the wedding party to the guests, pokes fun, and generally keeps the audience alert and entertained. The marriage service varies depending on whether the rabbi follows the traditions of the Bukharan synagogue or—those of the Lyubavitch. The food, too, runs the gamut from traditional Central Asian dishes like *plov* (rice pilaf) and *shashlyk* (shish kebab), to the cold vegetable salads that are ubiquitous in Soviet emigre cooking, to Leonard's more traditional "American Jewish" fare, much of which overlaps with what Bukharans are accustomed to eating. These dishes include lox (smoked salmon), roast chicken and jellied calves' feet. The music that follows the meal at Bukharan festivities is as mixed as that of the Russian restaurants in Brighton Beach. There is everything from ancient Bukharan wedding songs played by ensembles dressed in the multicolored silks that Jews in Samarkand have woven and dyed for centuries, to Neapolitan love songs and Israeli folk dances played by performers in tuxedos and flashy jewelry (Levin, 1997: 278–79).

In the larger Russian and Bukharan communities of Forest Hills are two much smaller Jewish ethnic groups, which also emigrated recently from the former Soviet Union—Mountain Jews from Azerbaijan and the Eastern Caucasus, and Georgian Jews. Both have unique cultures distinct from each other and from Ashkenazi Jews. Both were among the earliest residents of the Caucasus region, with roots dating back five to eight centuries before Christ. The Caucasian Mountain Jews are the smallest ethnic group among Soviet

Jewish emigres in New York, most having emigrated to Israel. Like other indigenous Central Asian Jews, they speak no Yiddish. Their Jewish dialect is called Judeo-Tat, a north Iranian language that uses some Hebrew words. Tat, like Yiddish and the Tajik dialect of the Bukharans, was, until the Stalin era, written in Hebrew characters.

The Mountain Jews, who are sometimes called Tats, believe they arrived in the Caucasus at the time of the Babylonian conquest of Judea. Two thousand years ago, this tribe of warriors swept across the region conquering and settling villages in the Caucasus mountains. They lived in low mud huts, like other Caucasian mountain dwellers, until the late 1920s, when Soviet authorities imposed a more modern way of life on them. In the Stalin era, local party leaders launched a fierce attack on Tat culture. In 1938 the Tats were forced to adopt the cyrillic alphabet. Stalinist officials attempted to purge the Tat language of its Hebrew words, and most Tat religious schools and synagogues were closed. Despite the repression, the Tats retained a strong sense of their religious, cultural and linguistic traditions. Intermarriage remains minimal and nearly all weddings are celebrated with ancient religious ceremonies. Their religiosity and independence, as well as their primarily rural lifestyle, prompted most Tats to emigrate to Israel. But several hundred have emigrated to the United States each year during the 1990s, many settling in the New York area ("Azerbaijan," *Virtual Jerusalem*, 1996).

Georgian Jews, perhaps the oldest indigenous Jewish community in the former Soviet Union, were also among the most devoutly religious. They too trace their origins to the beginning of the Jewish Diaspora, when Babylonian King Nebuchadnezzar scattered the Jewish tribes after sacking Jerusalem. Archaeological sites offer evidence of Jewish residence in the region of present-day Tbilisi from as early as the second century B.C. For millennia, Georgian Jews have referred to themselves as *hivri*, from the Hebrew for Jew, or *ebraeli*, which means Israeli in Georgian, and they call their community *dzhamaathi*, from the Arabic *djama'at*, which means community.

A strong sense of community and commitment to religious tradition was possible well into the 20th century as Georgia was one of the least anti-Semitic regions of the former Russian Empire and Soviet Union. Under the tsar, Georgian Jews did suffer legal and economic restrictions, and, despite their two-thousand-year residence in Georgia, they were declared foreigners, as opposed to "native" Georgians. This denaturalization, in the place they had occupied for so many years, sparked a great interest among Georgian Jews in early 20th-century Zionism. A handful emigrated to Jerusalem in 1926. By the 1930s, Soviet authorities tried to enforce assimilation of Georgian Jews by criminalizing Jewish customs and religious celebrations. Still, the repression did not take root as deeply in Georgia as in other parts of the Soviet Union because there was simply less native anti-Semitism. Though there were arrests during the purges of the 1930s, local officials were loath to enforce the anti-Semitic provisions of their native son, Joseph Stalin.

As a result, Jewish traditions continued to flourish in Georgia to a far greater degree than in other parts of the former Soviet Union. Congregations celebrated Passover communally in the courtyards of synagogues. Georgian Jews have long performed traditional wedding and funeral processions quite openly through the streets of Tbilisi and smaller Georgian towns, with music played by professional musicians and congregants singing Hebrew chants unique to their community. As late as 1979 half of all synagogues in the Soviet Union were located in the Republic of Georgia ("Festival," 1982; "Georgia," *Virtual Jerusalem: Jewish Communities of the World*).

Once the doors were opened, Georgian Jews poured into Israel, a few thousand in the 1970s, and more than 15,000 since 1989. Several thousand have also emigrated to the United States, many of them settling in Forest Hills, Queens, where they have their own synagogues, restaurants, businesses and community organizations. The Georgian Jews are largely well educated; many had been professionals prior to emigration. Among those from the capital of Tbilisi are a large number of physicians, engineers, artists and academics. Some have been able to find work in their fields. Others have fallen back on entrepreneurship, the immigrant's economic mainstay, or become computer programmers, a particularly popular option among Soviet emigres.

Like the Bukharan Jews among whom they live, many Georgian Jewish emigres have become more rather than less religious in the United States. They observe Sabbath in a synagogue decorated with the silverwork and embroidered cloth traditional to Georgian Jewish observance. Although *brit* (circumcision), wedding and *bar mitzvah* ceremonies were celebrated in the home prior to emigration, in New York, where almost as many Georgian women as men work outside the home, the burden of such celebrations has been shifted to local restaurants. Forest Hills has a number of Georgian and Caucasian restaurants, as does Brighton Beach. There immigrant families sit down at banquet tables to eat strongly flavored Georgian fare, which adds *lavash* (round bread), *sateni* (friend carp with pomegranates), yogurt and *brinza* (salted goat's milk cheese) to the usual Soviet favorites. Guests dance to Georgian Jewish melodies, and to the Russian, Israeli and American music found at the communal celebrations of other Jewish immigrants from the Soviet Union. The *tamada*, usually an older man whose job is to lead toasts, songs, and dances, tell stories and amuse the guests, is a Georgian version of the *vedushchii* who takes charge at Bukharan and other Soviet immigrant parties (Federation, "Festival," 1982).

In many ways the communal life-cycle celebrations that Soviet Jews hold in restaurants and catering halls throughout Brooklyn and Queens are an apt metaphor for their adaptation to life in this country. For the jarring, ebullient tapestry of sounds, tastes and sights that one finds at so many Soviet immigrant weddings, birthdays, and *bar mitzvahs* is a reflection of the fragmented process of change that dominates these emigre lives: uprooting and replanting, remembering and forgetting, negotiating the tension between preserving what each valued from the old land and embracing wholeheartedly the pleasures of the new. Since the 1970s, Soviet Jews of varied backgrounds have formed vibrant enclaves across the United States—most particularly in New York—where immigrants with limited command of English and little previous exposure to American culture can ease their adjustment to the new land. There is nothing ethnically or culturally pure about these enclaves, the hundreds of thousands of Soviet Jews who have settled in New York since the early 1970s came not from a homogeneous society but from an extraordinarily diverse continent that militaristic Russian rulers have dominated for 200 years. Well before their arrival in the United States the cultures of Soviet Jews in various republics of the Soviet Union were synthetic, shaped by a range of influences from Southern and Northern Europe, Russia, Asia and the Middle East. From that culturally mixed polyglot empire they came to what may be the most culturally, ethnically, linguistically diverse city in the world. Their process of adjustment has been correspondingly complex.

The impact of Soviet Jewish emigres on New York has been tremendous. Even with a sizeable number of children in private religious academies, Soviet Jews have become the second-largest group of foreign-born students in the city's public schools. Because nearly one-third of Soviet emigres in New York are elderly, they are also the largest immigrant consumers of government assistance in the city. But these newcomers have been a boon to the city's economy as well. The long hours and tireless labor of immigrant shopkeepers and restaurateurs have helped to revitalize flagging neighborhood economies across Brooklyn and Queens. And, with their superb educations in math and science, Soviet researchers, computer programmers and medical technicians have made their presence felt in New York area universities and hospitals, in the financial centers of Wall Street and corporate offices of midtown Manhattan. Continued immigration to New York in the next decades will reinforce all of these trends. And for as long as the immigration lasts, one thing is sure. The ethnic enclaves will continue to flourish as comfortable havens for some, sites of nostalgia for others and as claustrophobia-inducing nightmares to a third group of emigres who wish nothing more than to leave "the ghetto" far behind them (Tress and Gold, 1996).

BEYOND NEW YORK: URBAN AND SUBURBAN
SETTLEMENTS ACROSS THE UNITED STATES

Although the Soviet emigre community in the New York area is five to six times the size of the next largest settlement, nearly one in two Soviet Jewish immigrants now in the United States lives outside New York. The four cities with the largest concentrations of Soviet Jews are Los Angeles, San Francisco, Chicago and Boston. Smaller communities have settled in Philadelphia, Baltimore, Cleveland and Detroit. Smaller still, and quite different in feel, are the immigrant communities in American "heartland" cities, including Minneapolis, Cincinnati and St. Louis. The lives of Soviet Jewish emigres in these varied locales are shaped not only by the size and demography of each immigrant community, but also by the size and nature of each city's Jewish population and by the region's geography, economy, politics and particular quality of life. The similarities between Soviet Jewish emigre communities reflect the homogenizing power both of Soviet Russian culture and of American mass-market culture. The differences reflect the cultural and political complexity of an immigration that has drawn nearly half a million people from urban centers across one of the world's most diverse nations to make their new homes in another of the world's most ethnically and geographically varied nations (HIAS, 1996).

Since the late 1970s, the vast majority of Soviet immigrants to the United States have settled where they had family members who could sponsor them. Those with friends or family living in New York found homes there, while those with friends or family in Boston, Los Angeles or Cleveland settled in those cities. The issue of family sponsorship has been particularly important for Fourth Wave immigrants—post-1987 arrivals—most of whom applied for visas after the federal government ceased granting automatic refugee status to Soviet Jews. For the most part, these immigrants needed families to pay a portion of settlement costs, provide temporary housing and food, and sign guarantees that they would not allow the new immigrants to accept public assistance. In general, patterns of settlement in the 1990s followed those established in the 1970s.

How and why did those earlier immigrants choose to go where they did? The majority headed for New York because that was the first, the largest and the best-known of Soviet emigre settlements in the United States. Those who chose cities other than New York tended to do so for one of three reasons.

A small number had remained in contact with relatives whose ancestors had emigrated at the turn of the century. A slightly larger group chose cities with local economies best suited their job skills. But most Third Wave emigres who ended up outside New York were settled by the Hebrew Immigrant Aid Society and the Federation of Jewish Philanthropies as part of a strategy of broad dispersion.

When it became clear in the late 1970s that the numbers of Soviet Jews seeking refuge in the United States were going to be higher than anyone had anticipated, aid agencies tried to distribute the financial and social service burdens of resettlement among as many American Jewish communities as were willing to take in immigrants. Despite massive aid from the federal government, the cost of resettling hundreds of thousands of immigrants has been staggering. At $3,000 per individual or between $5,000 and $8,000 per family (not counting contributions by family members or refugee benefits provided by the federal government) the overall cost of this immigration to Jewish charitable agencies, synagogues, municipal and state governments has been in excess of $1.25 billion. There was simply no way that any city, even New York, could absorb everyone. Agents of the Hebrew Immigrant Aid Society, working in Rome and Vienna, offered emigres a variety of settlement options outside of the New York area. Boston, Chicago and Los Angeles were the most popular options.

The issue of resettlement costs became more urgent than ever in the early 1990s when nearly 220,000 Soviet Jews entered the country legally. By the fall of 1989, HIAS agents in Rome were working around the clock to help Soviet Jews enter the United States. The numbers leaving from Rome's Da Vinci airport for U.S. cities jumped 10 times from an average of 130 a day to 1,300 (*St. Louis Post Dispatch*, 9/26/89). When the flood continued into the '90s, Jewish agency and municipal social service providers began to panic. "A TIDE OF SOVIET EMIGRES THREATENS TO INUNDATE NEW YORK," blared a 1991 *Los Angeles Times* headline. "CITY SERVICES MAY BE SWAMPED" (*Los Angeles Times*, 1/02/91).

The numbers peaked at 69,000 Soviet immigrants entering the country in 1992. Jewish communities across the United States were taking in as many immigrants as they could but they were quickly overtaxed. Before the flood had even begun, most cities decided to accept only those immigrants who already had family living there. "Two years ago, we could manage with the kind of delivery system we had," said a weary Joel Carp, assistant executive director of the Chicago Federation of Jewish Philanthropies, in September 1989. "But this increase has been so dramatic and unexpected, we've had a financial emergency." There were simply not enough English teachers to accommodate so many new immigrants. And without English, the new immigrants had little chance of finding work. Neither were there enough apartments, jobs or medical professionals to handle the flow of emigres, which by 1991 reached about 2,000 per year (Oloroso, 1989; HIAS 1997).

In Los Angeles, immigrant aid workers and social service agencies were overwhelmed well before the arrival of an estimated 50,000 Soviet refugees in the early 1990s. With a vast population of illegal as well as legal immigrants, Los Angeles English classes were already overenrolled, and immigrants from across Asia, Latin America and Mexico lined up daily for medical, housing and vocational services. Prior to 1989 the federal government had shouldered a good deal of the cost of resettling Soviet immigrants, providing special allotments for those designated as refugees. After 1989, the U.S. government ended automatic refugee status for Soviet Jews, which did nothing to stop the flow of emigres into the coastal suburbs of Rome, where they besieged the U.S. Embassy, begging to be allowed to rejoin families in the United States.

Hoping to alleviate the pain of families like Alla and Boris Wayntrub, who waited miserably in a tiny Studio City apartment while their children and grandchildren paced the halls of the U.S. Embassy in Rome, the federal government in 1989 began admitting more than 2,000 Soviet Jews per month without refugee benefits. The official term for these immigrants was "parolees." Barred from seeking citizenship for several years, and from federally funded programs to help immigrants find housing, jobs and medical care, these "parolees" turned to local synagogues, private charities, social service agencies and family members (Chazanov and Schrader, *Los Angeles Times*, 1989).

In many cities, Third Wave immigrants shouldered much of the burden of resettling post-1989 arrivals. During 1989 and 1990, the Los Angeles-based Association of Soviet Jewish Emigres marshalled the resources of Soviet immigrants throughout Southern California to aid the newcomers. "We spent 10 to 15 years putting our roots in this country," said Association president Gregory Makaron. "We are ready to pay back whatever was done for us." Late in 1989, third wave emigres opened a drop-in center on Santa Monica Boulevard in West Hollywood, near the neighborhoods where more than 20,000 Soviet Jews had settled. Each day scores of dazed immigrants drifted into the drop-in center to seek comfort and advice in a familiar tongue from those who had already made the disorienting transition from the breadlines of collapsing Russian Communism to the traffic jams of triumphant American capitalism. Members of the Association handed out a Russian-language survival guide to Los Angeles and offered advice on how to apply for social services, look for housing and, most important, find jobs quickly. New emigres could also help themselves to a storage room full of food, clothing, furniture, mattresses and other household necessities donated by the established Soviet immigrant community (Steinberg, *Los Angeles Times*, 1989).

Los Angeles, like Chicago and New York, was initially a tough job market for many Soviet emigres. Competition for entry-level positions is particularly intense in Los Angeles County, which has perhaps the highest concentration of immigrants in the country. A 1996 study found that recently arrived Soviet Jews in Los Angeles and New York earned up to a third less than their fellow immigrants in other cities. The most intrepid immigrants have done fairly well. Indeed, a majority of Fourth Wave emigres to Los Angeles found some sort of work within eight months of their arrival. But a sizeable minority remained unemployed beyond their first year in the United States. They, along with more than 10,000 elderly immigrants in Los Angeles, have had to depend heavily on Supplemental Social Security, Medicare and food stamps (Tress, 1996; Soble, *Los Angeles Times*, 1989; Steinberg, *Los Angeles Times*, 1989).

The employment picture in San Francisco and Boston was quite a bit better, even during the peak years of immigration in the early 1990s. In these two smaller cities, extremely well-educated immigrants, a majority of whom had lived in Moscow and Leningrad, were easily integrated into booming high-technology industries. Immigrants to San Francisco did remarkably well, even with an estimated 2,500 people annually pouring into a city whose total population was far smaller than that of Chicago, New York or Los Angeles. The Jewish Vocational and Career Counseling Service in San Francisco placed more than a thousand immigrant workers in jobs each year, despite a deep state-wide recession and a hodge-podge of prior work experience among the emigres that ranged from highly specialized assembly-line work to cloud seeding to hide missile locations (Shaw, *San Francisco Business Times*, 1990; Collier, *San Francisco Chronicle*, 1993).

In a region with an ever expanding high-technology sector, these immigrants' skills fit labor market needs fairly closely. Eighty-five percent of employable adults between the ages of 18 to 55 were working within a year. About 40 percent of those early placements were in computer-related jobs. High-technology employment has been the most important wedge for young Soviet emigres across the United States who are seeking to break into the American job market. Excellent Soviet technical education can partly explain this phenomenon. Also, in the computer field, a limited knowledge of English does not impede advancement. Newly arrived Soviet emigres with strong technical backgrounds were snapped up by high-technology companies including Mitsubishi, IBM and National Semiconductor Corp. One result has been a growing concentration of Soviet immigrants in Silicon Valley (HIAS 1996).

Boston and its suburbs—particularly Newton—have proved to be perhaps the friendliest market in the country for Soviet emigres seeking work. Although it is one of the country's largest regions for Soviet settlement, with a population of more than 50,000 immigrants in the city and environs, employment counselors have consistently been able to place more than 95 percent of employable adults in jobs by the end of their first year. Even more remarkable, a full 50 percent of these placements have been in professional, health care or computer jobs. The Soviet immigrant community in Boston has provided the strongest evidence that an immigrant's city of origin and educational level play a powerful part in determining his or her success in this country. More than three-quarters of the immigrants to Boston came from Moscow and Leningrad; 63 percent had college degrees, and an astonishing 40 percent had post-graduate degrees (Franklin, *Boston Globe*, 1989; Anand, *Boston Globe*, 1995).

Soviet emigres to Boston have also had another advantage over their counterparts in New York, Chicago and Los Angeles. During the 1990s, Jews from the former Soviet Union were the largest group of immigrants entering Boston, which has fewer immigrants overall than these larger cities. Perhaps this is why they have encountered little of the hostility that has greeted these newcomers in other cities. If anything, the reception has been quite the opposite. In the early 1990s, the Massachusetts Bus and Transit Authority began printing Boston bus and subway maps in Russian, the first time those maps had ever appeared in a foreign language. Emigres in Boston found vocational, educational and social service counselors who were far less overwhelmed than their counterparts in cities with larger immigrant populations. And, once on the job market, they did not face the same kind of competition from Asian, Latin American, Caribbean and other Soviet immigrants.

The emphasis on science and technology in Soviet schools dovetailed with the surging demand in Massachusetts for high-technology workers in the 1980s, creating an ideal climate for this highly educated group of Soviet emigres. They have also found work in accounting and health care. Even as the Massachusetts economy spiraled downward in the 1990s, well-educated immigrants were able to find a toe-hold, even if not in their original fields. Some were forced, at least temporarily, to take low-skilled jobs. One Soviet physicist delivered pizza in his old station wagon for a while, but like many former Soviet academics, he later found work in health-care management (Sessler, *Boston Globe*, 1996).

Employment patterns for Soviet Jewish immigrants in mid-size cities such as Baltimore, Cleveland and Detroit have been more similar to those of Boston and San Francisco than to the larger cities like New York, Chicago and Los Angeles. The problem has been that these cities have nothing that compares with the California or Massachusetts high-technology industries. But energetic efforts by local affiliates of the Jewish Federation have resulted in very high employment rates—usually more than 80 percent—within the first year. Age seems to be the most important determinant in immigrants' success on the job market. Recent studies of the Detroit community, numbering just under 10,000, have shown a great deal of success among people 35 to 49 years old, who have median incomes of $35,000. Of these, 62 percent have bought or are in the process of buying homes, usually in neighboring suburbs. Those under 35 are doing equally well financially, although many are still living with their parents. Older working-age adults between 50 and 64 have had a much harder time, with 24 percent still unemployed three years after arriving in Detroit. And for those over 65 who wish to work, the success rate has been poor indeed: More than 75 percent of those wishing to work have been unable to find paid employment. As in other parts of the country, elderly immigrants in Detroit have been heavily dependent on public assistance (Becker and Isaacs, 1996; Gitelman, 1981: 11–28; Gilson, 1981: 29–56).

In some ways, the patterns of Soviet immigrant life have been consistent from New York to Chicago to Los Angeles. In every city with large numbers of Soviet emigres, there are colorful ethnic enclaves that make the immigration visible to outsiders. Los Angeles, Chicago, San Francisco and Boston all have neighborhoods that have been "Russianized." These communities had historically been home to East European Jewish immigrants. In the decade before Soviet immigration began, aging and suburbanization had sent those neighborhoods into decline. In Los Angeles, West Hollywood and Fairfax have now become Russian enclaves; in Chicago, it's West Rogers Park and Skokie. In San Francisco, the Richmond and Sunset districts boast thriving Russian communities. And in Boston, Brighton has become home to the city's largest Soviet community, with neighboring Brookline attracting more affluent immigrants. In each of these urban communities, the visitor can find shops with Russian names and signs in cyrillic lettering advertising food and clothing stores that cater to the newly arrived immigrants. Elderly men and women in leather coats and colorful scarves greet acquaintances on the street, jockey for the best piece of herring or sausage, or amble slowly arm in arm down crowded urban avenues. Although not as densely settled, these neighborhoods bear more than a passing resemblance to Brighton Beach and Rego Park.

Still, ethnic enclaves are not all there is to Soviet Jewish America. For many Soviet immigrants, city life and ethnic enclaves have started to lose their appeal. Whatever the factors determining their class status in the United States—the urbanity of a Moscow or Leningrad upbringing, a high level of education and accomplishment in the former Soviet Union, professional or financial success in this country—many middle-class Soviet emigres have become enthralled by the same vision of the "American Dream" that has drawn millions of other "new Americans" since World War II. During the last 15 years, growing numbers of Russian Jewish immigrants, particularly young families, have given up the cultural richness of the city for the relative safety and peace of tree-lined suburbs. The 1990s have seen the suburbanization of Soviet immigrant life, and the trend is becoming steadily more pronounced.

Not surprisingly, most of these immigrant suburbanites live near New York City, in the affluent sprawl of Long Island, Connecticut, Westchester and New Jersey. Some of these former city dwellers have simply sought greener ethnic enclaves. Perhaps the best example of this is the town of Fairlawn, New Jersey. Since the 1980s, growing numbers of emigre professionals like the Bienstocks of Lvov—he's an engineer working with air-conditioning systems, she's a computer programmer—have settled in Fairlawn. Young immigrant families have helped to make Fairlawn one of the country's first suburban Soviet Jewish enclaves. Some parts of Fairlawn feel rather like sanitized versions of Forest Hills or Brighton Beach. Local groceries and delicatessens sell East European foods and Russian-language newspapers. Large numbers of religious American-born Jews intensify the ethnic flavor of the place. The town has numerous kosher restaurants and eight synagogues to which religious families walk each Saturday, mingling with Russian emigres on their way to shop. But Fairlawn also has a strong flavor of Jersey mall culture. Alongside the poppyseed cake and sausages are kosher fast-food places, and American retail shrines like The Gap and Toys R Us offset more local businesses. In Fairlawn, as in many American towns of the 1990s, the urban ethnic island has been transformed into a suburban ethnic "mall land" (Interview with Regina Bienstock 1/27/97; Cheslow, *New York Times*, 1995).

While many Russian emigre suburbanites choose to live among their own, there are tens of thousands of others, like the Lunts of Leningrad and the Sperlings of Vilna, who have never had the desire to live in an immigrant community. Seeking escape from the ethnic enclaves they see as ghettos, whether in cities or suburbs, these financially comfortable Soviet Jewish immigrants are scattered throughout the manicured developments that ring New York City. These immigrant elites proudly claim friends from a wide variety of religious and national backgrounds. They host Fourth of July barbecues in their backyards. And they are quick to distinguish themselves from fellow countrymen and women who continue to live in Russian neighborhoods in Brooklyn and Queens.

But for all of their ambivalence about ethnic enclaves, these assimilated immigrants are often more closely tied to their land of origin than they are comfortable admitting. Many go regularly to visit parents or friends who live in Brighton Beach or Forest Hills; most attend family gatherings at Russian restaurants and nightclubs from time to time. Some have businesses on Queens Boulevard or Brighton Beach Avenue. Living in the New York area, they may claim to have assimilated completely, still they remain safely within the orbit of the second-largest concentration of Soviet emigres in the world. (Only Israel has more.) Like most suburbanites, they take comfort both in that closeness and in their self-imposed distance. Still, it is the children who are the measure of how quickly these suburban immigrants are becoming Americans. And these second-generation Soviet Jews, growing up amid split-level ranches and mega-malls, watching Barney and MTV, are shedding their distinctive Russianness as fast as any teen-ager sheds his or her parents' values and expectations.

In every city with a large Soviet Jewish population, the move to the suburbs and to less ghetto-like urban communities has already begun. In the Los Angeles area, parts of the San Fernando and Simi valleys have pockets of Soviet Jewish settlement. In the Bay area, Soviet Jews have moved to Berkeley, San Mateo and Hayward as well as the Silicon Valley. Soviet Jews can be found in the suburbs surrounding Hartford and New Haven, Connecticut, as well as the towns of Lynn, Needham and Swampscott just outside Boston. In Newton, a long-established, affluent Jewish town west of Boston, these young emigre families have transformed the landscape, creating another suburban ethnic enclave.

The Soviet immigrant populations in all of these major metropolitan areas are large enough that there can be no single Soviet Jewish community. There are pockets and subsets of immigrants, divided as they were in the former Soviet Union by economic and political differences as well as by region of origin. One can find more than a few neighborhoods or suburban streets where emigres from Kishinev or Minsk gather together in mini-communities. This splitting off into subgroups enables social services agencies to provide better adjustment counseling, to help immigrants deal with the traumas of uprooting and resettlement, loneliness, parent-child conflicts, marital tensions, and so on.

In virtually all of these cities, local Jewish agencies have launched successful "host family" or "one-on-one" programs matching immigrants with American Jewish families who have children of the same age and who share professional and social interests. These personal connections have eased the integration of Soviet Jewish families into many local Jewish communities. They have eased the shock of transplantation from one culture to another, helping new immigrants to make sense of the mundane but important rituals of American life: opening bank and credit card accounts, shopping in supermarkets, hunting for a job, getting telephone and heat and electricity service. And they have assuaged the pangs of loneliness of new arrivals who, through these programs, are much more likely to establish friendships outside the immigrant community than are those who do not participate (Heard, *Chicago Tribune*, 1989; Chazanov and Schrader, *Los Angeles Times*, 1989, 1992; Gitelman, 1981:72–82).

A PARTING SNAPSHOT: SOVIET EMIGRES WITH PALM TREES AND SMOG

While the patterns noted above illuminate the continuities and highlight the universal themes of Soviet immigrant life in the United States, such analysis obscures what is unique about daily life in each of these cities. There is not enough space in this small study to explore all of these differences, but it is worth a few pages to convey the flavor of life in the country's second-largest Soviet Jewish settlement, Los Angeles. Immigrants in the City of Angels have sometimes felt a world apart from newcomers in the older, industrial East Coast and Midwestern cities. Having begun this chapter with a focus on New York, the nation's early 20th-century immigrant capital, it is appropriate to end with the city that, as we reach the millennium, is the epicenter of international immigration.

All Soviet immigrants to the United States have described their first days here as confusing and disorienting, but perhaps none more so than the approximately 100,000 who settled in the Los Angeles area. New York, Boston, Chicago—cities with long histories, vibrant street life, public transportation and bleak, ugly housing projects—are at least somewhat reminiscent of the Soviet cities that they left behind. It is without question a stranger psychic journey from the cold, grey scarcity of Moscow or Kiev to the sunny, smoggy materialist fantasy that is Southern California. Sometimes the shock has been overwhelming.

Shortly after Sophia Belenky arrived in 1989, her cousin Adrian Lassman took her to an Encino beauty salon to get her first American haircut. It didn't occur to Lassman to explain to the new arrival that it was Halloween. On the street Belenky noticed people in heavy face makeup, men in drag or dressed as pirates and gorillas. Determined to take everything in stride, she said nothing. Entering the shop, Belenky was seated before a stylist dressed in white ghoul makeup, mask and wig. Feeling increasingly agitated, she bit her lips but remained quiet. It was the woman who rushed in dressed as a Vietnamese guerrilla fighter, with face paint and a frighteningly realistic plastic machine gun, who pushed Belenky over the edge. She fainted. When she regained consciousness in her cousin's bedroom, she sat up, swallowed and said quietly: "It is not another country. It is another planet" (Steinberg, *Los Angeles Times*, 1989).

The fear and disorientation that Belenky experienced were not uncommon. Many Soviet immigrants' early encounters with Southern California left them dizzy and gasping for air. The most frequently described trauma was learning to drive. The first time that he merged into traffic on the Santa Monica Freeway, former *refusenik* Ilya Levin gripped the wheel so tightly that his knuckles turned white. The Soviet police had nothing on L.A. drivers when it came to inducing fear. "Cars were coming from that side, from this side; it was a terrible situation," he recalled, able to laugh about it a year later. His wife, Yelena, remembered whispering reassurances as he inched the car into the torrent. "I kept saying, 'It's OK. It's OK.'" Meanwhile, she was imagining the worst. Over time Levin has become used to the traffic and the disregard for laws that characterize Los Angeles driving. "Now I drive normal," he said with a wink, leaving the details to the imagination (Soble, *Los Angeles Times*, 1989).

Levin had a license in the Soviet Union and knew how to drive before emigrating; it was simply a matter of adjusting to new conditions. For the large numbers of Soviet immigrants who had never driven before their arrival in Los Angeles, the freeway-linked sprawl presented a seemingly insurmountable problem. The most resourceful immigrants quickly adapted. Unfortunately for pedestrians and for other drivers, that did not always mean taking lessons at a legitimate driving school and then passing the driver's test. Instead, with their traditional disdain for bureaucracy and joy at beating the system, some emigres simply bought forged licenses and learned to drive while driving. Phony driver's licenses can be found in Soviet immigrant communities from New York to Los Angeles. It is quicker and easier to buy a license than to learn to drive and learn enough English to pass the test.

The results have been comical and dangerous. "They are driving on the wrong sides of the streets, knocking over fire hydrants, hitting telephone poles and no one even questioned the fact that they had come here without ever being behind the wheel," fumed one New Yorker in the early 1980s. If the situation was bad in New York, it was even worse in Los Angeles, where immigrants quickly realized that they had no choice but to drive. They could not shop, go to school, find or keep a job without possessing a car.

One solution to the problem of Los Angeles sprawl was to settle in the older, more densely populated parts of the city, where there is public transportation and at least some chance of walking to schools and shopping areas. Seventy percent of Soviet immigrants moved at least initially to the relatively urban and historically Jewish sections of West Hollywood, West Los Angeles and Fairfax. Here they have created a distinctly Southern California version of "Little Moscow," with smog-withered palm trees and neon signs. As in other parts of the country, it has been primarily the newest arrivals and the elderly who have remained for more than a few months in these New World ghettos.

Sadly, moving to West Hollywood did not save many elderly Soviets from Southern California traffic traumas. In 1996, the city of West Hollywood received a $79,000 grant to help elderly Russian immigrants learn how to cross a Southern California street safely. Largely because of jaywalking by newly arrived elderly, West Hollywood has the highest per capita incidence of pedestrian traffic accidents in California. The city's Russian outreach worker, Eugene Alper, tried to explain to community residents that "in Russia it's not so much about rules, but survival. Here, the traffic is much more ordered—here you don't have to risk your life every time you want to cross the street." The town posted Russian-language traffic-safety tips on billboards along Santa Monica Boulevard, ran public service announcements on Russian TV and radio stations, and conducted eight safety seminars in Plummer Park, the social heart of this elderly immigrant community (*Los Angeles Times*, 1996).

West Hollywood has also begun educational programs to ease tensions among its three major populations: Soviet Jewish emigres, elderly American-born and East European Jews, and gay men, who together constitute about two thirds of the city's population. Many Soviets have been openly hostile to gay men, reflecting the profound and historic intolerance for homosexuality rooted in Russian culture. Gay men in the former Soviet Union were often sentenced to hard labor camps and lesbians were forcibly committed to mental institutions. Discrimination against gay people persists in post-Soviet Russia. Soviet immigrants' homophobia has so alarmed many West Hollywood residents that the city has distributed leaflets in Russian promoting tolerance and explaining how AIDS is—and is not—transmitted. The city is also promoting sensitivity training for Russian teens. Whether or not such programs will work remains to be seen, but studies have shown that Soviet assimilation to American culture is often accompanied by greater tolerance for gays and lesbians (Goldberg and Saxe, 1996; Gross, *Los Angeles Times*, 1995).

Other groups in Los Angeles have sought to shape the attitudes and practices of Russian immigrants. The Lyubavitch Hasidic sect has taken as its mission to re-educate secular Jews to the ways of Jewish religious observance. And because the sect and its chief rebbe had their origins in the former Soviet Union, they have made the Soviet immigrant Jews a central focus of their work in Boston, New York, Chicago and Los Angeles, among other places. West Hollywood has been the site of one of their most successful projects.

In 1991 local Lyubavitchers opened the Chabad Russian Synagogue in a mostly renovated automobile-repair shop on Santa Monica Boulevard in the heart of the immigrant enclave. Much to their surprise, 1,400 people showed up for services on the synagogue's opening day, Yom Kippur, the Jewish Day of Atonement. Since fire laws permitted only 600 inside the building, the remainder lined up on the street to wait their turn to pray. Boris Minevich summed up the mood of the crowd when he joked that standing in a two-block-long line made him homesick for the former Soviet Union. But "in Russia they wait in line for food. Here we wait for synagogue," he said. Others were less jovial. Yom Kippur, when observant Jews fast and beg human and divine forgiveness for their sins, is a somber holiday under any circumstances. But those in line that day on Santa Monica Boulevard attached particular emotional power to their first Jewish holiday in the new land. For it is traditional on Yom Kippur to say *Kaddish* (the prayer for the dead) for one's parents, and many whose parents had been killed during the Nazi occupation had been unable to say *Kaddish* for nearly half a century (Martin, *Los Angeles Times*, 1991).

In this, as in every Soviet immigrant community, memorializing those lost in the Holocaust has played an extremely important role, particularly among the elderly. More than 700 mostly elderly Ukrainian Jews attended the 1991 unveiling of an outdoor memorial in Los Angeles's Plummer Park to honor the memory of the tens of thousands killed by the Nazis in Babi Yar. At the base of a black granite stone inscribed in Hebrew, Russian and English, gnarled fingers placed soil carried all the way from Kiev. Many in the crowd had personal losses to mourn. Gregory Makaron told of his grandfather's murder and burial in the mass grave that has lain unmarked for decades in the middle of an ordinary Kiev neighborhood. "Open the gates of history," he demanded, "and let us all behold the carnage of that morning." Remembering their murdered loved ones, middle-aged and elderly emigres wept openly in the Southern California sunshine as they listened to songs and stories of the massacre.

Sixty-seven-year-old Yevgeniya Podolskaya told the terrible and miraculous tale of how she survived Babi Yar. Pretending she'd been shot, the teenage Podolskaya had thrown herself on a pile of bodies in the forest ravine where the Nazis killed her parents and virtually everyone that she knew. She lay still as the soldiers walked down the rows of dead, shooting round after round to make sure that no one was left alive. "Hundreds of people were dying all around me," she said quietly. "I could see parents trying to cover children with their bodies." When it was all over, she wiped blood and bits of flesh from her eyes, nose and mouth and fled into the forest, believing that her entire family had been killed that day. When she returned to her home near Kiev at the war's end, she found that her sisters had somehow survived as well. "The people in the town called us the girls from another world, the girls who came back from the dead," she said. Many among the Soviet elderly in Los Angeles, who are survivors of Stalin's purges, of the Nazi genocide, of the gulags, feel that they have returned from the dead (Martin, *Los Angeles Times*, 1991).

The need to make sense of this loss is part of what drives some Soviet emigres to return to religion, or to practice Judaism for the first time. One charismatic emigre rabbi in Los Angeles, drawn into the Hasidic sect shortly after his arrival in the early 1970s, has ministered to many of them. Director of the Chabad Russian Immigrant Program in Los Angeles, Naftali Estulin trains adult men for their *bar mitzvah*, runs a day camp in Hollywood that serves 300 emigre children a month, and regularly performs mass weddings for emigre couples who had no chance of receiving a religious wedding in the former Soviet Union. These renewals of vows have been both moving and surreal. Held on the colorfully planted grounds of the Westin Bonaventure Hotel, hundreds of guests gathered at one 1991 ceremony to watch scores of spouses and as many as 20 Orthodox rabbis chant the ancient prayers above the not-so-distant hum of city traffic (*Los Angeles Times*, 8/25/91).

Circumcisions have been even more popular than weddings. Both adult immigrant men and the parents of young boys have asked Estulin to arrange the ritual. According to Jewish tradition, the operation is to be performed on eight-day-old babies. But, says Estulin, because circumcisions were outlawed in the Soviet Union, few Soviet Jewish males could be circumcised. Once in the U.S. some seek to rectify that. "If you are not circumsized," Estulin says, "there is constant conflict between your body and your soul. The soul is Jewish but the body is not." Wearing a fringed prayer shawl and

a skullcap over surgical greens, Estulin has personally overseen 3,000 circumcisions of Soviet immigrants. Although the vast majority of Soviet emigre
males do not choose this path, it is remarkable that so many do. In New
York, the Lyubavitch have overseen at least 10,000 circumcisions of males
between the ages of 10 and 62 (Haldane, *Los Angeles Times*, 1990; Sugarman,
Urban Gazette, 1992).

Still, those Soviet emigres who have embraced orthodox Judaism remain
a small minority. A far greater number seek to express their Judaism through
a celebration of Jewish social and cultural heritage. In Los Angeles it seems
appropriate that many of those affirmations of group identity have been built
around performance. Vera Pauker, an immigrant social worker who cares for
the elderly, noticed that the West Hollywood emigre community boasted
scores of aging singers and actors who were out of work and deeply depressed.
Believing that her elderly clientele would benefit emotionally from exposure
to the music and theater they remembered from home, Pauker began staging
showcases at the Westside Jewish Community Center. Simultaneously acts
of celebration and commemoration, these showcases became a beloved ritual
for the Los Angeles immigrant community (Beyette, *Los Angeles Times*, 1994).

Hundreds of elderly emigres came out regularly to support their stars from
home, such as famed classical performers Zlata Lyashkevich, Yuri Edelman
and Arta Shess. Lyashkevich immigrated in 1993 and was playing piano at
an Italian restaurant in nearby Glendale when Pauker first asked her to perform. Edelman, who had once sung with the Moscow Philharmonic, was
working as a carpenter. On stage at the Westside Community Center they
were stars once again, wringing tears and thunderous applause from the audience for their songs in Russian, Yiddish and Hebrew. Grey and white heads
bent to whisper explanations to small grandchildren through whom they
hoped to keep this language and culture alive. A light in some of the children's eyes suggested that maybe they would succeed. But these youngsters,
many of whom live in suburban San Fernando Valley developments far removed from their grandparents' immigrant world, wear T-shirts and sneakers
emblazoned with the names and images of newer pop icons. Their cultural
loyalties are already torn and the competition for their attention and identity
is sure to grow even fiercer. This is, after all, Hollywood, and Universal
Studios is just a short drive away (Beyette, *Los Angeles Times*, 1994).

If the attachment of Soviet immigrant children to American popular culture is a normal and benign part of the adjustment process, the infatuation
of some Soviet immigrant adults with Hollywood imagery of the gangster
playboy has had far more negative results. In the late 1980s, Los Angeles,
like Brighton Beach, became a national hub of Russian organized crime. By

1992, these immigrant criminals posed enough of a threat that federal, state and local law enforcement agencies created special units working in tandem to investigate and prosecute Russian crime syndicates in California (California Department of Justice, 1996).

The California Bureau of Investigation estimates that there are between 600 and 800 active members of Russian organized crime families in the Los Angeles area and more than 300 in San Francisco. As in New York, Russian immigrant syndicates in California have been most interested in white-collar crime, with fuel tax, credit card, art and Medicare fraud topping the list. However, more conventional organized crime activities such as extortion, loan sharking, drug trafficking and prostitution have been growing. And an entirely separate criminal infrastructure has grown up in California to steal, remodel and sell luxury cars. Rising levels of internecine as well as random violence have accompanied the growth of these crimes (California Dept. of Justice, 1996; Lieberman and Williams, *Los Angeles Times*, 1995).

While it would be silly to blame Hollywood movies for this surge in criminal activity by Soviet immigrants, the popularity of violent cinematic and musical depictions of U.S. life among young people in the former Soviet Union is indisputable. And it is not difficult to see links between popular culture portrayals of the American gangster hero and the self-images of some enterprising and amoral Soviet immigrants who slipped unnoticed into the United States during the years of mass immigration between 1989 and 1995. One such young man was Andrei Kuznetsov, a native of Leningrad who emigrated to Los Angeles in 1989 with a fascination for Hollywood-style glamour.

A child of the bleak, crumbling Zagrebsky factory district, Kuznetsov had, while still a teen-ager, found ways to indulge his taste for American designer jeans and sneakers. A charming hustler, the blue-eyed boy traded in foreign currency and procured women for foreign tourists. By the mid-1980s, he had perfected the look and talk of a beautiful young Californian and he was determined to find his way there quickly. In 1989, Kuznetsov ingratiated himself with a group of expatriate Soviet art dealers who'd returned to Russia looking for sales outlets. Through them he obtained a visa and a job at a gallery on Rodeo Drive that featured the works of Soviet emigre artists as well as those of David Hockney and Andy Warhol.

Kuznetsov made his way from a working-class section of Leningrad to the most famously wealthy neighborhood in America—Beverly Hills—and was earning thousand of dollars in commissions each month. But Rodeo Drive only sharpened his taste for luxury. He purchased a Mercedes-Benz, he wined and dined scores of women, and he soon needed more than the substantial salary that he was earning legitimately. Kuznetsov began copying credit card numbers from the gallery's customers. He returned to his old habit of procuring prostitutes for wealthy visitors (including visiting Russian mob members) until the gallery owner caught and fired him.

Undaunted, Kuznetsov shifted entirely to illegal activity, recruiting willing accomplices still living in St. Petersburg who desired a brief taste of the California good life. Shifting small amounts of money through a series of checking accounts so that there were always funds available if merchants called to inquire, Kuznetsov brought "shoppers" in from Russia for two-week stints to purchase goods from jewelry to electronic equipment worth tens of thousands of dollars. He quickly resold the goods, paid his "shoppers" a small cut and, by the time the bad checks were deposited in various banks, the perpetrators were safely back in St. Petersburg, well beyond the jurisdiction of American police. At its peak the scam was netting Kuznetsov more than $50,000 per month. But it all came to an abrupt end when two of Kuznetsov's temporary assistants murdered him in January 1992, in an attempt to take over his business. Kuznetsov would have appreciated the sensational coverage his murder received. Linked in print to Russian organized crime leaders in New York and Los Angeles, as well as to numerous women, Kuznetsov achieved in death the romantic playboy-gangster image he had for so long desired (Cullen, *Playboy*, April 1994; California Department of Justice, 1996: 15).

Mikail Markhasev, a Ukrainian teen-ager who emigrated to the San Fernando Valley in the late 1980s, is another of these young immigrant men fascinated with luxury and the romance of a gangster life. In March 1997, the eighteen-year-old Markhasev was arrested for the murder of entertainer Bill Cosby's son Ennis who was shot while changing a tire on his father's Mercedes. Although Los Angeles police did not find, or at least did not disclose evidence linking Markhasev to any specific Russian mob organization, they were led to Markhasev by an anonymous phone caller who claimed to know him as a member of a local Ukrainian immigrant car theft ring. There are several such rings operating in California; the best known, which the FBI calls the Northern California Auto Theft Group, is composed mostly of Ukrainian immigrants who steal, disassemble and rebuild luxury cars, then ship them through the ports of Oakland or Seattle to be resold in Russia (*San Francisco Chronicle*, 1995).

In Markhasev's 1998 trial, prosecutors argued that Markhasev may have committed the murder while attempting to steal Cosby's car. Russian car theft rings leave the stealing of luxury cars to young men around Markhasev's age, while older immigrants run the body shops that alter the cars and make the connections to the ports where the cars are shipped and received. Certainly Bill Cosby's $130,000 special-edition Mercedes would have been a prize in the new Russia, where money is flaunted by those few who have it. And stealing such a unique car would have established any young gangster's reputation. Markhasev had his brush with fame when he was tried in July 1998 for Ennis Cosby's murder. Convicted and sentenced to life in prison with no possibility of parole, his name quickly disappeared from the headlines. The brief criminal career of Mikail Markhasev, like the murder of Andrei Kuznetsov, may be seen as a tragic collision of Russian gangster fantasies, Hollywood romanticizations of violence and the American dream of riches and glory. In the unreal and spot-lit world of Los Angeles, young gangsters are able to enjoy a measure of glamour difficult to attain elsewhere. These are peculiarly Southern California immigrant tales (*Detroit Free Press*, 3/14/97; *People*, 3/31/97; *Los Angeles Times*, 3/13/97; *Time*, 6/02/97).

From Brooklyn, New York, and Fairlawn, New Jersey, to West Hollywood and the Silicon Valley, Soviet immigrants have created hundreds of communities of different sizes, economic bases and cultural characteristics. There are consistent themes and social patterns that tie these varied settlements together—Russian language, music, styles of dress; the growth of suburban settlements outlying more densely populated urban enclaves; the memories of Soviet Communism. But there are also particularities of region, economy, age and politics that separate these far-flung immigrant cities and towns. Together they constitute one of the largest new immigrant subcultures in the United States. But time and assimilation are fast diminishing the separateness of this immigrant culture. As with every immigrant group, adjustment and change have occurred in different ways and at different speeds for men and women, the old and the young. It is to those distinctions of gender and generation that we now turn.

Old and young Brighton residents under the "elevated" subway.

4

Gender and Generation: The Varied Rhythms of Acculturation

The old ones are like plants that have been taken from one soil, one kind of earth to another. They wither and are weak. And they need time to make new roots and to become strong again.

Sophie Spector, English teacher for
elderly immigrants in Brighton Beach.

We never dreamed it would be hard to find work in America. We thought in such a rich country as America, everyone works. I still don't really understand why this is not so.

Shura, a teacher in Kiev who emigrated to New York
in her mid-50s where she pieces together a living
from freelance translation work.

When you are thrown into the water and don't know how to swim, the survival instinct is what drives you. I did not have the slightest doubt that we would succeed.

Yuri Radzievsky, Moscow TV personality
who emigrated to New York at 28 and
became a millionaire advertising executive.

The first thing that appealed was the way people dressed. I thought that we had brought some foreign clothes that would make us look more like Americans but it didn't work out that way. Because no matter how I would dress up, I would look totally different from the streets.

Maxim Roisin, born in Kishinev,
emigrated at 16 to Brooklyn.

Yeah, I am an American . . . not Soviet American or Russian American, just American.

Yuri Feldman, born in Minsk, emigrated at
age three and grew up in Stamford, Connecticut.

Leaving one's nation of origin and learning to function in a new land, new climate, new culture is a complex process of change and adjustment that consumes all immigrants for at least a few years, sometimes more. Most Soviet Jewish immigrants are linked as well by their shared experience of Russian anti-Semitism and by a desire to, in one way or another, live a more Jewish life in the United States. Though, as we have seen, the nature and intensity of Jewish identification vary greatly among these immigrants, their encounters with American culture are shaped and colored by the intellectual and social training that they received in Soviet schools. But the rhythms and textures of Soviet immigrants' acculturation processes are largely determined by their gender, generation and class. Class distinctions have received some attention in previous chapters. Below is a brief exploration of the ways that elderly and middle-aged Soviet Jews, teen-agers and children, men and women have coped with starting again in America.

THE ELDERLY, A TRAUMATIZED POPULATION

In the 1970s and in the 1990s, Soviet Jews emigrated as entire families, bringing to the United States a much higher percentage of elderly than most immigrant groups before them. During the early years, nearly one-third of Soviet immigrants to the United States were over age 60. Various studies have shown members of the Fourth Wave to be even older. With the total number of Soviet Jewish immigrants in the United States nearing half a million, that means that an estimated 150,000 of these "new Americans" are senior citizens. Elderly immigrants face special problems. Past working age, or past the age when they can easily find work in the American job market, the vast majority require housing subsidies if they are to live on their own. Many need some sort of home care. All require more regular attention from physicians than do younger immigrants. (This is even more true of Soviet elderly than of Americans because they suffer from so many years of inadequate health care.) Almost all are dependent for their sustenance on Supplemental Security Income, Medicare and food stamps. And those are just their physical needs (HIAS 1996; Halberstadt, 1996; Solomon, 1996).

Soviet Jewish elderly carry to this country staggering emotional baggage. They have lived through Stalin's purges, the Nazi occupation, the so-called "Black Years of Soviet Jewry" after World War II. Some were sent into exile, and a smaller number were sentenced to time in the gulags. The oldest remember the bloody years of the Revolution and the Civil War that followed. Some were devout Communists, later disillusioned. Others were Zionists or Yiddish cultural nationalists and paid a price for their ethnic pride, persistent in the face of the homogenizing, often brutalizing force of Soviet culture. Almost all of them have lost loved ones to violent deaths. Many feel crippling guilt at having survived—and at leaving those graves behind.

Like Haitian, Vietnamese, Salvadoran, Guatemalan and Cambodian refugees in the United States, this is a traumatized immigrant population. Sometimes their hidden psychological damage manifests itself in communal panic. After the arrest of Mikail Markhasev in the slaying of Ennis Cosby, the Los Angeles news media were filled with stories of Russian gangs and crime activities. Elderly Soviet immigrants in West Hollywood reacted with the reflexive fear of those who have known real terror. Many locked themselves in their homes, calling Russian talk-radio programs to express fear that they might be attacked in retaliation. Few ventured to Plummer Park, their daily gathering spot. All they had ever known was gnawing insecurity, punctuated by periods of horrific violence against Soviet Jews. They could not easily distinguish between this coverage and the anti-Semitic news stories that would appear in the Soviet press as triggers for periods of heightened violence and discrimination. "For somebody who has gone through this kind of thing," said emigre outreach worker Eugene Alper, coverage of Markhasev's arrest was "like a red flag." Flashbacks and nightmares are never far away (Gold, *Los Angeles Times*, 1997).

These psychological disturbances augment the particular adjustment problems faced by any elderly immigrants. It is more difficult for elderly immigrants to master a foreign language and learn to navigate a new social system than it is for younger people. By not working outside the home, elderly emigres may be more isolated than their children and grandchildren. Their financial and physical frailties create heightened anxieties, sometimes leading to confusion and disorientation. To adjust at all, they need to live in areas with strong medical and social services (Solomon, 1996; Goldstein, 1979: 257–63).

Despite these very real difficulties, most elderly Soviet immigrants have adapted surprisingly well to life in the United States. This was to a great degree eased by their settlement in senior citizen oriented urban Jewish enclaves like Brighton Beach, West Hollywood, West Rogers Park and Allston/Brighton, where such medical, cultural and social service systems were already in place. These neighborhoods also offered familiar social and cultural environments, language accessibility and an abundance of inexpensive, subsidized housing that has enabled many Soviet elderly to live alone or just with a spouse for the first time in their lives. Living in housing complexes for the elderly, or at least in neighborhoods with a very high concentration of elderly Jewish immigrants, some emigres developed more active social lives and a stronger sense of community in the United States than they had in the former Soviet Union. This has been especially true for many who were retired prior to emigration. They felt less keenly the loss of prestige experienced by those who had to give up established careers to collect pensions in the United States. In that sense the retirees were better situated emotionally to enjoy the benefits of life in their new homes than those slightly younger at the time of their arrival.

One key to the relatively quick adjustment of the oldest emigres has been their ability to relate to Russian Jews from earlier immigration waves through the Yiddish language. Most Soviet Jews over the age of 70 learned Yiddish before speaking Russian. It was their *mamaloshn* (mother tongue). And for the next generation, those between the ages of 50 and 70, Yiddish was the language of their parents and grandparents. Some once knew how to speak it; some still do. But Yiddish for most of them is a dimly remembered music of their youths, laden with emotions, family memories, echoes of a world that disappeared during and after World War II. Encounters in Yiddish have been cathartic and moving for older Soviet emigres who have settled in communities with large populations of elderly Jews. Also, their knowledge of Yiddish puts them in a privileged position in their families during the early months in the United States, for they can make the first forays into the world of "American" Jewry. They can, in some cases, become the translators and mediators.

Speaking and hearing Yiddish is also a healing experience for many elderly Soviet immigrants, sparking memories of the prewar years. For Fanya from Odessa, who moved to the United States with her daughter and her two young granddaughters in 1978, landing in Brighton Beach felt like coming home. "The first time I heard Yiddish spoken on the street here," she recalled, still astonished a decade later, "I couldn't believe my ears. Then I saw little boys wearing *yarmulkes* [skullcaps worn by the religious], walking down the street unafraid, and I cried." Although Fanya's daughter, who owns a small grocery in Brighton, speaks no Yiddish, Fanya's grandchildren learned Yiddish when they attended yeshiva during their first two years in this country. "In the First World War," Fanya whispered sadly, "I lost my father; in the Second World War my husband. Since then I have had a bad heart. I could not cry at all. Here, for the first time, I cried. Here when my own little ones speak to me in Yiddish, my heart feels better."

Fanya's pleasure at the visibility of synagogues, of Jewish ritual items for sale in stores, of observant Jews like the Lyubavitch on the streets of her new neighborhood, was echoed by many Soviet elderly of the Third and Fourth Waves. For some, like Fanya, who saw the synagogues in her small town near Odessa destroyed first by the Communists and then by the Nazis, these sights feel like a revival of youth and a rising from the ashes. It is exhilarating, restorative. For others, like Grisha, a 65-year-old resident of Allston-Brighton who emigrated from St. Petersburg in 1989, it is a new and affirming experience to see so many synagogues in his neighborhood. "In a city like St. Petersburg," he recalled, "there was only one synagogue. And in Boston it is so different, you can't compare it. On one street there are four synagogues! *Chevo zedes evree dabilis* [It warms the heart]." Not surprisingly, in every ethnic enclave from Brighton Beach to West Hollywood, it is the elderly who have responded most enthusiastically to outreach efforts by the synagogues (Zaretsky, 1996).

Senior citizen centers sponsored by city funds, synagogues and the Federation of Jewish Philanthropies have also played an important role in the socialization of elderly Soviet emigres and in providing a social life for those who do not live in senior housing complexes. Senior centers like the one on the boardwalk in Brighton Beach provide daily lunches for members, getting them out of the house to a public setting where they can meet with friends, share news, tell jokes, even find romance. These senior centers also offer exercise classes, swimming pools and cultural events. Of all the services offered by these centers, English classes taught by fellow Soviet emigres have been perhaps the most vital resources, for they have been far more than language classes. The teachers, many of whom had taught English for a living in the Soviet Union, help their new students learn how to meet their needs in a dramatically different social and political system.

Sophie Spector, who taught English for more than 30 years in Odessa, was, during the early 1980s, the main English teacher for Third Wave elderly immigrants at the Shorefront Y in Brighton Beach. One of her primary responsibilities was to help new arrivals work through their fear of and frustration with the health care system. This wasn't simply crankiness or learned helplessness on the part of the aged immigrants; their fears were based in experience. Many of them remembered a time when people were hospitalized in the Soviet Union for political rather than health reasons, and many never left the hospital alive. "So, if they call an ambulance and a police car gets there first, they are terrified," said Spector. "They refuse to go. The medic tries to push them. It can be a mess." Spector and others like her across the United States try to teach their students how to explain themselves to police, ambulance drivers and physicians so that they don't find themselves in wards for the mentally ill.

Second, many of these older people have been treated at poorly funded and understaffed Soviet hospitals, particularly outside the major cities, where infection and mortality rates were extremely high. As a result, they viewed hospitals as a last resort, turning to home and herbal remedies before seeing a physician. Third and Fourth wave immigrants, particularly the elderly, continue to depend on herbal cures. As late as 1997, such remedies could be found in abundance in Soviet emigre enclaves. Elderly women in headscarves sell a wide variety of alternative ointments, herbs and oils on the streets of Brighton Beach, West Rogers Park and West Hollywood to immigrant residents still mistrustful of physicians and hospitals. The medicine cabinets of many immigrant seniors are filled with mustard plasters, garlic skin pastes, Siberian flowers, reindeer oils and homemade antibiotics. Staff members at Coney Island Hospital, the major public health facility in the Brighton Beach area, keep a Russian-language herbal remedy book in the Emergency Room so that they can figure out what emigre patients may have taken (Garrett, 1997).

Elderly Soviet immigrants also complain that it is impossible to find primary care physicians with whom they can establish a relationship. "In Russia," says emigre physician Marina Neystat, "each neighborhood has an outpatient clinic. Medical care is provided free of charge. When you get sick you can just go to the outpatient clinic and be seen the same day. If you are acutely sick . . . the doctor will make a home visit." Here elderly immigrants first face the difficulty of finding physicians who will accept Medicaid, publicly funded health insurance for the poor. (They do not qualify for Medicare, public health insurance for the elderly, until they have been in the country for five years.) And when they do find a physician who will treat them, they often find that the care they receive is cold and superficial compared with what they were used to in the Soviet Union (Carroll, *Newsday*, 1993).

Despite their feistiness in the face of ambulance attendants and their spirited attempts at medical self-help, the efforts by Soviet elderly to navigate in this confusing and alienating new culture have left many exhausted and depressed. Sophie Spector encountered feelings of helplessness and despair among many of her English students at the Shorefront Y. As a result English teachers like Spector—retired teachers, most in their late 50s and 60s, who came to the United States with more knowledge of English and of American culture than most immigrants—have assumed a special role. Formerly teachers of the young, they have become cultural guides, amateur psychologists and practitioners of "tough love" for the old.

Spector commented in 1983:

All of my work here, every step that I take, is to bring my people here to thinking about themselves in a positive way. There are many people who would like to go back. Yes! They remember the land where they were born. They remember that

Russian is the language they spoke all their lives and now they must work to learn English. It is hard for them. They complain about how dirty Brighton is and say that in Odessa you could eat off the street. So I tell them to clean it up. I tell them you must make Brighton really a little Odessa. I tell them: "If you think about those friends you left in Russia who are afraid to say that they are Jews, who are afraid to speak Yiddish, their mother language, who are not allowed to go to synagogue if they want to, and who give their children Russian names because they will be better off if they do not seem Jewish, then you will think about your own life in America and you will feel that you are happy."

I also explain to them that the way they think will affect their health. If they are nervous and upset all the time, they will become sick. I tell them about the old Russian woman who, every time she felt bad, went to the beauty parlor. One man asked me if there was a doctor in the beauty parlor. I said: "Look, if you see in the mirror a person who is a mess, you think you are old and ugly and sick. If you look in the mirror and see a person who is looking nice, you will think, 'I'm not so old.' " And then they come up to me at the end of a class and they all kiss me.

As noted, elderly Soviet immigrants combat depression and despair in a number of ways, including daily shopping trips to the large, crowded, immigrant-owned food stores that can be found in most Russian ethnic enclaves; attendance at cultural events where they can hear the music and language of home; and Jewish holiday celebrations sponsored by synagogues and senior centers. And always there are the public memorials. In this population that has seen so much violence and death, mourning and commemoration are not only central to the affirmation of collective identity. Many immigrants have come to feel that this is their essential task as survivors. As we have seen, these communal days of mourning have helped to forge bonds of kinship and to ease survivor guilt among elderly Soviet immigrants from Brighton Beach to West Hollywood. Babi Yar, the worst of the mass slaughters of Jewish civilians by Nazi forces, has become an occasion for immigrants of that generation to mourn their losses and to do what they could not in Russia or Ukraine: create physical memorials that they can visit, where they can reflect and cry. But mourning is not the only route to community-building.

Celebrations of past victories are also crucial to the affirmation of collective identity. Minsk-born Natasha Zaretsky, a young scholar of Soviet Jewish immigration and identity formation in the United States, has found that *Dyen Pobedi* (Day of Victory) celebrations have become a central communal ritual among Soviet elderly in this country.

Dyen Pobedi was the official Soviet holiday celebrating, each May 9, the Red Army's defeat of the Nazi Army. It is the only Soviet holiday honored by Jewish immigrants now in the United States. Immigrant newspapers like *Novaya Russkaya Slovo* (The New Russian Word) and *Bostonskoye Vremya* (Boston's Time) run front-page stories honoring World War II veterans, immigrants' recollections of the war and Jewish contributions to the defeat of the Nazis. The latter is the key difference between the official festivities in the former Soviet Union and the commemorations held by elderly immigrants in the United States. In parties at restaurants, gatherings at senior centers, marches down the main avenues of the ethnic enclaves, Soviet Jewish immigrants remember the terrible price paid by the Soviet people as a whole, 20 million dead. But they also rebuke those in the former Soviet Union who accused Jewish soldiers of cowardice and profiteering, who built public markets on mass Jewish graves, and who defaced Jewish tombstones and memorial plaques.

Like other elderly people on veterans' days around the world, some men and women squeeze bulky bodies into old uniforms, or balance lovingly preserved military caps and medals on heads of snow-white hair. But the strange symphony of national symbols gives the particular nature of this veterans' day celebration away. Along with Soviet military regalia, the veterans carry American and Israeli flags. They sing not only in Russian but in Hebrew, Yiddish and English. The Russian-language anthem of the day reflects the bittersweet nature of any military victory: "This is *Dyen Pobedi*, propelled by gunpowder. This is *Dyen Pobedi* with gray hairs on our temples. This is happiness with tears in our eyes. *Dyen Pobedi, Dyen Pobedi*." But there are also militant expressions of survival that mark these aging veterans as Jews and as Americans. "Hatikvah" (Hope), the haunting Israeli national anthem, is often sung at immigrant Victory Day festivities. So too is the anthem of the Jewish anti-Nazi resistance: the Yiddish "Partisan's Song." And at one Boston celebration in 1996, elderly Russian veterans chose as their American theme the messianic Civil War marching song "The Battle Hymn of the Republic." Seeming not to mind either the wordy verses or the Christian allegory, the vets sang the words with verve and thick accents: "Glory hallelujah, His truth is marching on!" (Zaretsky, 1996).

Caring for family has been at least as important in the daily lives of many Soviet immigrant elderly as finding community among other older immigrants. The suburban migration of the 1990s has diminished this somewhat, creating a new family dynamic in which the grandparents often live in the city while the children and grandchildren live in the suburbs. However, in the early days after immigration, when parents are struggling to find work or are consumed with studying for licensing exams or for new careers, grandparents have often played a vital role in child care and child-rearing. In many

A young Odessan immigrant in her grandfather's store.

neighborhoods in New York, the role of grandparents in caring for the young is still highly visible. Interestingly, there seems to be little gender differentiation in this. Elderly men and women both can be seen pushing a stroller with one hand and a wire shopping cart with the other, purchasing the day's groceries and caring for the babies while their grown children are at work. When the shopping is done, but before it is time to pick up older children at school, the grandparents congregate in parks and on beaches to talk or play chess, or turn ruddy faces to the sun while their charges play. On a cement walkway by the ocean in Manhattan Beach, Brooklyn, scores of elderly immigrants have gathered daily for years, impervious to wind and cold, rocking bundled infants as they sleep in their carriages, warning running preschoolers not to let the waves wet their clothes.

This traditional closeness of different age groups within the Soviet Jewish family greatly diminishes the isolation of elderly immigrants and ties the grandchildren to Russian-Jewish traditions and history. Though Soviet Jews vary widely in their stated reasons for immigrating to the United States, most have expressed a desire for their children to develop a Jewish identity of which they can be proud. For many youngsters, that identity is anchored in the experiences of their grandparents as conveyed through the stories their grandparents tell. Second, grandparents act as mediators between irreligious parents and those children who are developing an interest in Judaism through the myriad teen programs, Sunday schools and day camps sponsored by Jewish charities for Soviet Jewish immigrants. Much of what immigrant youngsters learn in those programs is new to their parents. It is often grandparents who find ways to integrate Jewish ritual into family life.

It is difficult to know how much the suburbanization of Soviet Jewish immigrants will alter this close-knit family structure. In many families, the grandparents move to the suburbs with the rest of the family, taking a nearby apartment or condominium. But just as often, the grandparents remain in the city, where they have the amenities they need to live independently. Living alone and relatively far from family, perhaps for the first time in their lives, some elderly experience depression and a loss of self-esteem that come months or even years after emigrating.

Their children, particularly young professionals, have begun to move toward a more American nuclear family lifestyle that may provide a refreshing sense of freedom for these increasingly independent and assimilated young families. However, it strips their elderly and middle-aged parents of a caretaking role that has long been traditional in Soviet Jewish fimilies. It leaves some of these older immigrants feeling unmoored and unneeded (Brodsky, 1998).

STRUGGLES IN THE WORKADAY WORLD: ADULTS FROM 25 TO 60

Soviet Jewish immigrants of working age brought with them a wide array of skills and an unusually high percentage of university and graduate school degrees: They were also highly professionalized, with more than half having previously held academic, scientific or technical jobs. Many adult immigrants in their 20s and 30s have been able to reap the benefits of their educations, rising quickly in American business and soon earning comfortable salaries (Tress, 1996). Most of these 20- and 30-something emigres were able to pick up the English language easily, to retool for new careers if necessary and to adapt themselves to the competitive nature of job-hunting in the United States, so different from the system in the Soviet Union, where high school and college graduates are placed in one job that they will most likely keep for the rest of their careers. By the early 1980s, these young Russian professionals had begun to make their presence felt across the United States as physicians, entrepreneurs, stock analysts, industrial researchers, accountants and computer specialists.

Some have had remarkable success. Of the fortunes made by this immigrant group, most were amassed by people who were young adults when they arrived. Zindel Zelmanovitch, age 25 when he moved to New York, took whatever kind of work he could find, from clerking to plumbing, eventually making his way into venture capitalism. He began a company called Fresh Start to provide loans mostly to immigrant entrepreneurs. By the time he turned 40, his company held $3 million in loans to over 150 companies. Yuri Radzievsky, a former Soviet TV personality with a degree in electronics, re-created himself as an advertising executive when he came to New York in his late 20s. By his early 30s, Radzievsky had made his first American million. There are more than a few similar stories of entrepreneurial conquest by young Soviet immigrants. Most, of course, did not end up as millionaires. However, there is a common theme in the recollections of many of those who arrived in the United States while still in their 20s: They enjoyed the challenge of remaking themselves, of testing their mettle in a new land (Taylor, *Fortune*, 1986).

Former teacher Sophia Shkolnikov left Minsk for New York during the summer of 1979, when she was 27 years old. Young, energetic and undaunted by the pace or the crowded streets, Shkolnikov immediately liked the new city. Recognizing that her lack of English would prevent her from getting a teaching license, she decided to retrain as a computer programmer.

I felt comfortable. I'm used to living in the city. I never lived in the country, so it was familiar. At first I went to get some training in typing. My first job was in a bank. And then I was taking some computer classes in Brooklyn College. I was thinking that I need to have some profession here because I wasn't planning to be a teacher. And I needed something that will give me enough money to live on, so at first I started computer and economics. I took one year of introductory courses just to get oriented. And then I got my job at Smith Barney [a Wall Street brokerage house] doing programming. I've been there 10 years.

What Zhana R. accomplished was even more difficult. In her late 20s when she emigrated, Zhana had been practicing medicine for four years in Moscow when she came to New York. Despite some difficulties with English, Zhana passed her AMA licensing exams within a few months and won a prestigious residency at a New York hospital. Within a few years she had recouped whatever career losses her decision to emigrate had cost her.

Older working-age immigrants, especially those who are 50 and older, have had a much harder time picking up their careers where they left off in the Soviet Union. They are less able to master the language but they are far enough along in their careers that they apply for extremely competitive high-level job openings, which they are unlikely to get. In a Catch-22, they are also considered overqualified for lower-level professional positions. While social workers and vocational counselors argue that the "unrealistic expectations" of highly educated immigrants have constituted one of their major obstacles in finding employment, the emigres refer to "an intellectual holocaust" forcing physicians and lawyers, Ph.D.s and musicians to exchange their vocations for clerical positions and manual labor (Rubin, 1975; Holden, 1990).

In 1990, *Science* magazine estimated that approximately 15 percent of Fourth Wave immigrants arrived in the United States with Ph.D. equivalents in science or engineering. (That number doesn't include those who have Ph.D.s in humanities and social sciences.) Despite U.S. government warnings about an impending shortage of scientists with doctorates, most of these Soviet scientists and engineers have been unable to find high-level work in their fields. The top Soviet mathematicians and theoretical physicists were quickly hired by U.S. universities, and some talented graduate students and recent Ph.D.s have been able to find short-term positions. But thousands were forced to drive taxis, walk dogs, or work as store clerks, doormen and companions to the elderly. "In Russia," one engineer commented bitterly, "we had to hide that we are Jews. Here, to get a job, we have to hide that we have a Ph.D."

Age discrimination has been a key factor, especially in the rapidly changing high-technology fields in which young people with fresh degrees are a hot commodity, and people over age 35 are generally thought to be out of touch with the latest developments. Leonid V., a ceramics engineer from Kiev, was told at age 36 that he was too old for one research job he particularly wanted. George L., 40, was told by potential employers at several California universities: " 'You are too old.' They don't believe you can keep up with younger people." Emigre mathematician Vladimir Naraditsky claims that some Soviet research scientists "are dyeing their hair to hide their age" (Holden, *Science*, 1990.)

Gender bias in the U.S. labor market has also forced former Soviet professionals to settle for lower-level jobs than they had hoped for prior to emigration. If the situation has been hard for male professionals in their 40s and 50s, it has been doubly difficult for older women, who face discrimination both because of their sex and their age. Of all post-1965 immigrant groups, Soviet Jews have the largest gender-based wage gap, with the median hourly wage for men (as of 1996) $9.75 per hour and for women $7.00. Among those earning $15 or more per hour, men outnumber women by nearly two to one (Tress, 1996).

For the large number of middle-aged women immigrants who worked as pediatricians in the Soviet Union, the loss of professional status and job satisfaction has been particularly devastating. Pediatrics was seen in the Soviet Union as a "women's field" and the general perception among U.S. physicians is that the training of these women pediatricians was of a lower grade than that of other Soviet doctors. Of all the emigre physicians to enter the United States since the 1960s, these women have had the least success in rebuilding their careers. Sonya, 51 when she arrived in 1979, had practiced medicine for many years in Leningrad. She took a job in Brighton Beach as a paid companion to the elderly, a minimum-wage position. She comforts herself with the thought that her son, an electronics engineer in Houston, has done far better for himself in the United States than he could have in her home city. Still, she often finds her life in Brighton Beach drab and boring. "As for myself," she says wistfully, "I could be more fulfilled."

Bertha Klimkovich, who came to Brooklyn with her daughters and grandchildren in 1979, found herself working in a garment sweatshop after 32 years of pediatric practice in Borisov. She recalled her first years in New York:

The first days were very hard because I worked 32 years [as] a doctor and now I must work in a factory. Very hard. But I understand that I don't have my English. My English is nothing, zero. And to begin to study to take the exam to be a doctor was too hard for me. I was 55 years old, without language. So I began working in a factory because my youngest daughter was with me. And she was at that time not married. She was a musician in Russia. This was not a profession for her. She must study something to be in America. So I must work in the factory. I cried so much. But I know that for the children it will be better here. And now I am happy because the children are working and the grandchildren go to college.

Such dramatic loss of professional status, coupled with frustration over the inability to speak English and initial incompetence at basic tasks—job-hunting, shopping, meeting with children's teachers, reading official mail—have caused severe emotional and psychological problems for many older working-age immigrants who had been accustomed to occupying respected positions in the workplace and in their families. The process of uprooting and resettlement is akin to the experience of mourning. The disorientation of loss, the profound sense of missing old friends, relatives and familiar places hits many immigrants soon after the euphoria of "starting over" wears off. For adult immigrants this mourning period is intensified by the loss of their professional selves. Adustment means not only grieving external losses but rebuilding their egos (Yaglom, 1996).

Adele Nikolsky, coordinator of Russian immigrant services for a Brooklyn community clinic, noted in 1996 that area mental health clinics were seeing "overwhelming numbers of middle-aged immigrants" with debilitating symptoms of depression and anxiety. She identified some common characteristics among those severely afflicted. All had achieved career success in the former Soviet Union and had identified strongly with their work roles. They had been relatively content under the Soviet system but felt forced to emigrate for one or more reasons: because their children had already emigrated; because of anti-Semitism, or because of the social and economic chaos that followed the dissolution of the Soviet Union. Once in the United States, many of these middle-aged emigres experienced poor health and a tight American job market that prevented them from finding work in their fields. These patients all described suffering from feelings of exclusion and humiliation (Nikolsky, 1996).

The psychological problems of these middle-aged immigrants were related not only to their stage of life at the time of emigration but also to the period in Soviet history into which they were born. The oldest of this generation witnessed as children the bloodshed and torture of the Nazi occupation. All were old enough to have had parents who experienced those terrible years; many lost fathers and grandparents in very early childhood. This deprivation created in them a determination to shield their own children from suffering. That protective role continued into their children's adult years, when many provided grown children with financial and political aid, scrounged special kinds of food and clothing, or called in favors to get their children apartments or their grandchildren into good schools. One of their feelings of loss as immigrants has been that they no longer know how to assist their children, and that they no longer need to; in general, their young adult children have adapted more easily than they to the complexities of American life (Nikolsky, 1996).

This generation of immigrants has also experienced an internal tug-of-war between a desire for independence and a lifetime of training to passively accept what they are told by an authoritarian state. Many feel a sense of shame that they "went along to get along," trading silence for the hope of professional success. Once in the United States, this habit of hiding was hard to break. When explaining why she did not want her real name used for this book, Irena Lunts said: "You can take the girl out of the Soviet Union, but you can't take the Stalin out of the girl." Emigre psychiatrist Edgar Goldstein has written about this phenomenon: "A Soviet immigrant carries within himself a totalitarian state, a system of inner dictates reinforced by all his experiences in a totalitarian society." One emigre scientist treated by Goldstein complained after three years in the United States: "I still feel the policeman inside of me." Goldstein interpreted this remark as indicative both of the lasting damages inflicted by a repressive system and of the human capacity to resist brainwashing.

It shows that in spite of cultural reinforcement, the totalitarian system has not been completely internalized. If it had been the scientist would not feel that there was a "policeman inside" of himself, but would, perhaps, have become a policeman and never have left the Soviet Union. What he perceives as a "policeman inside" himself is actually the conflict between his dependency and his quest for freedom. (Goldstein, 1979)

That conflict between accepting, even valuing, dependence and striving for freedom has created strong feelings of guilt and humiliation in many middle-aged immigrants. Some express it as shame at having been duped by Soviet ideology; others feel ashamed at having been made victims, unable to help others. "That is the ultimate triumph of the system," emigre poet Joseph Brodsky wrote in 1986. "Whether you beat it or join it, you feel equally guilty. . . . Ambivalence I think is the chief characteristic of my nation. There isn't a Russian executioner who isn't scared of turning victim one day, nor is there a sorriest victim who would not acknowledge (if only to himself) a mental ability to become an executioner" (Brodsky, 1986: 10).

Ambivalence around Jewish identity has created an equally and tenacious set of psychological and emotional problems for middle-aged immigrants. Soviet emigres of all ages have issues around being Jewish. The particular cast that these identity issues take among the middle-aged is related to their central concern with loss of status and respect. Because this generation was born after the destruction of most visible remnants of Soviet Jewish culture, few among them have much knowledge of, or positive identification with, their Jewishness. They know that their parents suffered horribly for being Jewish but, unlike their parents, they have only faded and tenuous connections to the world of Russian Jewry that was annihilated in the 1930s and '40s. For them, being Jewish was an almost exclusively negative reality, the root of their parents' terror, a cause of the subtle and overt discrimination that they themselves experienced in school and at work, and the reason that their children might be prevented from achieving their full potential professionally.

Indoctrinated as young people with the Soviet internationalist ideology— which rejected as retrograde all national and religious attachments, but simultaneously inculcated an ethnocentrism toward all things Russian—many of these middle-aged immigrants are quite confused about their identities.

They genuinely believe that religion is silly; they identify strongly with Russian culture and feel a gnawing sense of inferiority about being Jewish. But they also deeply resent non-Jewish Russians for their treatment of Jews. In the Soviet Union, psychologist Goldstein has argued, this confusion sometimes bred a neurotic aggressiveness—what we might, in colloquial English, call "a chip on the shoulder." Driven to prove that they were not inferior, some Soviet Jews remained unsatisfied no matter how much they accomplished in the Soviet Union because they never felt respected or accepted. In the United States, this nervous aggressiveness and inability to trust have continued—often, ironically, in their interactions with American Jews, who have sometimes made them feel unworthy of American efforts on behalf of Soviet Jewry. Many American Jews have indeed said: "These are Russians. They're not really Jewish." This is frustrating and upsetting to adult immigrants who feel that they will never fit in: "In Russia," they say, "we were Jews, not Russians. And here we are 'Russians,' not Jews" (Goldstein, 1979; Nikolsky, 1996).

GENDER AS A FACTOR IN ADULT ADJUSTMENT

The identity crises faced by older immigrants have been complicated by the differences between men's and women's experiences of the transition to American life. As has often been the case with new immigrant groups to the United States, Soviet Jewish women have generally been able to find work more quickly than have men. The primary reason for this has been their greater willingness to accept lower-paid, lower-prestige work as a means to feed and clothe their families. Psychologists Ben-David Amith and Yoav Lavee have found that in some Soviet immigrant families where the wife finds work before the husband, the feelings of helplessness and incompetence common among adult male immigrants are intensified, leading to conflict between spouses. Even when the father has found work quickly, his frustration over status loss is sometimes taken out on the family. Rates of divorce are relatively high among Soviet immigrant families, though still not as high as the overall American divorce rate of 50 percent (Amith and Lavee, 1994).

As the case of women pediatricians makes clear, women in the Soviet immigrant community have experienced severe status loss of their own, and that too has placed stress on their marriages and family relations. Reflecting the general pattern in the former Soviet Union, where women made up 51 percent of the labor force, almost all Soviet Jewish women worked outside the home prior to emigration. And they were as likely as men to have earned graduate degrees and achieved professional success. Sixty percent of emigre women held jobs in the former Soviet Union that were classified as academic, scientific, professional or technical. Once in the United States they have been far less likely than adult men, even over time, to continue their careers. Only 31 percent of Soviet immigrant women, mostly the young, have found employment in their fields here. More than 55 percent have had to take jobs in service or clerical work. After the initial months of family elation following arrival in the United States, and the next period when most mothers are too busy meeting the immediate needs of their families to worry about themselves, many adult women have gone through periods of profound depression, mourning the loss of respect and professional identity, grieving the careers that they will probably never have again. Like Bertha Klimkovich, many formerly professional women in the Soviet immigrant community recall months and even years when they cried each day on their way to their new menial jobs (Halberstadt, 1996).

In some senses, then, the position of Soviet immigrant women, as women, was superior prior to emigration. Communist ideology condemned "male chauvinism" and placed women workers on a par with men, striving together toward a bright and productive future for "the worker's state." Women in the Red Army saw combat as early as World War II. Abortion was available on demand. There was no parallel in the Soviet Union to the debate that still rages in the United States about whether mothers should work outside the home, but rhetorical equality was not the same as equality in practice. As in the United States, a Soviet woman worker on average earned just two-thirds the salary of her male counterpart, and, no matter how long her working hours, she was expected to perform virtually all of the labor in the home: cooking, cleaning and child-rearing. The average Russian mother spent 40 hours a week caring for her home and family, compared with her husband, who spent fewer than five hours. In recent years, she had to add to that time an indeterminate number of hours spent on food lines to provide even basic nutrition for her family. Her work hours then were probably twice those of her husband's and there was no public debate about it (Bennett, *Los Angeles Times*, 1997; Lissyutinskaya, 1993).

Underlying women's inequalities was a deeply entrenched set of beliefs, unchallenged by the Soviet Revolution, that the sexes are fundamentally different. A woman's professional achievements in no way changed the dominant cultural view that her role as wife and mother was primary. In everything from sociological studies to children's school books and popular films, women were portrayed as healthy only when married with children. The single, childless woman was seen as hardened, unnatural and unfulfilled. This view made it extremely difficult for women to choose not to have children, and it endowed men with the power to "save" even women more educated than they from an embittered spinsterhood (Markowitz, 1993: 180–82).

Many Soviet men felt frustrated by their lack of power in the larger society. In two-earner families, some men felt denied their place as primary provider. In addition living in a dictatorship, they could not protect their loved ones from external threats. The state protected, and the state punished. Some analysts have linked that sense of male helplessness and frustration to an epidemic of alcoholism and domestic violence among Soviet men. I. A. Kurganoff commented in 1971 that "officially the husband has neither economic, cultural nor political advantages over the wife, but he does have the advantage of physical strength and uses it indiscriminately when drunk" (Kurganoff, 1971: 118).

According to the Moscow Center for Gender Studies, a *perestroika*-era creation, the power of husbands over their wives in the former Soviet Union was aggravated by a long-term "shortage" of men that is the legacy of World War II casualties. Women raised in the 1950s and '60s were taught to be grateful to have any husband, no matter how he behaved, and were encouraged to remain silent about dissatisfactions in their marriages. Their reluctance to discuss problems at home was reinforced by the Soviet government's practice of censoring any information that could be construed as damaging to the state. Feminism was viewed as dissidence, and the few womens'-rights activists feared arrest and imprisonment. There could therefore be no counterpart to the 1970s movements in the United States and Western Europe that politicized marriage, the family and violence against women. But since the fall of Communism, Russian feminism has come out of the closet and the epidemic of violence against women has become a political issue. At the request of activists, statistics have been gathered by the U.S. State Department's Division of Human Rights. They are staggering: In the United States, one of the world's most violent societies, approximately 1,100 women are killed each year by husbands or lovers. By conservative estimate, as many as 14,000 Russian women were killed by their abusers in 1994 alone. In 1996, the Russian government estimated that women were the victims of violence in one of every four Russian homes (Mantilla, 1997; U.S. State Department, 1996; Yoon, 1996).

It is difficult to know to what extent that culture of violence has affected women in Soviet Jewish households. Many, if not most, Soviet Jews were highly assimilated and it is logical to assume that they absorbed prevailing gender norms, to some degree at least. And certainly Jews shared the privations, helplessness and frustration of other Soviet citizens. On the other hand, most Soviet Jews were highly conscious of being different from the ethnic majority groups in Russia, Ukraine and Central Asia. Many Jewish families maintained a separate subculture built around distinct moral as well as behavioral codes. According to Jewish law, women's contributions to family life are highly valued and any assault on the wife's body is grounds for a religious divorce. Of course, theory and practice often diverge.

Assuming that the problem of domestic violence existed in some Soviet Jewish families prior to emigration, the next question is whether the stresses of immigrant life have increased or diminished its frequency and intensity. There are no statistics on rates of domestic violence in Soviet Jewish households, either in the former Soviet Union or in the United States. However there is anecdotal evidence that battering remains an issue for Soviet Jewish emigres. In Israel the problem reached serious enough proportions by 1994 that the Knesset, Israel's parliament, convened a committee of inquiry into the murder of women by their spouses. The Knesset Committee to Advance the Status of Women emphasized that, while violence against women was a problem among all classes and nationalities, it seemed particularly severe among recent immigrants to Israel, especially those from Russia and Ukraine. It is important to note here that the numbers of recent immigrants to Israel from the former Soviet Union dwarf those from other countries. It is not surprising that there are more cases of battering found in that community. While many cases were linked to the stresses created by immigration—including loss of status, financial hardships, quicker adjustment by the woman than by her husband—there was a link to the epidemic of violence in the former Soviet Union and abuse of alcohol (Izenberg, *Jerusalem Post*, 1994; Prince-Gibson, *Jerusalem Post*, 1996).

Although law and culture in Israel and the United States are kinder to victims of domestic violence than the former Soviet Union, where it has been next to impossible for women to bring charges against their abusers, many immigrant women remain unaware that they can report the violence to police. Prosecution of abusers has also been hindered by the Russian-language press in the United States and Israel, which has maintained silence on the issue of domestic violence. But serious flaws in the American legal system have also made immigrant women fear the outcome if they report their batterers. The New York case of Galina Komar, 33, was a tragic illustration of the failure of American courts to protect one battered immigrant. Komar did go to the police to press charges against her abuser, a non-Russian immigrant. But because she had neither broken bones nor visible bruises by the time the case came to court, her batterer was released. Three weeks later he followed Komar to her job and shot her to death. The publicity surrounding this case has intensified the fear that many immigrant women have about reporting domestic violence and about leaving their husbands or abusers. In the United States, as in the Soviet Union, a woman is most likely to be killed by her batterer after she has pressed charges and attempts to leave (Yoon, 1996).

Recently, several high-profile court cases have begun to raise awareness among Soviet immigrant Jews about domestic violence in their community. In Chicago, Russian immigrant Yechiel Abramov was convicted of conspiracy to murder his wife, and the immigrant press did cover the trial. In Cleveland, the 1996 murder of community leader Bella G. Leybovitch by her estranged boyfriend galvanized women volunteers to publicize Project Chai, a Jewish Family and Children's Services program for women battered by husbands and boyfriends (*Jewish Advocate*, 11/30/95; *Cleveland Jewish News*, 2/21/97).

One particular concern of battered women's advocates is low self-esteem among Soviet immigrant women. Russian culture's denigration of single women has carried over to the United States, and there is strong community pressure on women to find a mate and marry young. "American women are more independent," commented Sonya Krasnanskaya, a single 35-year-old emigre living in Brooklyn. "They have a higher opinion of themselves. Russian women are afraid of being alone. They want to be at home with a husband. Perhaps God made them that way." Fear of being single sometimes results in relationships and marriages in which immigrant women are physically and/or verbally abused (*Newsday*, 6/19/96).

In New York, Anna Halberstadt of NYANA runs a support program for battered Soviet women that seeks to build their self-confidence in a culturally sensitive way. While insisting that all women have the right to live free from violence, NYANA counselors recognize that the triggers for domestic violence vary from one Soviet Jewish immigrant group to another. In a Ukrainian or Russian home, the trigger might be the father's occupational status loss or alcoholism. In a Bukharan home, where there is less relative status loss or alcoholism, the trigger would more likely be the wife or daughter's deviation in dress or behavior from culturally accepted norms.

With their millennia-old links to Central Asian Islamic culture, Bukharan immigrants have leaned far more heavily on traditional social roles to root them in the United States than have Soviet Jewish immigrants from the European republics. This has been particularly true in regard to accepted behavior for women and girls, and in laying out the rights and responsibilities of children and adolescents. In the United States, with its more fluid relations between men and women, and parents and children, the expectation of many Bukharan elders that all family members will adhere to "the old ways" has sometimes created family conflicts and tensions requiring the intervention of social workers, therapists or even police.

Halberstadt and Nikolsky argue that gender conflict has become a major issue for Bukharan immigrants because of the traditionally low status of women in Bukharan families: "Neither education nor the professional status of the women can necessarily provide her with the respect of her family. Except for the most progressive families, Bukharan women always live under the power of men—their father, brothers and then husband. Verbal and physical abuse of women are frequent and not seen as something especially cruel or unusual." The Soviet immigration coincided with the politicization of violence against women in the United States and the emergence of legal and institutional aids for battered women. As a result, the acculturation process for many Bukharan women, as for women of many other immigrant groups, has included learning to claim their rights in a society that does not accept wife-beating or child-beating as "normal" or "natural." Many women have sought assistance through NYANA. Although Bukharans represent just 10 percent to 15 percent of the Soviet immigrant community in New York, Bukharans constitute more than 50 percent of the participants in NYANA's battered women support groups. Victoria Neznansky, a NYANA counselor, says that many of these women have been able to take only the first steps, coming to treatment but refusing to leave their marriages for fear of being cut off entirely from their communities and bringing shame on their children (Halberstadt and Nikolsky, 1996).

Daughters of abused women have often gone further, running away or in other ways asserting their right to be free of domestic violence. Their rebellion is echoed by other Soviet children and teen-agers, who, in various ways, resist parental pressure to conform to communal norms. While conflicts within Bukharan families provide some of the most dramatic examples of intergenerational tensions faced by Soviet immigrants, generational problems can be found across Soviet Jewish America. Nevertheless, the stridency of their teenage revolt is probably more muted than in most American homes. These youngsters feel a high degree of loyalty to their parents, for they are keenly aware of the sacrifices made to bring them here.

ADOLESCENTS AND CHILDREN: THE 1.5 GENERATION

The Americanization of the youngest Soviet Jewish immigrants, who were still children when they arrived in the United States, has been marked by a fundamental contradiction. Although they were given little say in the decision about whether to leave the country of their birth, they have been told time and again that their parents undertook the hardships of immigrating so that they, the children, could have a better life. Once in the United States, the pressure is on them not only to succeed, first academically and then financially, but to be happy as well. Whether their parents have said so explicitly or not, they feel that they cannot fail; that they cannot take time to explore their career options; and that they cannot express dissatisfaction with their new lives. In the back of their minds, even if they only imagine these words, they can always hear the stressed and tired voices of their parents, whispering "We did this for you. Don't blow it."

As with working-age immigrants, the adjustment of Soviet emigre children has been strongly affected by their age at the time of arrival. Those who came to the United States as young children, age 5 or less, have had a fairly easy transition to American life. They had few memories of the Soviet Union, positive or negative, to color their perceptions of this country. They arrived at an age when language acquisition is still natural and unforced. Beginning their educations and their conscious lives in the United States, most of them have grown up with English as their first language. Many speak little or no Russian. Indeed some immigrant parents have had to send their youngest children to "Russian" schools (immigrant-run afternoon programs) so that they can communicate with elderly relatives who have not learned much English (Bychov-Green and Bychov, 1996).

Even young immigrants raised partly in ethnic enclaves display little confusion about their national identity. Sam Gurevitch, Polina Globerman and Regina Bienstock—each of whom emigrated before age five—spent several years of their childhood living in or around Brighton Beach, among tens of thousands of Soviet emigres. All nevertheless identify themselves as natives. Regina is clear that she is "just American." And she is, in her dress, her bearing, her idiomatic English. There is no way to tell that she was born in Minsk. Polina says she is "American with a Russian background, but definitely more American, . . . much more American." And Sam, who is proud of his Russian Jewish heritage, sees himself as little different in that way from so many Americans with immigrant forebears. "I certainly feel American," he concludes. As conversant with American popular culture as any native, the youngest Soviet immigrants have usually had little trouble making friends with American-born children. Their adjustment problems usually arise during adolescence, when parents less comfortable with American culture try to force them into "Old World" behavior patterns, or when these children try to use their knowledge of American culture to circumvent parental authority (Baptiste, 1993: 341–63; Pawliuk et al., 1996).

Those who were age 11 or older when they left the Soviet Union have

Teenage girls out on Saturday night.

often had difficult periods of adjustment to American life. With several years of Soviet schooling behind them, they were accustomed to a far more rigid and specialized education system than they found in this country. To succeed in American schools, which emigre children feel they must do to justify their parents' sacrifices, they have had to negotiate the distance between their parents' Soviet-trained understanding of the purpose of education and the often competing expectations of their American teachers and peers. Social conflicts arise as well. Most adolescent immigrants had already begun to separate socially from their parents and to create autonomous lives and personalities. Many had to leave behind valued circles of friends, and older teens may have had boyfriends or girlfriends from whom they were abruptly separated. In short, Soviet immigrant teens have had to struggle simultaneously with the complex of psychological and emotional issues facing every adolescent and with the problems of adjustment that plague every immigrant.

In immigrant families it is not only the teen who is just learning to navigate the world outside the familial home, but parents and grandparents as well.

And if that process has always been painful and humiliating for adolescents, it is even more so for adults. The normal teen-age rebelliousness that creates tension in non-immigrant families becomes magnified and distorted by the social, emotional and financial stresses of immigration. Natural parental fears of what teen-agers will encounter in a hostile world are sharpened. So too is the normal adolescent need for a stable home environment to rebel against. Adolescence is difficult enough under the most stable family circumstances, but the psychological and financial uncertainties of immigrant life, the role reversals that occur when children and teens learn the new language more quickly than parents and are forced to become translators and mediators, the resultant parental anxieties and depressions combine to make many adolescent immigrants feel more alienated and disoriented than they otherwise would (Baptiste, 1990).

NEW ARRIVALS: MAKING FRIENDS AND REBUILDING IDENTITIES

Many Soviet immigrant teens new to the United States describe an intensified experience of that primary teenage anxiety: worry that they will never fit in or make friends. For Soviet Jews, these very normal adolescent fears are aggravated not only by the experience of immigration but by memories of schoolyard anti-Semitism. Even among the youngest immigrants born in the 1970s or later, memories of childhood are shadowed by painful recognitions of their difference. "I was six when my parents first told me I was Jewish," Sergey Shapner recalls. "I was extremely upset. *Ivrey* [Jew] was the word used to insult other kids in the kindergarten." Artyem Lifshitz first found out that he was Jewish when he was baited by fourth-grade classmates: "The word they used was *Yid*. And I didn't know what that was. So I remember asking my parents about it and my parents said, 'Oh, boy. Here we go.' " Rebecca Pyatkevich remembers being taunted regularly throughout her childhood, not just by other children but also by adult neighbors: "Maybe it was just the part of Moscow where we lived, but my brother and I experienced a lot of anti-Semitism of all kinds. Just pure verbal 'Jews get out of here.' If we were in the playground, for example, some of the ladies sitting there would start shouting at us: 'Go back to your part of town. Go away.' It was not a very pleasant thing to grow up with."

Well before the pangs of adolescence, most Jewish children in the former Soviet Union felt a sense of alienation. Perhaps to convince them that they too could survive the fights and name-calling, many Jewish parents shared with their children their own memories of anti-Semitic teachers, neighbors and schoolmates. And because they had taken strength from the bits and pieces they knew of Russian Jewish history, some parents tried to instill in their children a sense of ethnic pride, a belief that they were the inheritors of a special legacy of Jewish courage, talent and intellect. Some Soviet Jewish children did learn to take pride in their differentness. Sergey recalls bonding with the handful of Jewish children he found in his Kishinev elementary school: "We had our little clique. If one of us learned a new Yiddish word from our grandparents, he became the hero of the day." Still, they could never forget that being Jewish made them vulnerable. "It was a hidden pride," says Sergey, "because you couldn't exhibit it around others. You had to be very careful."

Those feelings of danger and "otherness" were empowering to some Jewish children. At age 10 Sergey and some elementary school friends produced a parody of the official Soviet press that displayed a taste for irony far beyond their years: "We called it the 'Bubliedzh Post,' the official organ of peasant hedgehogs." At 13, Sergey, now militantly Jewish, asked his mother to find him a Star of David pendant to wear. Simply locating the forbidden piece of jewelry required courage and ingenuity on his mother's part. After being told that she was crazy by jewelers who nervously asked her to lower her voice when discussing the Jewish star, she found an old Rabbi who gave Sergey the necklace he himself had worn for many years. Sergey wore the star proudly and began to attend illegal Hebrew classes.

Channeling teen-age anger toward the state and anti-Semitic neighbors strengthened bonds between Soviet Jewish adolescents and their parents. In most families that loyalty and intimacy persisted through the immigration process. Still, life in an anti-Semitic society created a sense of relentless pressure and vulnerability that left many young Soviet Jews feeling constantly angry at their peers and ambivalent about their ethnic heritage. Says Artyem: "Coming from Russia, being Jewish has nothing to do with religion. It has to do with being caught after school and beaten. Or being called names and stuff. Or being threatened every day. And having your path sort of chosen for you, not having all the opportunities open." Miriam Yaglom, who counsels Soviet immigrant teens in New York, found that many of her young clients were worn out by such internal conflicts well before their parents decided to emigrate. They arrived in the United States already edgy and defensive, especially anxious about how their new schoolmates would perceive them (Yaglom, 1996).

Thrust into public schools within weeks after their arrival, some went into shock. Ilya, who moved to Brooklyn from a comfortable Moscow neighborhood where he had many close friends, began attending a huge, chaotic public high school less than a month after landing in New York. He did not know a soul. His traumatized response, not uncommon among teen-age immigrants, was to stop speaking entirely until he could get his bearings.

There were probably three or four thousand students in a three-story building, so every time a class was over it was very hard to move around. Just being in that atmosphere of everybody screaming and shouting and not being able to tell where you were going was a little overwhelming. So I spent my first year just getting used to the whole thing. I didn't speak until three or four months into being here. I honestly tried not to talk at all because I was scared of saying something wrong.

Despite his confusion, Ilya became aware fairly quickly that many of the other students in his school were also immigrants—some from the former Soviet Union, many from the Dominican Republic, Central America, China and Korea. He began to feel a kinship with them. These feelings grew into friendships when he transferred the following year to a high school for the intellectually gifted. There he became best friends with a child of Greek immigrants and found romance and friendship with a Chinese immigrant girl in his class.

Soviet adolescents whose families moved directly to the suburbs entered public schools that were smaller, less frightening and less diverse than those in big cities like New York or Los Angeles. The dearth of other immigrants made for a difficult emotional transition. The relative homogeneity of the student population in suburban schools left many immigrant adolescents feeling even more like outsiders than they had in the former Soviet Union. Some emigre children looked back with longing; even the anti-Semitic name-calling seemed more bearable than their new social isolation, for it was at least familiar. Artyem, who quickly took the American name Tim, was 11 when he emigrated from Minsk to Newton, Massachusetts. He felt miles apart from his American classmates and frighteningly unmoored when he realized that his parents had no idea how to help him transcend the social boundaries that he encountered each day at school.

I didn't have the clothes they wore. The clothes were different. Styles were different. There are certain things you just don't do, colors you don't wear if you are a guy. There is all this stuff that is just not an issue at all in Europe. In Russia you didn't change your clothes every day. It wasn't a necessary thing. And you know, it takes a couple of weeks to catch up on these things. And my parents weren't working at that point or anything so they didn't know. I guess that's the hardest part, when you start learning more than your parents about this stuff. Because they were trying, but they didn't know what the right things were.

Rebecca Pyatkevitch, who left Moscow for Newton at the age of 12, traded in the anti-Jewish taunts of her former neighbors for the anti-immigrant barbs of her new schoolmates. Like any early adolescent, she was anxious about her physical appearance and worried about whether her peers would accept her. Feeling lost and awkward in her new environment, she became a target for other 12- and 13-year-olds, with their radar-like sense for anyone who is different and vulnerable: "It was rather unpleasant because kids tended to be mean and they didn't want to understand. And they'd say things. They would tease me about my clothes and the way I spoke or didn't speak. And the girls would come up and ask me if I'd ever been on a date. And I didn't know what a date was then. I didn't know English."

Although there were only a few other immigrants in her school, they comforted one another. "In seventh grade," says Rebecca, "my friends were basically my ESL [English as a Second Language] class. We had a group of about 10 people who spent half the school day together. About half were Russian. There was an Asian girl, a guy from El Salvador, a guy from France. It was interesting."

Sergey, who moved to Bradenton, Florida, from Kishinev when he was 14, was the only immigrant in his school. He made no friends at all during his first four years in the United States. Although he learned English quickly, Sergey found that fluency did not help him to cross the social chasm that separated him from other students. It is not just language that creates barriers for teen-age immigrants, he says: "A lot of it is cultural. There are idiomatic expressions and all of the other things that language carries." Little things, he says, like never having seen the "Flintstones" cartoon series, made him seem like "a KGB spy" to his schoolmates.

I make friends very slowly in general. And there I guess it was even slower because I had no peers with the same cultural experience to talk to. Literally nobody my age in Bradenton spoke Russian. And that may have contributed to it. It would have been nice to have had three or four kids to hang out with. I think that anything else would have been unproductive with respect to introducing me to American culture. I mean, I am glad about having assimilated to some extent.

Once in college, Sergey began to make non-Russian friends for the first time, but most of them were from other immigrant groups. "I've had an awful lot of friends from China," he grins. "I will leave it to you to see what's in common between the Soviet Union and China."

Tim found friends only when he was invited to join a program for Soviet immigrant teens at the Newton Jewish Community Center. Though he deeply loves his immigrant friends, he has not forgiven his American class-mates. "I'm bitter," he says. "I'm very bitter at all of the American kids." After nine years in the United States Tim still sees American young people as cliquish and superficial. By contrast, Tim says he and his immigrant friends are intellectuals, interested in books and ideas, not pop culture, sports or fashion. "[Italo] Calvino is popular with my friends right now," he says when asked what his friends talk about when they're alone. "[Vladimir] Nabokov is big. [Marcel] Proust. Just many things that when you tell [American] kids you read them, they say: 'Oh, wow, you read that?' " Still, Tim understands that his anger and his impulse to caricature American young people arise out of his hurt at being unable to fit in.

There's a different set of values that you have and a different set of standards. It's very easy to classify the people here as people who just don't live up to those stan-dards. It's a simple dismissal instead of somehow trying to work your way in, which is very difficult. I haven't done it even now. I still don't laugh at the same jokes for example. I still can't keep up a conversation about baseball or about TV or about pop music. There's all this stuff that, to gain, is extremely difficult. But to say, "Oh these Americans are dumb," that's extremely simple.

Max Roisin, who at 16 left Kishinev for the epicenter of Soviet Jewish life in the United States, Brooklyn, New York, never tried to make friends with the native-born Americans in his new high school. He didn't need to. He attended Edward R. Murrow, a large city school with hundreds of Soviet immigrant students. In a community that size, Max had little trouble finding friends whose experience was close to his. Indeed, many of his friends in the United States are also from Kishinev and emigrated to this country in their teens. Like Tim and Sergey, Max felt that he had little in common with his American classmates, who seemed to him emotionally remote.

My perception of what I like in people was pretty much built in Russia. There was something in Americans that I didn't feel comfortable with. And so I think it was not so much the language barrier as the psychological barrier that prevented me from making friends. I think that my relationship with Russians, even Russians who I didn't know before—I've made some really good friends here—those relationships are much more personal. My Russian friends, I think, devote much more of them-selves to their relationships than Americans do. At least that's my feeling.

Perhaps there is a cultural basis for Max's view. Russians do place a high value on friendship, while Americans tend to focus their emotional lives on the nuclear family. Perhaps language creates more of a barrier than these young people are willing to admit. As Rebecca points out, "You kind of change your personality when you change languages." Or maybe Soviet immigrant teens simply feel a deep loyalty toward friends who have shared the traumas of uprooting and immigration. Whatever the reason, Russian emigre youths frequently claim that intimate friendship is more important to them than it is to their American counterparts. "I'm quite different from American people," 20-year-old Rebecca says after eight years in New England. "I don't really interact at all with Americans so I don't really know what American teen-age culture, or college culture is like." Still, she insists: "I'm a lot closer to my friends than American teen-agers would be. And we're more aware of our closeness." Rebecca does not claim a Russian identity but rather a transitional one. Her friends' willingness to show emotions publicly and to express love openly, she says, is a positive result of living in a free society: "We're willing to verbalize our love and make it explicit, which a lot of people who are more Russianized are not willing to do."

Studies have found that in some cities, more than three quarters of Soviet immigrant teens report that "most or all" of their friends are other Russian immigrants. On the surface, such in-group socializing would seem to impede acculturation because it makes it emotionally unnecessary for immigrant teens to have American friends. In one study, 37 percent of Bay Area Russian immigrant teens said that they had no American friends at all. Even Tim is critical of a group of fellow emigres he knows at Brandeis University who associate with each other so exclusively that their English is deteriorating. But young immigrants do not simply wallow in nostalgia for their Russian past. They also help each other to function in a strange, new environment. The Brandeis emigres are hardly social misfits. Indeed, they would be considered successful by most measures; they attend a first-rate university and are doing well academically. They are close to their parents and respectful to their grandparents. But their friends provide practical and emotional support that family members cannot. For their elders are consumed with their own social and career concerns and cannot be expected to understand the intricacies of American youth culture (Strasser, 1995).

Finally, there are important emotional and psychological benefits that young emigres derive from these long-lasting friendships. Socializing with peers enables Soviet immigrant adolescents to forge complex cultural identities that are reflective of their experiences. "What I went through when I came here has made me what I am," says Tim. "And I'm not unhappy with what I am. I'm Soviet Jewish and American somehow. I'm all of those things." Even Max, who believes that his personality, morals and philosophy were fully developed by the time he left Kishinev at 16, understands that immigration has transformed him. "I guess I feel American in a certain way," he admits. "When I came to this country, I had to change in many things. And if I went back I would have to change again and I don't think I could find the strength."

PARENTS, GRANDPARENTS AND TEEN-AGE REBELLION

Difficult as it has been for Soviet immigrant teens to find a niche for themselves among American youth, many have found strained relations at home to be the hardest part of adjusting to U.S. life. Tensions among teenagers, parents, grandparents and siblings have developed around a variety of issues that are found in immigrant families of many ethnic backgrounds. Most common sources of intergenerational conflict among Soviet immigrant teens have been: linguistic gaps between the generations; cultural gaps around issues such as dress style, dates, night-time curfews, marriage, child-rearing and over the amount of freedom an adolescent may have to shape his or her own life and future.

Different rates of language acquisition can create serious emotional problems between young immigrants and their elders. One of the most painful is the barrier that arises between grandchildren and their grandparents when the young immigrants cannot or will not speak Russian at home. Given the important role that grandparents have historically played in raising Soviet Jewish children, this refusal is particularly hard for the elderly to bear. Egos already damaged by their dislocation are further unsettled by their inability to communicate with young members of their own families. Helen Ekmechi, an emigre resettlement worker in Swampscott, Massachusetts, considered the problem significant enough that she created a Russian culture club for children of immigrants to teach or reacquaint them with the Russian language. "Children speak Russian badly," she says, "and can't communicate with their grandparents. My kids, 17 and 11 years old, speak only English between themselves. And I'm yelling at them to speak Russian at home." Across the country, immigrant parents echo that complaint (Sessler, *Boston Globe*, 1996).

An equally common language issue is the adult-child role reversal in the months after arrival. In many immigrant families, the children learn English faster and more thoroughly than their parents. As a result the children have to take on the adult responsibility of mediating between their relatives and the outside world, from supermarket cashiers to government authorities.

Children worry that they will not perform as well as they need to. In addition, they find the sudden shift from ward to caregiver unnerving. Ilya recalls:

My sister knows English as well as I do and the two of us were the support of our parents. We had to deal with all the forms and all the appointments. And we were the only interpreters for that. And they would constantly tell us: "You have to help us. It's your duty." That kind of pressure didn't make it better. I felt, not used . . . abused? Just in the sense that I had to do all these things that I didn't want to do. Part of it was the fact that for the last 14 years these people took care of me. And now I had to take care of them. I wasn't ready for the responsibility and I didn't want to make any mistakes in front of people. And worrying that I would say something wrong in front of my parents made it even worse. I felt pressure from all sides.

Immigrant children are also deeply affected by their parents' depression and anxiety. General studies of immigrant children and those that focus on Soviet Jewish emigres have shown a correlation between emotional disturbance in parents and poor adaptation among their children. Studies of the New York area and other cities with high proportions of immigrants suggest that these symptoms are widespread among adult immigrants of all kinds, and that children absorb and reflect their parents' emotional state. Children whose parents suffer from depression, sleep disorders, severe headaches and other symptoms of serious anxiety are much more likely to have academic difficulties and/or behavioral problems themselves. When parents are experiencing severe depressions, the children can become immobilized by depression. When parents project onto children their own anxieties by telling them horror stories about the cruelties that await them on streets of American cities—sometimes recycling sensational crimes of violence played up in the Soviet press—some immigrant children grow fearful of leaving their homes at all. "I have seen teenagers who believed they could be kidnapped or mugged every day," says therapist Miriam Yaglom. Paralyzed by fear, these teens are unable to enjoy the growing sense of independence so essential to the teen-age experience (Barnakin et al., 1989; Yaglom, 1996).

When children do reject their parents' characterizations of American life, tensions arise as well. Soviet immigrant parents often feel that their children are taking too many liberties, while the child sees in American culture an escape from a stifling or authoritarian home culture. The close-knit community and highly ritualized life that Bukharan Jews have created in New York has enabled them to achieve economic success and community cohesion. But it has also generated many conflicts when children are drawn to

American notions of individualism. Among boys the most frequently heard complaint is that they do not wish to enter the family business. With their long history of entrepreneurship in the former Soviet Union, many Bukharan emigres in New York have opened businesses that are intended to provide job security for the entire family. The son who chooses to do something other than work in the family store alongside his father, uncles and brothers may be seen as ungrateful and selfish.

Rebelliousness among adolescent girls in the Bukharan community has been even more common and certainly more roundly condemned. Expected to marry and bear children young, some Bukharan girls instead have claimed their right to be "free" American women. In a community that takes family honor very seriously, parents may believe such girls are besmirching the family's reputation. Occasionally, frustrated parents who are unable to control their children lash out violently. In extreme cases, it is a prior history of domestic violence that makes the teenage girls rebel in the first place.

After years of watching her father beat her mother, one 17-year-old daughter of a Queens emigre family refused to accept his authority any longer. Although he beat her to make her stop, she began wearing miniskirts and red lipstick to school. Then she announced that she would never marry a Bukharan man because Bukharan men abuse their wives. In a similar case, 15-year-old Nellie called New York City Child Welfare Services and asked to be placed in foster care because she could no longer stand watching her father beat her mother. Both girls expressed pity toward their mothers, who were sending them mixed messages of approval and fear. Frustrated and infuriated that they could not help their mothers escape, the girls swore that they would never let themselves be beaten (Halberstadt and Nikolsky, 1996).

Like the older women who have flocked to NYANA's battered-women's groups, these young girls cling to the hope that intervention by social workers will bring an end to the battering of Bukharan women. NYANA caseworkers are also hopeful. The prevalence of domestic violence seems to be diminishing in the Bukharan community over time. Some traditional Bukharan elders have attempted to prevent change by rushing youngsters into adulthood, trying to marry off girls still in their mid-teens, or pushing boys to drop out of school and take their places in the family business. But the most rigid parents have usually had difficulty themselves making the financial, social and psychological transition to American life. In the Bukharan community, as in the larger Soviet emigre society, most parents are proud of their children's accomplishments and believe that the children will bring honor and prosperity to the family.

Ironically, even those Soviet emigre children who have adapted well sometimes feel guilty about being happy when their parents may still be struggling emotionally, if not financially. Their guilt is manifest in the conviction that they must allow their parents to live vicariously through them, and that only if they achieve great success can their parents' sacrifices be made worthwhile. Tim believes that his "parents are not very happy people. I think they have a lot of problems, because they feel that their potential has not been realized somehow, in a broader humanitarian, intellectual sense." He and his Korean girlfriend talk about the sense of responsibility that they both feel for their parents. They believe that this dynamic is common to immigrant families. Tim says:

The parents made this big, big struggle to come across and then they can't ever fit in completely. They feel it, and once you grow up enough, you feel it. Then the pressure's on you. Some families are very explicit about it: "We emigrated so that you could have a chance here." My parents are extremely liberal. They're not explicit about it. And I don't know if that makes it worse for me or not. Because I feel it's true.

One result of this guilt has been that Soviet immigrant teens and young adults feel compelled to pursue only those careers that will bring prestige and financial security to their families. The combination is seen as important to restore a family's lost status and to "pay back" parents for getting the family out of the Soviet Union. Says Max:

In Russian Jewish families, it's a common trend that parents do expect their children to get a high level of education. In the Russian language there is a term "intelligentsia," which means a class that has some intellectual kind of profession. In Russia this kind of profession was considered a teacher, an engineer, a doctor, a professor. And this is the sort of values that they're looking for here. I would say that commonly in Russian families this is what they would expect

But most Soviet immigrants in colleges and universities do not pursue intellectual fulfillment, taking subjects like English or history; neither do they pursue teaching degrees. The issue is not just honor but money. Although Max does not believe that material success would, in and of itself, make him happy, he feels that he owes it to his parents to enter a high-paying profession. "At this point in my life, what I worry about most is family," he says, "and my material success would really be important for my family. And so in that sense, material success is important. Right now my parents support me. But in the future, I plan to support my parents." That is a very common goal among immigrant children.

Psychologists see among many Soviet Jews, and other immigrants in the United States, what they call an "enmeshed family," in which parents and children are much more deeply involved in each other's lives than is the norm in American families. That level of intergenerational interdependence can create the sense of pressure that Tim described. Catering to their parents' desires, some Soviet young people have given up their career preferences in favor of their parents.' Fran Markowitz's study of teen-age Soviet girls in Chicago shows this to be common: Julia gave up music to become a computer scientist, while Alexandra abandoned her artistic aspirations and took up marketing. Shirley Sperling found the same to be true at Dartmouth College, where most Soviet emigre students that she interviewed said they would not dream of calling home and saying, "Hey, Mom, I'm majoring in drama" (Markowitz, 1994; Sperling, 1997).

But close, engaged relationships between parents and children can also provide immigrant youngsters with the support, role-modeling and motivation that enable them to make a successful transition to American life. Like the deeply loyal friendships that young immigrants form, the "enmeshed family" both impedes and accelerates adjustment. Just as Soviet emigres argue that Americans care less about friendships than they do, many also say that the tradition of intimacy between Russian Jewish parents and children, and between grandparents and grandchildren, is a value worth keeping, even if the American way tends more toward segregating the generations.

And as immigrant families are here longer, many children are striking a balance—preserving closeness with their parents, while asserting their freedom of choice. Rebecca is extremely close to her father and mother. Although she left town to attend college, she says, "I'm home every other weekend and when I'm not there, they come here." Still, she resists her parents' attempts to dictate her studies. Her father wants her to be a physician, while her mother wants her to be a computer programmer. Neither is happy about her decision to major in history. But, says Rebecca: "They know they can't tell me that I can't because they know that I won't listen to them. When my mother says, 'Be a computer programmer,' that seems like an absurd thing for me to do. I've been a humanities and social sciences person since I was seven." Rebecca reminds them that freedom of choice was part of the reason that they came here.

Achieving balance is a big part of the immigrant adjustment process for every generation. And although the demands that the close-knit Soviet Jewish immigrant family places on its children are sometimes so intense as to be damaging, for most immigrants the emotional and psychological benefits far outweigh the harm. Learning to function in a radically different environment is exhausting work, and the love of family is a rejuvenating balm that gives people the strength to remake themselves and their lives daily. Male and female, working- and middle-class, elderly, middle-aged and young Soviet immigrants have grappled with the problems of acculturation in their own ways. But they have all found in family an emotional resource, for some a safe space to test their new American personalities, for others a place where they can relax into accustomed ways of being. There is inestimable value for the weary immigrant in being able to do that now and then.

Certainly there is conflict between Soviet emigre children who are changing quickly and older relatives for whom the past will always be more compelling. But even among those gripped by nostalgia, there are few who regret the decision to leave; for being Jewish in Russia has never been easy. There are many Jewish emigres, the old as well as the young, who would agree with Rebecca that "Russia never felt like my country. I always felt like I wasn't wanted there." Their struggle now is to find ways to make the United States feel like home.

Epilogue: Personal and Political Transformations— Soviet Jewish Life in the United States After 25 Years of Immigration

Since 1972, when the first Soviet Jewish emigres arrived on American shores, a tiny community of exile dissidents has grown into a massive nationwide immigrant presence numbering nearly half a million people. Dramatically varied in class, education, region of origin, age, degree of religiosity and personal temperament, Soviet Jewish Americans defy broad generalizations or simple characterizations. Since they, like most immigrant groups, have been subjected to crude and reductive stereotyping that paints them all as criminals, or rude, gold-bedecked welfare cheats, that in itself is an important point to make. It is not possible to understand this immigration without noting the many significant differences among the emigres. But students of this emigration must also mark changes over time. In the 25 years since the immigration began, there have been some important transformations.

Most of those who came in the 1970s have by now grown accustomed to life in the United States. Whether they speak flawless, barely accented English or continue to communicate primarily in Russian, it has been at least twenty years since most of them held Soviet citizenship. They have come to feel settled in their American lives. "America is my country, not Russia," one Brighton businesswoman replied impatiently when asked whether she continued to follow the news from home. "I have no one left there to worry about. My family is all here or in Israel."

Her final comment highlights an important factor distinguishing this immigrant group from many others who have arrived since 1965. Like the Jewish immigrants from Russia who flooded into this country a century ago, and the Holocaust survivors who arrived here after World War II, most

Jewish emigres from the former Soviet Union feel that there is nothing left of the world they once knew, nothing left to go back to. During the painful years of the 1980s, when the doors of the Soviet Union were bolted against those who wished to leave, Third Wave immigrants paid close attention to any news about political shifts in the Soviet regime, for many had family members still living there. But since the Gorbachev era, more than 300,000 Soviet emigres have moved to the United States. Most immigrant families here have been reunited with friends and loved ones. When asked why they came, more than a few Soviet Jews who emigrated in the mid-1990s have replied succinctly: "There was nothing to stay for. Everyone I know is here."

Although most came to be reunited with family, the Fourth Wave immigrants were different from those who came before, and one of the key distinctions was political. The first emigres were passionately anti-Communist; many admired President Ronald Reagan for his hard-line stands on military preparedness and Soviet expansionism. They saw him as standing up to the leaders of "the evil empire" and they loved him for it. Many Soviet Jews applied to become citizens as soon as they were eligible and almost immediately thereafter registered to vote as Republicans. This attraction to Republican politics was strengthened by the immigrants' fear of becoming victims of violent crime in the American cities where they lived, and by their horror at the "lawlessness and lack of discipline" in American schools. Perceived as the law-and-order party, the Republicans won a majority of Soviet immigrant votes through the 1980s. Then, however, the political profile of the immigrant community began to change. By 1992 polls showed that Soviet Jews, like other immigrants, were voting overwhelmingly for Bill Clinton (Lin, *Newsday*, 1992).

The arrival of hundreds of thousands of Fourth Wave immigrants in the 1990s was partly responsible for the political shift. Traumatized by the economic chaos in the former Soviet Union, by the frightening rise in violent crime, and the resurgence of anti-Semitism since the fall of the Communist regime, Fourth Wave immigrants tended to be far less idealistic about capitalist democracy than their Third Wave counterparts. Some even looked back with a certain amount of nostalgia on the Communist era, when at least the streets of Soviet cities were safe. Having witnessed the power vacuum and the widespread suffering that followed Communism's end, many of them came to this country as strong supporters of generous state subsidies for housing, education, health care and the elderly, as well as for more police and prisons.

Third and Fourth Wave immigrants became increasingly drawn to the Democratic Party in the 1990s for two reasons. In the 1992 and 1994 elections, conservative Republican candidates promised to place new limits on legal immigration and to gut social welfare programs that buffered tens of thousands of Soviet Jewish immigrants from poverty. Republican vows to cut or end federal housing and health care subsidies, stipends for elderly immigrants, Food Stamps, Legal Services, Head Start and other programs terrified newly arrived, low-income and elderly Soviet Jews. Extremely sensitive to any hint of a *pogrom* in the making, many Soviet Jews were also upset by the party's anti-immigrant stance. California Governor Pete Wilson's campaign for Proposition 187 (to prohibit health care and educational services to illegal immigrants), the strident anti-immigrant speeches of maverick Republican presidential candidate Patrick Buchanan, and Senator Alan Simpson's proposed 1995 Immigration Reform Act (which would have made it more difficult for the family members of legal immigrants to enter the United States) frightened many Soviet Jewish emigres and moved them to organize politically.

After years of allying primarily with American Jewish groups in efforts to preserve refugee status for Jews from the former Soviet Union, Soviet community leaders began to make common cause with Americans of other ethnicities to preserve the rights of all legal immigrants. Several times during the 1990s, Soviet Jewish federations such as the Union of Councils for Soviet Jews and the American Association of Russian Jews allied with the Mexican-American Legal Defense Fund and other Latino and Asian groups to campaign against Republican attempts to restrict legal immigration to the United States. This is a significant shift from earlier years, when advocates for refugees from Mexico, Central and South America complained that Cuban refugees and Jews from the Soviet Union received preferential treatment from the U.S. State Department.

During the 1994 and 1996 election seasons, Soviet emigres worked with Asian, Caribbean and Latino groups across the United States to protest immigrant bashing in political campaigns and to defeat proposed legislation restricting legal immigration. In San Francisco's Chinatown in 1995, Soviet Jews joined Chinese, Filipino, Mexican, Irish and Italian immigrants at a rally to celebrate the contributions made by immigrants to U.S. life and culture. The Soviet emigres were represented on the speaker's platform by Michael Shapiro, a Fourth Wave immigrant from Moscow who organized a letter-writing campaign to Bay Area legislators out of fear that the proposed 1995 Immigration Reform Act would prevent him from bringing his adult son to this country. Standing under a banner that said "Immigrants Are Good for the U.S.," Shapiro addressed the multiethnic crowd by singing the praises of American pluralism. "This country has been created by immigrants," he said forcefully, "and the diversity and the richness of their ideas and their talents has made this the greatest country in the world." Shapiro's sentiments reflect a growing pan-immigrant political identity among post-1965 immigrants across the United States (Katz, *Jewish Bulletin of Northern California*, 1995).

During the 1996 election most Soviet Jews joined other immigrant groups to re-elect Bill Clinton. They did so without enthusiasm and only because they feared that a Republican victory would make things worse for the country's legal immigrants. Clinton had already shown himself quite willing to restrict the rights of legal immigrants. That September he had signed the Illegal Immigration Reform and Immigrant Responsibility Act, which gave the Immigration and Naturalization Service [INS] the right to deport long-time legal residents for minor crimes and placed unprecedented restrictions on an immigrant's right to appeal INS deportation orders. He also signed the Personal Responsibility and Work Opportunity Act which cut off Supplemental Security Income and cash assistance for legal immigrants who have not yet become citizens. Many immigrants, particularly the elderly, feared disaster once these laws went into effect. They hoped that they could believe Clinton's pre-Election Day promise to reverse the most harshly anti-immigrant provisions of the bills. Still, they feared a rising tide of anti-immigrant sentiment. After all, legal immigrants accounted for just 5 percent of those who received public assistance in the United States, but 44 percent of the program cuts in the welfare reform bill targeted them directly (Glasser, 1996).

The summer of 1996 and the winter of 1997 saw widespread panic among elderly Soviet emigres, nearly 100,000 of whom faced the loss of SSI, Medicare, food stamps and housing benefits. At senior centers and housing complexes across the country, overwhelmed social workers tried to explain the coming legal changes to terrified crowds of elderly immigrants. "This seems unbelievable," 76-year-old Boris Leybovich screamed in Russian at the Forest Hills Community House Senior Center in New York. "How can they accept us here, then throw us to the garbage? If this happens, will we live in the street? This can't be happening." At the Menorah Park houses in San Francisco, 69-year-old Ukrainian immigrant Maria Gorinshteyn described the mood of her neighbors: "People are panicking; they are very worried. One is having chest pain" (Ramirez, *Newsday*, 1996; Gelbwasser, *The Jewish Advocate*, 1996; Josar, *Detroit News*, 1996).

In Los Angeles County, a crisis loomed as officials estimated that 430,000 legal immigrants faced the loss of SSI, food stamps and Medicare. "Why us?" asked 76-year-old Kosaya Nina, who had fled Ukraine in 1991 to escape neo-Nazi gangs. "Haven't we suffered enough?" In Los Angeles, as in cities across the country, many of those who had been in the country five years or longer tried to stave off disaster by studying for the U.S. citizenship test. But thousands of elderly feared that their English was simply not strong enough to pass. In the West Hollywood area, Jewish social service workers worried that there were at least 10,000 elderly immigrants who would not be able to pass an exam in English. Nervously, aged men and women gathered in West Hollywood's Plummer Park and whispered horror stories. One woman they knew went to sleep convinced that she had failed the test and died of a heart attack before morning (Rojas, *San Francisco Chronicle*, 1997).

This fear prompted an unprecedented event in the history of Soviet Jewish America: its first mass march on Washington to protest U.S. government policy. On April 14, 1997, more than 10,000 Soviet Jewish emigres from New York, Boston and Philadelphia attended a Washington, D.C., protest march sponsored by the Union of Councils for Soviet Jews (UCSJ) and the American Association of Jews from the Former Soviet Union. "We firmly believe that the United States' welfare laws should never be based on a social Darwinist theory where only the strong, young and healthy survive," the protesters declared in a petition that they presented to Clinton and the U.S. Congress. "Food stamps, assistance for needy families and children and Supplemental Security Income should be reinstated for the most vulnerable." The angry demonstrators were met by Minnesota's Senator Paul Wellstone, a Democrat who read a "sense of the Senate" resolution passed that morning that called for the restoration of benefits to elderly and disabled legal immigrants. The demonstrators cheered, enjoying their first taste of political empowerment. Two of the rally's organizers, UCSJ Director Micah Naftalin and President Yosef Abramowitz, called on those gathered to hold politicians' feet to the fire. Abramowitz warned that the 1996 Personal Responsibility Act was a "ticking time bomb" that would explode that summer, hurting millions of legal immigrants (Union of Councils for Soviet Jews, 1997).

With the cuts scheduled to take effect during the summer of 1997, Jewish social service agencies launched intensive citizenship classes for elderly Soviet immigrants to enable as many as possible to keep their benefits. All that spring, buses arrived six days a week to take aged immigrants from housing complexes, like Ivy Hill in Newark, New Jersey, to area synagogues where they could study English and American history in preparation for the citizenship exam. The ages of the students ranged from early 60s to the upper 80s. The older the immigrants, the more fear they had about the exams. Eighty-one-year-old Isylya Berdichevskaya, a retired bookkeeper who emigrated from Minsk in 1992, joined a citizenship class offered by the Jewish Community House of Bensonhurst, Brooklyn, in 1997. She studied furiously and wrote down details about American and local government: How many

Supreme Court justices are there? Who is the head of city government? Despite her preparation, she says with a warm smile, she is still too fearful to take the citizenship exam. She makes appointments, but, sleepless with anxiety, she can never quite make herself go. In scores of U.S. towns and cities that summer, however, many other elderly Soviet immigrants did take the exam and passed. Emotional citizenship ceremonies followed, like one in Whippany, New Jersey, in June 1997, where Democratic Senator Frank Lautenberg administered the oath to 149 Soviet emigres, most of whom were well past 70. In New York City, the United Jewish Appeal raised over $1.2 million to train 7,000 elderly emigres for the test (Brown, *The Jewish Week*, 1997; Banner and Ramer, *Metro West Jewish News*, 1997).

In the end, as part of a balanced-budget agreement passed early in August 1997, Clinton negotiated the restoration of cash assistance for elderly immigrants who were receiving SSI at the time that the original welfare reform bill was signed. For tens of thousands of Soviet elderly, like 75-year-old Ukrainian emigre Yevgeniya Kaster, who lived alone in Chicago, the last-minute reprieve meant the difference between careful budgeting and homelessness. Still, Kaster, like all legal immigrants who had not become citizens by summer 1997, did lose her monthly allotment of food stamps—amounting to more than 10 percent of her income. Nine state governments, including New York's, voted to continue offering food stamps to legal immigrants, to be paid for with state funds. In states like Illinois, where no such arrangement was made, synagogues, social service agencies and private charities scrambled to fill the pantries and the stomachs of the immigrant poor. The Jewish Federation of Metropolitan Chicago made plans to open a food pantry and a free kosher kitchen called the Uptown Cafe. In the San Francisco Bay Area, local Jewish groups gave Soviet immigrants food vouchers that could be exchanged for groceries at several supermarket chains (Dorf, Jewish Telegraphic Agency, 1997).

Grateful for yet another outpouring of support from American Jews, Soviet emigre leaders nevertheless continue to express deep-seated ambivalence toward what they call "the American Jewish establishment." There have been tensions between Soviet Jewish immigrants and American Jews since the emigres began arriving in the mid-1970s, and relations have not improved all that much.

Many Soviet Jewish emigres continue to feel judged by American Jews and largely unwelcome in their synagogues and community centers. Mark Handelman of NYANA argues that some of that hostility is imagined. Many American Jews were and are interested in reaching out to their Soviet Jewish neighbors. Still, those feelings of rejection are rooted in a real experience. In every city where Soviet Jews settled, there were American Jews who openly expressed a sense of disappointment when Soviet emigres turned out to be different from what they had expected. In most cases, says Handelman, these criticisms said less about the behavior of the immigrants than about American Jewish stereotypes.

American Jews expected the Russian Jews to fall into two categories, either to be Natan [Anatoly] Sharansky or to be their own grandmother from the *shtetl.* Unfortunately the great majority who arrived were neither Prisoners of Zion or *bubbe* and *zeyde* [grandma and grandpa]. These people had to endure under a police state for 70 years, which prevented observance of Jewish customs. . . . But we expected to meet Tevye [the folksy protagonist of the Broadway musical "Fiddler on the Roof"]. (cited in Ruby, 1995)

By the late 1980s, such persistent cultural and identity differences convinced many Soviet Jewish Americans that they should play a more central role in welcoming and helping to settle their countrymen. Nationwide, the American Association of Russian Jews (AARJ) trained immigrants as Jewish teachers and community outreach workers. They also ran Jewish education programs for immigrant children and teens. On a local level, the New American Organizations and Communities of New York was formed to coordinate social, cultural and political activism in the city's vast Soviet immigrant community. The Association of Soviet Jewish Emigres of Southern California does similar work. There are also new vocational self-help groups, many of which were modeled on the Association of Engineers and Scientists for New Americans, which was founded in 1981.

All of these groups express frustration with the large American Jewish charitable agencies, especially the United Jewish Appeal (UJA) and the Federation of Jewish Philanthropies, which they say have been very slow to fund their proposals. "We feel like there is a glass wall between American Jewry and Russian Jews," says Inna Arlovich, vice president of the AARJ. Vladimir Epshteyn, co-founder of New American Organizations, put it this way: "What has been exceedingly difficult to get through to the American Jewish organizations is that the leadership of the Russian community should be in the hands of native Russians" (Ruby, 1995).

UJA and Federation officials counter that they have spent enormous sums on Soviet Jewish resettlement and cultural programs, $40 million in 1993– 1994 alone. But Soviet immigrant leaders insist that such responses miss the point. Says Pereytz Goldmacher, president of the Association of Engineers, "Yes, NYANA works with Russian Jews, but we *are* Russian Jews. We have to build our own community from the grassroots up, and we can't develop leadership from employees of agencies." Increasingly, there are signs that Soviet emigres are reaching accord with American Jewish leaders. In New York, emigres founded a Russian division of the Federation of Jewish Philanthropies that raised $350,000 in 1994 to fund local immigrant projects. And in Los Angeles, says Eugene Levin of the Association of Soviet Emigres, relations have improved because Soviet Jews have become active members of Jewish charitable organizations.

As for relations between Soviet emigres and American Jews more generally, time will probably be the most important healer of resentments and misunderstandings. Older American Jews still remember when German and East European Jews associated little with one another. German Jews, with a longer history in the United States, tended to be wealthier, better educated and more assimilated that the newly arrived East European Jews. The German Jews felt uncomfortable with the newcomers and tried to Americanize them as quickly as possible. *Litvak* (North-East European) and *Galizianer* (Central-East European Jews) were considered to be so different that many parents would balk at "intermarriage." There has never been a monolithic American Jewish community, and there will never be one. As this book has attempted to illustrate, even Soviet Jewish America is far too large and too diverse to be summed up simply or to be represented by leaders of one political caste. From New York to Seattle, Soviet Jews are becoming American but what that means to each is as varied as the immigration itself.

Just after New Year's Day 1998, I visited the boardwalk in Brighton Beach. It was a cold, sunny day and there were hundreds of Soviet immigrants walking arm in arm, pushing baby strollers, lining the benches, pulling berets and fur hats down over their ears to block the wind, squinting against the sun glinting off the sea. But even there, in that most stereotyped and reviled of Soviet Jewish communities, the diversity was striking. Middle-aged women with proud bearing and intent eyes ambled slowly along, deeply engaged in Russian conversation. Chic young couples walked briskly, speaking perfect English with just a hint of an accent. Young men in black leather and middle-aged men in wool overcoats stood with their thumbs clasped behind their backs, discussing business in a random and rambunctious mixture of Russian and English.

In the Gastronom Moscow, a boardwalk snack bar, old men in wool caps played dominos beneath a startlingly good painting of Russian men drinking. Creases in the painted canvas were still visible; someone had obviously folded it very small to get it out of the Soviet Union. The air was warmed by the smells of frying chicken cutlets and cheese blintzes, and filled with rhythmic clicking of dominos and vodka glasses. This was a male enclave, almost exclusively, and I was feeling a little out of place, standing there with my baby daughter in my arms. Then one of the men, still wearing his coat and cap though indoors, smiled broadly at my daughter and in Russian, then Yiddish, praised the sweetness of her face. An emigre from Minsk, he was still quite pleased that he had decided to come to America although, after 26 years in Brighton, he spoke no English. "Here family can be together," he said in a husky, emotional Russian whisper, gesturing at my child. And then in Yiddish: "Family is the most important thing. Family is life."

Leaving the restaurant I saw a group of young boys playing tag on the beach, shouting to each other in ebullient tones, joking in slang English, wearing baggy jeans and running shoes. I was a little surprised when one of the old women standing outside the Gastronom spoke sharply in Russian to one of the boys who stopped to listen, dancing in place, anxious to get back to his friends just as any 10-year-old would be when being lectured by an elder. He answered her sweetly in perfect Russian, then turned back to his friends. "Let's go," he said in English, and they ran off to climb a nearby jungle gym, once again indistinguishable from any other group of American kids at play.

Appendix: Noted Soviet Jewish Americans

Joseph Brodsky, poet (1940–1996): The best-known of all Soviet Jewish emigres to the United States, Brodsky was born in Leningrad on the eve of World War II. Brodsky left school at age 15 and worked as a laborer, a millhand and a mortuary assistant, among other jobs. He began publishing poetry at age 18 and won praise from some of Russia's greatest poets. Anna Akhmatova, Osip Mandelstam and Boris Pasternak all hailed the young writer. The praise of such well-known dissidents and his "decadent, Western" poetic style soon earned him official censure. In January 1964, he was put on trial for "social parasitism." When the judge asked him who had authorized him to be a poet, he uttered the famous response: "No one. Who was it who decided I was a member of the human race?" Sentenced to a five-year exile in Siberia, he was released early but faced continued government harassment until he was expelled in 1972, ostensibly to emigrate to Israel. Brodsky chose instead to live in the United States, where he enhanced his literary reputation by publishing three collections of poetry in English: *Selected Poems* (1973), *A Part of Speech* (1978) and *To Urania* (1988). His essay collection, *Less Than One* (1988), also won him great acclaim. In 1987, he was awarded the Nobel Prize for literature, the youngest recipient in the history of the award. In 1991 he was appointed Poet Laureate of the United States. On January 28, 1996, he died of a heart attack at age 55.

Bella Davidovich, pianist (1929–   ): World-renowned classical pianist, Bella Davidovich was born in the Azerbaijan capital of Baku into a family of musicians. She was admitted to the Moscow Conservatory at age 18. Three years later she won the prestigious International Chopin Competition in Warsaw. Davidovich was awarded the coveted designation "Deserving Artist of the Soviet Union" and a professorship at the Moscow Conservatory, through which she had the opportunity to train the best young Soviet musicians. One of these was her son Dmitry, a violin prodigy who won the International Concertino Competition in Prague when he was 12. Though Davidovich had an international reputation in the classical music world, the Soviet government did not permit her to perform overseas. This became intolerable after her son Dmitry left for New York in 1977, and she emigrated in 1978. She made her Carnegie Hall debut shortly after her arrival and quickly became one of the best-known solo pianists on the international classical circuit. She gives more than 100 concerts annually, as a solo performer and with her son.

Nachum Kaziev, community activist and entrepreneur (1970–   ): A prodigy among Soviet emigre notables, Kaziev was born in Tashkent, Uzbekistan, and immigrated to Rego Park, Queens, with his family in 1986. At age 21, he helped found the Educational Center for Russian Jewry, which offers classes in Jewish topics. Kaziev publishes *Druzhba* (Friendship), a Soviet Jewish emigre magazine with subscribers in seven states, Israel and Australia. He founded the Russian Language Directory, a yellow pages for the Soviet Jewish community, and a Russian-language radio program, "Mir Shalom" (world peace), which airs on WKDM-AM in New York.

Fatima Kuinova, singer (1917(?)–   ): Born in Dushanbe, Tadjikistan, Kuinova learned to sing from her father, who was a cantor in a Bukharan synagogue. She quickly revealed her gift in many Central Asian musical styles, including the classical *maqam*, Bukharan liturgy, and Tadjik, Uzbek and Tatar folk music. A popular performer in the years after World War II, she was named a "Merited Artist of the Soviet Union" in 1948. She had a prolific television, recording and concert career for the next quarter-century. During the 1970s, Kuinova joined the Bukharan emigration to Rego Park, Queens, where she continues to perform.

Ilyas Malayev, musician and poet (1936–   ): A child star, Bukharan emigre Ilyas Malayev has performed classical Bukharan and Uzbek music since he was nine years old. Gifted on many stringed instruments including the *tanbur*, violin and *tar*, Malayev moved from the Uzbek Ensemble of Song and Dance in the Philharmonia Society to a solo career that won him great fame. Before he emigrated to the United States in 1992, Malayev was playing stadium concerts that drew standing-room crowds of more than 25,000 people. Now living in Rego Park, Queens, Malayev continues to teach and perform poetry and music in the ancient Central Asian tradition.

Ernst Neizvestny, sculptor (1927–   ): The son of renowned poet Bella Dizhur, Neizvestny served in the Red Army during World War II and received a Red Star for heroism. He and his unit were among the liberators of the Nazi concentration camps, an experience that left a lifelong imprint on his art. He began painting and drawing Holocaust-related scenes in 1947 to accompany a poem written by his mother about a rabbi who perished in the camps. He soon became known as a leading figure in the Russian avant-garde. In 1962, Soviet Premier Nikita Khrushchev denounced a Neizvestny exhibition as "filth." Neizvestny's response earned Khrushchev's respect, and he was later commissioned to sculpt a bust for Khrushchev's tomb. During the Brezhnev years, Neizvestny was hounded by the government and denied official commissions. In 1976 he and his mother emigrated to Brooklyn. On his arrival in the United States, he was hailed as one of the masters of modern art. Since 1991, his work has been greatly in demand in the republics of the former Soviet Union. Massive sculptures dedicated to victims of Soviet repression are installed in St. Petersburg, Odessa and several Siberian cities, and one of his small sculptures is the prototype for the Teffie, the Russian equivalent of the Emmy Awards. His latest works are a monument to the victims of fascism to be installed in Riga, Latvia, and a 14-story "Tree of Life" to be displayed at the United Nations.

Greogoriy Pogrebetsky, structural engineer (1927–   ): Formerly a high-ranking Soviet engineer who specialized in the reinforcement of building foundations for government and military structures, Pogrebetsky has waged a one-man campaign since his emigration to Philadelphia in the late 1980s to convince the Ukraine government that the Chernobyl nuclear power plant remains extremely dangerous. No nuclear power plant in the former Soviet Union was constructed on sound foundations, Pogrebetsky argues, and there is a potential for devastating disasters in the future. His analysis of the continuing dangers at Chernobyl has been published in the *Bulletin of the New American Association of Scientists and Technicians*, a journal of Soviet emigre scientists, and his proposals for strengthening the foundations of nuclear power plants are on record at the Library of Congress.

Yuri Radzvievsky, television star, entrepreneur (1945–   ): Born in Moscow at the end of World War II, Radzvievsky made his first fortune as the host of a Soviet television program that mixed American game show, talk show and comedy formats. Emigrating to the United States in 1973, at age 28, Radzvievsky began a commercial translating and advertising business geared to Russian immigrants. When advertising giant Ogilvy and Mather bought him out in 1981, Radzvievsky became one of the Soviet immigrant community's first millionaires.

Alexander Sirotin, theatrical director, radio journalist (1943–   ): Born in Moscow during World War II, Sirotin spent his early years living in the shell of the famous Moscow Jewish State Theater, where his mother, Nechama Sirotina, was a leading actress. During the 1960s, Sirotin spent several years as a television actor and announcer, but was ultimately fired because he "did not have a Russian face." Thereafter, Sirotin became a satirist and playwright, forming a dissident theater company and directing numerous plays. After emigrating to Brighton Beach in 1978, Sirotin became a radio and print journalist, and occasionally appeared in Yiddish and Russian theatrical productions. During the 1980s, he was host of a Russian-language radio show, "Gorizont" (Horizon). Today he is a correspondent for Radio Liberty and Voice of America, broadcasting to Russian speakers across the United States and around the world.

Nechama Sirotina, actress (1919–1991): One of the best-known Yiddish actresses in the Soviet Union, Sirotina was a child student of Solomon Mikhoels, famed director of the Moscow Jewish State Theater and the moving spirit behind Jewish art theater in pre–World War II Russia. Sirotina played leading roles in Yiddish classics by Shalom Aleichem and in more contemporary Soviet Jewish plays by Peretz Markish and others. She participated in the revival of Jewish theater in the Soviet Union during the 1960s, as one of the founders of a traveling Yiddish drama company. She and her son emigrated to Brighton Beach in 1978. There she formed a small troupe of emigre Yiddish actors that performed locally and she starred in several productions staged by New York's pre-eminent Yiddish company, the Folksbiene Theater.

Bibliography

BOOKS

Jews in the Soviet Union

Altshuler, Mordecai. *Soviet Jewry Since the Second World War: Population and Social Structure.* Westport: Greenwood Press, 1987.

Eckman, Lester. *Soviet Policy Towards Jews and Israel, 1917–1974.* New York: Shengold Publishers, 1974.

Freedman, Robert O. ed. *Soviet Jewry in the 1980s: The Politics of Anti-Semitism and Emigration and the Dynamics of Resettlement.* Durham and London: Duke University Press, 1989.

Gilbert, Martin. *The Jews of Hope.* New York: Viking/Penguin, 1985.

Gilboa, Yehoshua A. *The Black Years of Soviet Jewry: 1939–1953.* Boston: Little, Brown and Co., 1971.

Klier, John Doyle. *Russia Gathers Her Jews: The Origins of the 'Jewish Question' in Russia.* Dekalb: Northern Illinois University Press, 1986.

Klier, J. D., and Shlomo Lambroza eds. *Pogroms: Anti-Jewish Violence in Modern Russian History.* Cambridge and New York: Cambridge University Press, 1992.

Kochan, Lionel ed. *The Jews in Soviet Russia Since 1917.* Oxford and New York: Oxford University Press, 1978.

Korey, William. *The Soviet Cage: Anti-Semitism in Russia.* New York: Viking Press, 1978.

Kurganoff, I. A. *Women in the U.S.S.R.* London: SBONR Publishing, 1971.

Lenin, V. I. *Collected Works,* 2nd edition, vol. 17. Moscow: Gosudarstvennoe Izdatel'stvo, 1961.

Levin, Nora. *The Jews in the Soviet Union Since 1917,* 2 volumes. New York: New York University Press, 1988.

Low, Alfred D. *Soviet Jewry and Soviet Policy.* New York: Columbia University Press, 1990.

Luckert, Yelena. *Soviet Jewish History 1917–1991: An Annotated Bibliography.* New York and London: Garland Press, 1992.

Mandelstam, Nadezhda. *Hope Against Hope.* New York: Atheneum Books, 1970.

Nudel, Ida. *A Hand in the Darkness: The Autobiography of a Refusenik.* New York: Warner Books, 1990.

Pinkus, Benjamin. *The Soviet Government and the Jews, 1948–1967.* Cambridge and New York: Cambridge University Press, 1984.

Reznik, Semyon. *The Nazification of Russia: Anti-Semitism in the Post-Soviet Era.* Washington: Challenge Publishers, 1996.

Sawyer, Thomas E. *The Jewish Minority in the Soviet Union.* Boulder: Westview Press, 1979.

Schwartz, Solomon. *Jews in the Soviet Union.* Syracuse: Syracuse University Press, 1951.

Solodhuko, Yu. A. *Soviet Views of Talmudic Judaism.* Leiden: E. J. Brill, 1973.

Vaksberg, Arkady. *Stalin Against the Jews.* New York: Alfred A. Knopf, 1994.

Wiesel, Elie. *The Jews of Silence: A Personal Report on Soviet Jewry,* expanded edition. New York: Schocken Books, 1987.

Young, Cathy (Ekaterina Jung). *Growing Up in Moscow: Memories of a Soviet Girlhood.* New York: Ticknor and Fields, 1989.

The Emigration Struggle

Olitsky, Kerry ed. *We Are Leaving Mother Russia.* Cincinnati: American Jewish Archives, 1990.

Orbach, William. *The American Movement to Aid Soviet Jews.* Amherst: University of Massachusetts Press, 1979.

Ro'i, Yaacov. *The Struggle for Soviet Jewish Emigration, 1948–1967.* Cambridge and New York: Cambridge University Press, 1991.

Sanders, Ronald. *Shores of Refuge: A Hundred Years of Jewish Emigration.* New York: Henry Holt, 1988.

Soviet Jews in the United States

Brodsky, Joseph. *Less Than One: Selected Essays.* New York: Farrar, Straus and Giroux, 1986.

Gold, Steven J. *Soviet Jews in the United States.* ERIC Document Reproduction Service, 1990.

———. *From the Worker's State to the Golden State: Jews from the Former Soviet Union in California.* Needham Heights, Mass.: Allyn and Bacon, 1995.

Howe, Irving. *World of Our Fathers.* New York: Harcourt, Brace, Jovanovich, 1976.

Jacobs, Dan N., and Ellen F. Paul. *Studies of the Third Wave: Recent Migration of Soviet Jews to the United States.* Boulder: Westview Press, 1981.

Markowitz, Fran. *A Community In Spite of Itself: Soviet Jewish Emigres in New York.* Washington: Smithsonian Institution Press, 1993.

Ripp, V. *From Moscow to Main Street: Among the Russian Emigres.* Boston: Little, Brown & Company, 1984.

Rothchild, Sylvia. *A Special Legacy: An Oral History of Soviet Immigrants in the United States.* New York: Simon and Schuster, 1985.

Simon, Rita J. *New Lives: The Adjustment of Soviet Jewish Emigres in the United States and Israel.* Lexington, Mass: Lexington Books, 1985.

———. *In the Golden Land: A Century of Russian and Soviet Jewish Immigration in America.* Westport: Greenwood Press, 1997.

Soviet Jewish Emigres and Crime

Rosner, Lydia S. *The Soviet Way of Crime: Beating the System in the Soviet Union and the USA.* South Hadley, Mass.: Bergin and Garvey, 1986.

Bukharan Jewish Emigres and Music

Levin, Theodore. *Thousand Fools of God: Musical Travels in Central Asia (and Queens, New York).* Bloomington: Indiana University Press, 1997.

ESSAYS/CHAPTERS IN EDITED COLLECTIONS

Abramsky, Chimen. "The Biro-Bidzhan Project, 1927–1959." In *The Jews in Soviet Russia Since 1917,* ed. Lionel Kochan, 64–77. Oxford and New York: Oxford University Press, 1978.

Ainsztein, Ruben. "Soviet Jewry in the Second World War." In *The Jews in Soviet Russia Since 1917,* ed. Lionel Kochan, 281–99. Oxford and New York: Oxford University Press, 1978.

Aronson, I. Michael. "The Anti-Jewish Pogroms in Russia in 1881." In *Pogroms: Anti-Jewish Violence in Modern Russian History,* ed. J.D. Klier and Shlomo Lambroza, 44–61. Cambridge and New York: Cambridge University Press, 1992.

Ettinger, Shlomo. "The Jews at the Outbreak of the Revolution." In *The Jews in Soviet Russia Since 1917,* ed. Lionel Kochan, 15–30. Oxford and New York: Oxford University Press, 1978.

Friedgut, Theodore. "Passing Eclipse: The Exodus Movement in the 1980s." In

Soviet Jewry in the 1980s: The Politics of Anti-Semitism and Emigration and the Dynamics of Resettlement, ed. Robert O. Freedman, 3–25. Durham and London: Duke University Press, 1989.

Gilson, Jerome M. "The Resettlement of Soviet-Jewish Emigres: Results of a Survey in Baltimore." In *Studies of the Third Wave: Recent Migration of Soviet Jews to the United States,* ed. Dan N. Jacobs and Ellen F. Paul, 29–56. Boulder: Westview Press, 1981.

Gitelman, Zvi. "Soviet Immigrants and American Absorption Efforts: A Case Study in Detroit." In *Studies of the Third Wave: Recent Migration of Soviet Jews to the United States,* ed. Dan N. Jacobs and Ellen F. Paul, 11–28. Boulder: Westview Press, 1981.

Goldman, Marshall. "Soviet American Trade and Soviet Jewish Emigration." In *Soviet Jewry in the 1980s: The Politics of Anti-Semitism and Emigration and the Dynamics of Resettlement,* ed. Robert O. Freedman, 141–59. Durham and London: Duke University Press, 1989.

Haberer, Eric. "Cosmopolitanism, Anti-Semitism and Populism." In *Pogroms: Anti-Jewish Violence in Modern Russian History,* ed. J.D. Klier and Shlomo Lambroza, 98–134. Cambridge and New York: Cambridge University Press, 1992.

Hirszowicz, Lukasz. "The Soviet-Jewish Problem: Internal and International Developments, 1972–1976." In *The Jews in Soviet Russia Since 1917,* ed. Lionel Kochan, 366–409. Oxford and New York: Oxford University Press, 1978.

Kenez, Peter. "Pogroms and White Ideology in the Russian Civil War." In *Pogroms: Anti-Jewish Violence in Modern Russian History,* ed. J.D. Klier and Shlomo Lambroza, 243–313. Cambridge and New York: Cambridge University Press, 1992.

Klier, John. "The Pogrom Paradigm in Russian History." In *Pogroms: Anti-Jewish Violence in Modern Russian History,* ed. J.D. Klier and Shlomo Lambroza, 13–38. Cambridge and New York: Cambridge University Press, 1992.

Korey, William. "The Soviet Public Anti-Zionist Committee." In *Soviet Jewry in the 1980s: The Politics of Anti-Semitism and Emigration and the Dynamics of Resettlement,* ed. Robert O. Freedman, 26–50. Durham and London: Duke University Press, 1989.

Lambroza, Shlomo. "The Pogroms of 1903–1906." In *Pogroms: Anti-Jewish Violence in Modern Russian History,* ed. J.D. Klier and Shlomo Lambroza, 195–247. Cambridge and New York: Cambridge University Press, 1992.

Levenberg, S. "Soviet Jewry: Some Problems and Perspectives." In *The Jews in Soviet Russia Since 1917,* ed. Lionel Kochan, 30–46. Oxford and New York: Oxford University Press, 1978.

Lewis, Phillipa. "The Jewish Question in the Open, 1968–71." In *The Jews in Soviet Rusia Since 1917,* ed. Lionel Kochan, 349–65. Oxford and New York: Oxford University Press, 1978.

Lissyutinskaya, Larisa. "Soviet Women at the Crossroads of Perestroika." In *Gender*

Politics and Post-Communism, ed. Manette Funk and Magda Mueller, 274–86. New York: Routledge, 1993.

Lubin, Nancy. "Small Business Owners." In *New Lives: The Adjustment of Soviet Jewish Immigrants in the United States and Israel*, ed. Rita J. Simon, 151–64. Lexington, Mass.: Lexington Books, 1985.

Spier, Howard. "Soviet Anti-Semitism." In *Soviet Jewry in the 1980s: The Politics of Anti-Semitism and Emigration and the Dynamics of Resettlement*, ed. Robert O. Freedman, 51–57. Durham and London: Duke University Press, 1989.

Weinberg, Robert. "The Pogrom in 1905 in Odessa." In *Pogroms: Anti-Jewish Violence in Modern Russian History*, ed. J.D. Klier and Shlomo Lambroza, 248–90. Cambridge and New York: Cambridge University Press, 1992.

Weinryb, Bernard. "Anti-Semitism in Soviet Russia." In *The Jews in Soviet Russia Since 1917*, ed. Lionel Kochan, 300–331. Oxford and New York: Oxford University Press, 1978.

SCHOLARLY ARTICLES AND ADAPTATION STUDIES

Amith, David, and Yoav Levee. "Migration and Marital Distress: The Case of Soviet Immigrants." *Journal of Divorce and Remarriage*, 21, No. 3–4 (1994).

Baptiste, David. "Immigrant Families, Adolescents and Acculturation." *Marriage and Family Review* 19, No. 3–4 (1993): 341–63.

———. "The Treatment of Adolescents and Their Families in Cultural Transition." *Contemporary Family Therapy* 12, No. 11 (Spring 1990): 3–22.

Barnakin, Tamara, Mary Konstantareas, and Bosett de Farideh. "Adaptation of Recent Soviet Jewish Immigrants and Their Children to Toronto." *Canadian Journal of Psychiatry* (August 1989): 512–18.

Becker, Patricia and Judah Isaacs. "A New American Acculturation Study: Five Years Later." *Journal of Jewish Communal Service* (Summer 1996).

Birman, Igor. "Jewish Emigration From the USSR: Some Observations." *Soviet Jewish Affairs* 9 (September 1979): 46–63.

Brodsky, Betty. "Mental Health Attitudes and Practices of Soviet Jewish Immigrants." *Health and Social Work* (Spring 1988): 130–136.

Bychkov-Green, Sonia, and Ida Bychkov. "Bilingualism in Immigrant Children." *Journal of Jewish Communal Service* (Summer 1996): 339–343.

Chiswick, Barry R. "Soviet Jews in the United States: An Analysis of Their Linguistic and Economic Adjustment." *International Migration Review* 27, no. 2 (1993).

Cullen, Robert. "Soviet Jewry." *Foreign Affairs* 65 (Winter 1986–87).

Fisher, Leon D. "Initial Experiences in the Resettlement of Soviet Jews in the United States." *Journal of Jewish Communal Service* (March 1975): 267–69.

Gidwitz, Betsy. "Problems of Adjustment of Soviet Jewish Emigres." *Soviet Jewish Affairs* 6 (Spring 1976): 27–40.

Gitelman, Zvi. "Soviet Immigrant Resettlement in the United States." *Soviet Jewish Affairs* 12, no. 2 (1982).

Goldenberg, Victor and Leonard Saxe. "Social Attitudes of Russian Immigrants to the United States." *The Journal of Social Psychology* 136 (August 1996): 421–35.

Goldstein, Edgar. "Psychological Adaptations of Soviet Immigrants." *American Journal of Psychoanalysis: 39/3* (1979): 257–63.

Halberstadt, Anna and Adele Nikolsky. "Bukharan Jews and Their Adaptation to the United States." *Journal of Jewish Communal Service* 72, no. 4 (Summer 1996): 244–55.

———. "A Model Assessment of an Emigre Family From the Former Soviet Union." op. cit. pp. 298–309.

Hawks, Irene Kaminsky. "The New Immigrant: A Study of the Vocational Adjustment of Soviet Jews." Presented at the Annual Meeting of the National Conference of Jewish Communal Service, June 7, 1976.

Jacobson, Gaynor. "Spotlight on Soviet Jewry: Absorption in the U.S.A." *Journal of Jewish Communal Service* (December 1975): 190–194.

Lissyutinskaya, Larisa. "Soviet Women at the Crossroads of Perestroika." Funk, Manette, and Magda Mueller eds. *Gender Politics and Post-Communism.* New York: Routledge, 1993.

Markowitz, Fran. "Family Dynamics and the Teenage Immigrant." *Adolescence* 29, no. 113 (Spring 1994): 151–61.

Nikolsky, Adele. "An Adaptation Group for Middle-Aged Clients From the Former Soviet Union." *Journal of Jewish Communal Service* (Summer 1996): 316–25.

Orleck, Annelise. "The Soviet Jews: Life in Brighton Beach, Brooklyn." Nancy Foner ed. *New Immigrants in New York.* New York: Columbia University Press, 1987, pp. 273–304.

Pawliuk, Nicole, Natalie Grizenko, Alice Chan-Yip, Peter Gantous, Jane Mathew, and Diem Nguyen. "Acculturation Style and Psychological Functioning in Children of Immigrants." *American Journal of Orthopsychiatry* 66, no. 1 (January 1996): 111–21.

Rubin, Burton. "The Soviet Refugee." *Journal of Jewish Communal Service* (December 1975).

Scherbak, Yuri. "Ten Years of the Chernobyl Era." *Scientific American* (April 1996): 44–49.

Schnur, Elizabeth, Rebecca Koffler, Nicola Wimpenny, Helayne Giller, and Eileen Rafield. "Family Child Care and New Immigrants: Cultural Bridge and Support." *Child Welfare* (Nov–Dec. 1995): 1237–48.

Simon, Rita, Louise Shelley, and Paul Schneiderman. "The Social and Economic Adjustment of Soviet Jewish Women in the United States." Rita Simon and Caroline Brettell, eds. *International Migration: The Female Experience.* Boston: Rowman and Allenheld, 1986.

Sluszki, Carlos E. "Migration and Family Conflict." *Family Process* 18, no. 4 (December 1979): 379–90.

Solomon, Linda. "Providing High Quality Service to Elderly Soviet Emigres." *Journal Of Jewish Communal Service* (Summer 1996): 326–34.

Tress, Madeline. "Refugees As Immigrants: Revelations of Labor Market Performance." *Journal of Jewish Communal Service* 72, no. 4 (Summer 1996): 263–79.

Tress, Madeline and Steven Gold. "Immigration, Acculturation, Integration and Other Questions: A Review of the Recent Literature on Soviet Jews in the United States." *Journal of Jewish Communal Service* (Summer 1996).

Weinberg, Armin, Sunil Kripalani, Philip L. McCarthy, and Jack Schuli. "Caring for Survivors of the Chernobyl Disaster: What the Clinician Should Know." *Journal of the American Medical Association* 274, no. 5 (August 2, 1995): 408–12.

Weinstein, Lewis. "Soviet Jewry and the American Jewish Community." *American Jewish History* (June 1988).

Yaglom, Miriam. "The Impact of Loss and Mourning on Soviet Emigre Teenagers and Their Families." *Journal of Jewish Communal Service* (Summer 1996): 311–15.

NEWSPAPER AND MAGAZINE ARTICLES

Anand, Geeta. "A Russian Evolution." *Boston Globe.* July 5, 1995.

Anonymous. "I'm Not Fleeing, I'm Being Evicted." *Harper's.* June 1991.

Antonelli, Judith. "We Must Get Real About Spousal Abuse." *Jewish Advocate.* November 30, 1995.

Banner, Lori, and Alia Ramer. "The Road to Citizenship Reaches Its End." *Metro West Jewish News.* June 12, 1997.

Bennett, Vanora. "Russia's Ugly Little Secret: Misogyny." *Los Angeles Times.* December 6, 1997.

Berry, Steve. "Cosby Case is No Celebrity Circus." *Los Angeles Times.* May 4, 1998.

Beyette, Beverly. "A Time for Songs, for Joy, for Sorrow." *Los Angeles Times.* March 3, 1994.

Blume, Howard. "Red Army Jews Toast Defeat of Nazis." *Los Angeles Times.* November 16, 1992.

Brown, Elicia. "How Many Supreme Court Justices Are There?" *The Jewish Week.* May 9, 1997.

Bryant-Friedland, Bruce. "Russians Perplex Their Bronx Brethren." *Bronx Beat Online.* November 13, 1995.

Burstein, Daniel. "The Russian Mafia: A New Crime Menace Grows in Brooklyn." *New York.* November 24, 1986.

Caroll, Linda. "Seeking Care in A Strange Land: Medical Culture Shock. *Newsday,* October 10, 1993.

Chazanov, Mathis and Esther Schrader. "Southland Not Prepared for Soviet Emigres." *Los Angeles Times.* February 19, 1989.

Cheng, Mae. "Immigration Most in Decades." *Newsday.* January 9, 1997.

Cheslow, Jerry. "Fair Lawn: A Suburb With Some Surprises." *New York Times.* January 8, 1995.

Collier, Robert. "Russia West." *San Francisco Chronicle.* June 13, 1993.

Corwin, Miles and Matt Laitt. "Suspect in Cosby Slaying Identified." *Los Angeles Times.* March 14, 1997.

Cullen, Robert. "Russian Mob." *Playboy.* April 1994.

Dawsey, Darrell. "2,000 Rally for Emigration of Jews From Soviet Union." *Los Angeles Times.* March 19, 1990.

Dorf, Matthew. "With Food Stamp Loss, Emigres in Bay Area Worry About Hunger." *Jewish Telegraphic Agency.* August 22, 1997.

Drinan, Robert. "Soviet Jews." *Christian Century.* November 1, 1983.

Dugger, Celia. "Immigrant Influence Surges." *New York Times.* January 9, 1997.

Franklin, James. "As Soviets Allow Jews to Emigrate Hub Supporters Feel Urgency to Act." *Boston Globe.* September 24, 1989.

Friedland Ellen. "NJ State Welfare Reforms Threaten Russian Jewish Emigres." *Ethnic News Watch.* October 12, 1995.

Friedman, Robert I. "The Russian Mob." *New York.* November 7, 1994.

———. "The Money Pit." *New York.* January 22, 1996.

Garrett, Laurie. "Crumbled Empire, Shattered Health." *Newsday.* October 28, 1997.

Gelbwasser, Michael. "Worry Over Welfare Reform." *The Jewish Advocate.* August 15, 1996.

Glasser, Ira. "Scapegoating Immigrants Again." *Visions of Liberty,* no. 17. November 17, 1996.

Gold, Matea. "Russian Mafia Label Denounced." *Los Angeles Times.* March 21, 1997.

Goldberg, Carey. "Tidal Wave of Immigration Carries Off Soviet 'Brains'." *Los Angeles Times.* October 8, 1990.

Gorin, Julia. "Along the Bukharan Broadway." *Newsday.* July 23, 1995.

Goshko, John. "U.S. Plans To Bar Thousands of Soviet Jews." *Washington Post.* September 7, 1989.

Gross Jane. "City's Tolerance Is Tested at Park in West Hollywood." *Los Angeles Times.* September 5, 1995.

Haldane, David. "Immigrants Fulfill a 'Covenant' With God." *Los Angeles Times.* November 24, 1990.

Hartstein, Larry. "Relearning Passover Traditions." *Chicago Tribune.* April 10, 1995.

Heard, Jacquelyn. "Family Program Aids Soviet Jews in City." *Chicago Tribune.* December 1, 1989.

Holden, Constance. "No American Dream For Soviet Refugees." *Science.* June 1, 1990.

Howells, Polly. "Bad Jews: Good Jews: The Story of Soviet Jewish Immigrants in the Promised Land." *In These Times.* September 11–17, 1985.

Izenberg, Dan. "MKs Get Tough With Domestic Violence." *Jerusalem Post.* November 23, 1994.

Jacoby, Tamar. "New Deal for Soviet Jews?" *Newsweek.* November 2, 1987.

Josar, David. "Push For Citizenship Soars." *Detroit News.* January 22, 1996.

Katz, Leslie. "Rally Unites Interethnic Voices to Support Immigrants." *Jewish Bulletin of Northern California* (on-line). 1995 digest.

———. "As Welfare Shrivels, Local Emigres Chase U.S. Citizenship." *Jewish Bulletin of Northern California* (on-line). 1996 digest.

Kempster, Norman. "U.S. Moves to Speed Soviet Immigration." *Los Angeles Times*. April 6, 1989.

Kreimer, Susan. "From Russia With Love." *Newsday*. June 19, 1996.

Lee, May. "House Panel Votes to Aid Soviet, Asian Immigrants." *Los Angeles Times*. April 27, 1989.

Lieberman, Paul and Williams, Frank. "FBI Arrests 11 in Black Market Fuel Ring." *Los Angeles Times*. September 13, 1995.

Lin, Wendy. "Immigrants Back Clinton." *Newsday*. November 3, 1992.

Lubetkin, Jordan. "Trial Begins for Killer of Bella Leybovich." *Cleveland Jewish News*. February 21, 1997.

Mantilla, Karla. "Russian and American Women Battle Domestic Violence." *Off Our Backs*. November 1, 1997.

Martin, Hugo. "Lines Form For Faith Not for Bread." *Los Angeles Times*. September 19, 1991.

———. "Sad Reminder of Slaughter Unveiled." *Los Angeles Times*. September 30, 1991.

McCleod, Ramon. "Surge in Soviet Immigration to U.S." *San Francisco Chronicle*. July 4, 1990.

Oloroso, Arsenio. "Moscow on the Lake: Soviets Pour into City." *Crain's Chicago Business*. September 25, 1989.

Pevtzow, Lisa. "45 Years Later Soviet Jews Share Holocaust Secrets." *Detroit News*. January 1, 1996.

Prince-Gibson, Eetta. "Battered Lives." *Jerusalem Post*. December 6, 1996.

Ramirez, Margaret. "Welfare Fears: No Refuge for Elderly Refugees." *Newsday*. August 4, 1996.

Ribadeneira, Diego. "Awakening to a Heritage." *Boston Globe*. April 4, 1996.

Rojas, Aurelio. "Immigrants Worried About Reform." *San Francisco Chronicle*. February 13, 1995.

Rozenblit, Amir, "The Mean Streets of Ofakim." *Jerusalem Post*. December 9, 1994.

Ruby, Walter. "The Abandonment of Soviet Jewry." *Moment*. April 30, 1995.

Sawyer, Susan. "Apple Pie and Affiliation: Soviet Jews Try Religion American Style." *The International Jewish Monthly*. Reprints 1995.

Schuss, Deborah Gastfreund. "Russian Emigres Discover A Home for the Spirit." *Boston Globe*. September 10, 1995.

Sessler, Amy. "Emigre Enclave Arises in North." *Boston Globe*. September 15, 1996.

——— "Three Immigrant Families Share One Reason for Leaving." *Boston Globe*. September 15, 1996.

Shaw, Jan. "Soviet Emigres Grabbing Bay Area Jobs." *San Francisco Business Times*. November 2, 1990.

Soble, Ronald. "Postscript: Our Family Made the Right Choice." *Los Angeles Times*. April 11, 1989.

Stanglin, Douglas, with Jeff Trimble and Charles Fenyvesi. "The Soviet Gate Opens a Bit." *U.S. News & World Report.* June 22, 1987.

Steinberg, Lynn. "Perestroika Fallout." *Los Angeles Times.* December 15, 1989.

Strasser, Teresa. "Russian, American Teens Move in Separate Circles." *Northern California Jewish Bulletin* (on-line digest), 1995.

Sugarman, Rafael. "The Kindest Cut of All." *Urban Gazette.* December 10, 1992.

Taylor, Alex. "Entrepreneurs: Russia's Newest Export." *Fortune.* December 8, 1986.

Tanner, Adam. "A School For Wives." *Newsday.* November 14, 1994.

Vandenberg, Martina. "Fighting Rape and Trafficking of Women." *Networking For Women.* October 1, 1997.

Wallace, Bill. "Hot Overseas Market for Stolen Cars." *San Francisco Chronicle* (on-line digest), 1995.

Yoon, Cindy. "No Broken Bones, No Justice for Battered Women." *Interpress News Service Wire.* March 29, 1996.

Zundelevich, Natalie. "The Waiting Has Finally Ended." *New York Times Magazine.* January 1, 1989.

Not Bylined

"The Arrest of a Troubled Teenager." *People.* March 31, 1997.

"Bush OKs Sharp Increase in Soviet Refugees." *Chicago Tribune.* October 16, 1990.

"Gorbachev Opens the Doors for Jews: The U.S. Prepares for An Influx." *World Press Review.* November 1989.

"Helping Jews in Distress." *Jewish Advocate.* March 9, 1995.

"Old Refugees Find New Ones Wanting." AP wire. January 31, 1995.

"Our Story, Our Towns/Queens." *Newsday.* February 22, 1998

Also Cited

Jerusalem Post. July 5, 1995.

Jewish Samizdat. 8 (1975):255–70.

Los Angeles Times. December 1, 1989; January 2, 1991; August 25, 1991; October 25, 1991; November 23, 1992; March 3, 1994; March 16, 1996; December 14, 1996.

Macleans. January 19, 1987.

New York Times. January 11, 1997.

St. Louis Post Dispatch. September 26, 1989.

Time. June 2, 1997.

U.S. News & World Report. October 23, 1995.

ORGANIZATIONAL NEWSLETTERS AND GOVERNMENT PUBLICATIONS

Congressional Quarterly Weekly Report. September 16, 1989; May 26, 1990.

Federal Bureau of Investigation. *Crime in the U.S.: Uniform Crime Reports,* 1996.

Federation of Jewish Philanthropies of New York. *Festival of Soviet Jewish Traditions of Central Asia, The Caucasus, and the Western Republics.* 1982.

HIAS Annual Reports, 1972–1997.

HIAS Statistical Surveys, "Case Employment Rates at Six Months After Arrival," 1996; and "The HIAS Statistical Abstract," XXI, no. 6 (April 1997).

International Conference One Decade After Chernobyl. *Summary of the Conference Results.* Vienna: August 8–12, 1996.

NYANA. "Starting Over: The NYANA Resettlement Process." 1996.

Office of the Attorney General of the State of California. *Report on Russian Organized Crime.* March 1996.

United States Department of State. *Human Rights Country Report 1996: Russia.* January 30, 1997.

World Jewish Congress. *Machon Policy Dispatch,* no. 9. May 22, 1997.

UNPUBLISHED PAPERS AND THESES

Carfora, John. "Soviet Immigrants in America: An Introductory Reading for Volunteers Involved With Resettling Soviet Emigres." M.A. thesis, Dartmouth College, 1985.

Sperling, Shirley. "The 1.5 Generation of the Soviet Jewish Immigration to the U.S." Independent study, Dartmouth College, May 1997.

Zaretsky, Natasha. "Elderly Soviet Jewish Immigrants in Boston." Seminar paper, Dartmouth College, June 1996.

INTERNET RESOURCES

"Archive of Jewish Immigrant Culture": <*http://arts.ucsc.edu/faculty/efimova/archive*>. The Archive is a project of emigre Professor Alla Efimova and artist Marina Tempicka. It is both a virtual and a paper archive. The paper archive can be visited at 309 W. 30th St. No. 1A, New York, New York 10001.

"Beyond the Pale: The History of Russian Jews": <*http://www.friends-partners.org/partners/beyond-the-pale*>.

Carr, Donna. "The Jews of Bukhara": <*byblos@getnet.com*>, 1997.

"Children, Chernobyl and the Internet": <*http://prism.prs.k.12.nj.us:70/0/WWW011/Chernobyl.html*>.

"Discovery Channel Online—Chernobyl Victims Speak Out": <*http://eagle2.online.discovery.com/DCO/doc/1012/world/science/chernobyl/chernobyl3.2html*>.

"Jewish Communication Network": <*http://www.jcn18.com/newstand/roundup*>.

"New York Association for New Americans": <*http://www.nyana.org/home.html*>.

"Russians in America": <*http://ourworld.compuserve.com80/homepages/V__Feshchenko*>.

"Union of Councils for Soviet Jews": <*http://www.serve.com/ucsj/frames/alert.html*>.

"U.S.A.-Canada Chernobyl Immigrant Registry": <*http://radefx.bcm.tmc.edu/usacir/bcm-cr.htm*>.

"World Jewish Congress on-line, Virtual Jerusalem: Jewish Communities of the World—Commonwealth of Independent States": <*http://www.virtual.co.il./communities/wjcbook/commonw.htm*>.

AUTHOR'S INTERVIEWS

*Bela. White Lake, New York, August 12, 1996.

Regina Bienstock. Hanover, New Hampshire, January 27, 1997.

*Fanya. Brooklyn, New York, March 15, 1983.

*Marya Frumkin. Brooklyn, New York, July 14, 1980; July 15, 1980; September 20, 1983.

Samuel Gurevich. Hanover, New Hampshire, February 24, 1997.

Lyuba Halberstam. Brooklyn, New York, July 5, 1981.

*Ilya Hanover. New Hampshire, February 24, 1997.

Rose Kaplan. Brooklyn, New York, August 9, 1980.

Igor Katyn. Brooklyn, New York, September 9, 1980.

Tamara Katyn. Brooklyn, New York, September 9, 1980.

Yenta Katz. Brooklyn, New York, August 15, 1980.

*Khaya. Jerico, Long Island, August 8, 1996.

Bertha Klimkovich. Brooklyn, New York, August 13, 1996.

Semyon Kommissar. Brooklyn New York, September 22, 1980; April 5, 1983.

Artyem Lifshitz. Hanover, New Hampshire, February 9, 1997.

*Irena Lunts. Jericho, Long Island, August 8, 1996.

Victor Ourin. Brooklyn, New York, September 10, 1980.

Rebecca Pyatkevich. Hanover, New Hampshire, February 14, 1997.

*Zhana R. Brooklyn, New York, August 13, 1996.

Maxim Roisin. Hanover, New Hampshire, February 5, 1997.

Sara Rovenski. White Lake, New York, August 12, 1996.

Sergey Shapner. Hanover, New Hampshire, February 3, 1997.

Maya Shkolnikov. Brooklyn, New York, August 13, 1996.

Sophia Shkolnikov. Brooklyn, New York, August 13, 1996.

Edith Shvartsman. Brooklyn, New York, August 13, 1996.

Alexander Sirotin. Brooklyn, New York, May 8, 1981; September 7, 1985; May 5, 1993; August 9, 1996.

Nechama Sirotina. Brooklyn, New York, May 10, 1981.

Sophie Spector. Brooklyn, New York, April 23, 25, 1983.

Bela Sperling. Edgewater, New Jersey, August 9, 1996.

Izak Sperling. Edgewater, New Jersey, August 9, 1996.

Names marked with asterisks were changed, or the last name omitted, at the request of the interview subject.

Index

AARJ (American Association of Russian Jews), 191
Abramov, Yechiel, 168
Acculturation, 3–4, 170, 171, 173–174, 176–177, 178–183, 185
Activism, 54–56, 64, 68. *See also* Dissidence; Politics; *Refusenik*
Adolescence, 170–183. *See also* Children
Age, 136, 160
Agron, Evsei, 115, 116
Alexander II, 13, 14
Alexander III, 14
American Association of Russian Jews, 191
Amith, Ben-David, 164
Andropov, Yuri, 65, 66
Anti-Semitism: and Bolshevism, 25–26; and Brezhnev era, 49–51; and Caucasian Mountain Jews, 128; and contemporary Russia, 74–76; and economy, 15; and education, 51, 52; and elderly immigrants, 150–151; and Georgian Jews, 128–129; and Gorbachev era, 69–70; and immigration, 5; and Krushchev, 40; and

Marx, 26; and mental health, 163; and 1905 Revolution, 15; and Pamyat, 69–70; persistence of, 6; and post-war Russia, 31–39; and pre-revolutionary Russia, 13–16; and Public Anti-Zionist Committee, 66; and religion, 164; and Russian Revolution, 18; and Stalin, 23, 26, 33–34; and teenagers, 172; and United States, 67; and Uzbek Jews, 122–123; and World War I, 17; and Zionism, 64. *See also* Nazis, Nazism
Arts, 41–48, 87, 121, 127. *See also* Yiddish Theater
Assimilation, 26, 53
Association of Engineers and Scientists For New Americans, 191
Association of Soviet Jewish Emigres, 133–134, 191
Association of Soviet Lawyers, 67

Babi Yar, 102–103, 142–143, 154. *See also* Holocaust
Balagula, Marat, 115
Bar mitzvah, 110–112, 126
Begun, Iosef, 67, 68

About the Author

ANNELISE ORLECK is associate professor of history and women's studies at Dartmouth College. She is the author of *Common Sense and a Little Fire: Women and Working Class Politics in the U.S.* (1995) and co-editor of *The Politics of Motherhood: Activist Voices from Left to Right* (1997). Her next book is a study of women and welfare activism in Las Vegas, Nevada. She is a native of Brighton Beach, Brooklyn, home to a large community of Soviet Jewish Americans.